Praise for *Year of No Clutter*

"With vivacity and wit, Eve Schaub embarks on a year of decluttering that yields profound insights into the grasp of things on our lives. Thanks to this stunningly object-rich memoir, I will certainly never look at stuff in quite the same way again."

—Abigail Carroll, author of *Three Squares:*
The Invention of the American Meal

"This book not only offers practical tips and advice on letting go and clearing out, but some really interesting insight into the psychology of 'stuff.'"

—Cwtch Up Books

"Everybody's got a Hell Room in their house. *Year of No Clutter* is a witty, touching, and sympathetic account of a woman and her family's attempt to deal with the chaos of familial collections accrued over more than a decade. If you struggle with clutter, you will surely take heart, and maybe even resolve to give more than a few things away."

—Lisa Kotin, author of *My Confection:*
Odyssey of a Sugar Addict

"A fascinating window into the life of a would-be hoarder. Eve Schaub has written a parable for modern life and the stuff we accumulate. [The book] prompted me to set a goal of ruthlessly cleaning out stuff I can live without."

—Tom Rosenbauer, author of *Casting Illusions*

Praise for *Year of No Sugar*

"A funny, intelligent, and informative memoir."
—*Kirkus Reviews*

"I certainly learned a lot about the benefits of reducing sugar, but the best part was how much I laughed!"
—Melissa Sorrells, associate editor of *FIRST for Women*

"Delicious and compelling, her book is just about the best sugar substitute I've ever encountered."
—Ron Powers, Pulitzer Prize–winning author

"Shine[s] a much-needed spotlight on an aspect of American culture that is making us sick, fat, and unhappy, and it does so with wit and warmth."
—Suvir Saran, author of *Indian Home Cooking*

"The diary I wish I had kept...the adventures of her family, the roadblocks they encountered, and the sheer daily difficulty of overcoming a national obsession."
—David Gillespie, author of *Sweet Poison*

ALSO BY EVE O. SCHAUB

Year of No Sugar

YEAR OF NO CLUTTER

a memoir

EVE SCHAUB

This book is not intended as a substitute for medical advice from a qualified physician. The intent of this book is to provide accurate general information in regard to the subject matter covered. If medical advice or other expert help is needed, the services of an appropriate medical professional should be sought.

This book is a memoir. It reflects the author's present recollections of experiences over a period of time. Some names and characteristics have been changed, some events have been compressed, and some dialogue has been re-created.

All brand names and product names used in this book are trademarks, registered trademarks, or trade names of their respective holders. Sourcebooks, Inc., is not associated with any product or vendor in this book.

Published by Sourcebooks, Inc.
P.O. Box 4410, Naperville, Illinois 60567-4410
(630) 961-3900
Fax: (630) 961-2168
www.sourcebooks.com

Library of Congress Cataloging-in-Publication Data

Names: Schaub, Eve O.
Title: Year of no clutter : a memoir / Eve O. Schaub.
Description: Naperville, Illinois : Sourcebooks, [2017]
Identifiers: LCCN 2016028643 | (pbk. : alk. paper)
Subjects: LCSH: Hoarders--United States--Biography. | Schaub, Eve O.--Homes and haunts. | Housekeeping. | Storage in the home.
Classification: LCC RC569.5.H63 S33 2017 | DDC 616.85/2270092 [B] --dc23
LC record available at https://lccn.loc.gov/2016028643

Printed and bound in the United States of America.
UGI 10 9 8 7 6 5 4 3 2 1

To Dr. F,
who gave me back my life.

⚠ WARNING ⚠

Reading, perusing, or glancing at this book may be disturbing or traumatic to those with fastidious constitutions, those with meticulous sensibilities, and/or Martha Stewart.

My aunt Mill, for example, must never, under any circumstances, be encouraged to read this book.

"Nothing heals us like letting people know our scariest parts."

—Anne Lamott

CONTENTS

A NOTE FROM
THE HUSBAND

BY STEPHEN SCHAUB

I love my wife.

    I *really* love my wife.

Okay. So now that I have gotten that out of the way, let me go where no husband with any common sense should *ever* go and talk about my wife's big hidden problem…clutter.

Ever since I have known Eve she has always been a collector. I always felt that the word *collector* seemed about right: she loved to collect all sorts of things, both tangible and abstract, from souvenirs and photos to antiques and family memorabilia to travel experiences and relationships with friends. She revels in the tiny details that other people might miss, cherishes things other people might toss away without a thought.

I recall the first time that I realized she kept more than most people. It was before we were married, and we were out to dinner somewhere. Spontaneously I wrote "I love you" on a paper sugar packet and passed it to her across the table, and of course she smiled at me. Then she slipped the sugar packet into her purse. I made a joke that she'd have to keep the package forever now—seeing as how it was a declaration of love.

"Yes. I *will* keep it forever," she said, looking at me, still smiling but serious. After we were married and moving into the house where we live now, I recall coming across that sugar packet and being a little astounded. She really meant it.

I now realize that using that word—*collector*—is perhaps my own way of not dealing with a big problem. Eve loves to collect, but for some time now her collections have in many ways controlled her.

Living in a house that has one room or several rooms (depending on the day) that are nearly impossible to navigate due to the piles of unorganized objects is exhausting…for everyone. But because most of the clutter is either Eve's or under Eve's jurisdiction, it seems by far worst for her. Surrounded by Stuff, she lives with the constant reminder of failure: failure to finish a project, failure to make a decision, failure to have a functioning space free of clutter. I know Eve feels this very keenly. There have been days when to her the weight of it was overwhelming, and as her husband it was very hard to see her feeling powerless, hopeless, in the face of her belongings.

I've known Eve now for more than twenty years, and I've watched her grapple with the problem of "letting go" for all of them. Upon occasion it has worried me. Part of her personality is to carry with her a tremendous sense of obligation not only to her friends and to her family but also to her objects. Some people can just let it go and move on. Not Eve. These emotionally perceived failures and shortcomings cling to her like award ribbons you never wanted to win.

When Eve told me about this project, I was hopeful. Hopeful not only that would we regain control over our house and get back some of our living space but more importantly that it would provide Eve with a greater sense of empowerment in her life.

I love my wife, and I love her collections… I'm just happy that they now occupy a much smaller part of our life.

I hope you enjoy her story.

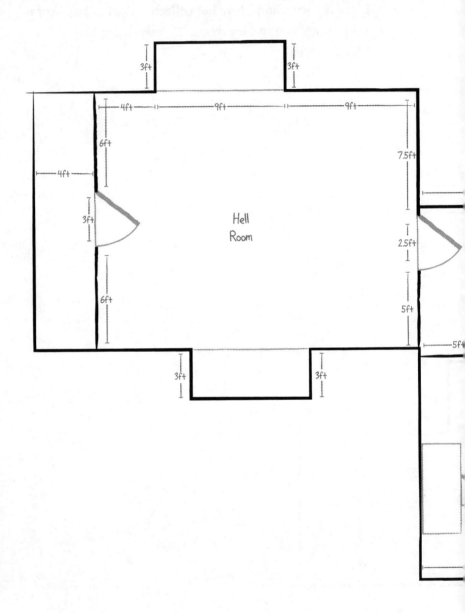

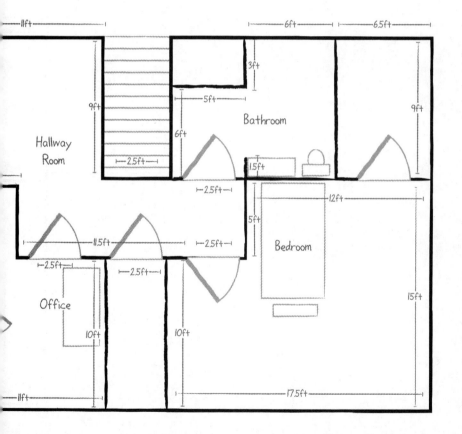

IT'S ONLY STUFF

"Have nothing in your houses that you do not know to be useful, or believe to be beautiful."

—William Morris

I put up a pretty good front. To the average visitor, my house resembles a normal—if slightly disheveled—home for a family of four. Sure, piles of clothes creep, amoeba-like, into the hallway from the laundry room, and it's not completely unheard of for me not to get *all* the dishes done before bed.

But generally speaking, most of the time my house looks neat. Ish. If, at a moment's notice, we were to be informed of the president and First Lady's imminent arrival, a laundry basket would materialize to sweep away the random school papers, summer camp projects, and squadrons of fleece jackets that seem magnetically attracted to my floor. In the grand scheme of things, it's all fairly manageable.

If, however, when the president and the First Lady arrived they asked to be given a tour of the house, we might have a tiny problem. Having seen the rather unremarkable first floor, we'd ascend the stairs and, if it was just the right day, we'd peek through doorways at the top to see a clean bathroom sink and a made bed. Let's assume I'd even finished filing papers the day before, so just down the hall and to the left we'd glimpse a fully visible office floor. Further down the hallway opens into a small room lined with bookshelves and, at the far end of that, a closed door. It is at this point that our tour would abruptly conclude.

"*Thank you,* Mr. President and Mrs. First Lady, for visiting our humble home," I would say, with a small head gesture that indicated deference if not an actual curtsy.

"But…what's in *there?*" the First Lady would inquire, pointing to the closed door directly behind me.

"What? Where? Oh, in *there?*" I'd say innocently, opening my eyes a tad wider than necessary. "Oh, that's *nothing.* It's…a closet. A *half*-closet, really. Practically a dead end. Probably a builder's mistake. Actually the door doesn't even open—it's not even really a door—it's more like a *painting* of a door. Very trompe l'oeil, isn't it?"

There would be some whispering between the First Lady and her security detail, the president looking on with a slightly furrowed brow. Despite my warm smile, tiny beads of sweat would be starting to form on my forehead.

"Open the door," one of the men in sunglasses would say firmly, stepping in front of the first couple.

"But…" I'd try to protest.

"Mrs. Schaub, it's *the biggest room in your house,*" another agent would say, edging around me and reaching for the doorknob. "Clearly, you're hiding something."

"Ha! Ha ha!" I'd laugh a little hysterically. "*Some*thing? Some*thing?* Go ahead—*open* the door! I dare you!"

The door would fly open, and audible gasps would be heard. Immediately, the First Lady would be hustled away by her agents, the president looking shaken.

"My God," he would say, slowly. "*How...did it...ever get...to this?*"

It's a question I've asked myself a lot. When the largest room in your house—a full 567 square feet—is filled from top to bottom with so much *Stuff*—detritus, things, excess, clutter—that all you can seem to do about it most days is close the door and hope it will somehow resolve itself—you can't help but occasionally wonder, *How?*

Not to mention that it's a secret. Beyond the four members of our household, the number of people who have been heretofore aware of my—err—eccentricity can be counted on one hand. A hand that is wearing a mitten. Like I said, *most* of our house is fine. We find things we're looking for, we eat, clean up, go to bed, and start all over again. It functions, and sometimes it even exists as that sort of island of tranquility we all ideally want our homes to be. But...*the Room*?

How shall I describe it? It's my picture of Dorian Gray. It's the room that proves I am not, nor ever may I remotely (even for five consecutive seconds) pretend to be, Martha Stewart. It's my Fibber McGee's closet. It's the room that I—I am not kidding—*lock* when the babysitter comes for fear she will see it.

It is the largest room in our house, and it is entirely unusable. The Hell Room, as we have come to know it, is really a world unto itself, a sort of Land of Misfit Belongings. Somewhere in that room, for example, I have my fifth-grade report card, three sheep's worth of wool fleece, and a desiccated dead mouse in a box. Somewhere in that room I have a never-played board game based on wine trivia, a hook rug I made of Garfield the cartoon cat when I was nine, a series of photos of me with the date who dumped me on prom night, and two large shoeboxes filled with actual pieces of wall from a house renovation. I could mount an impressive retrospective at the Louvre, drawing from my vast collection of children's finger paintings, homemade puppets, and lopsided ceramic pinch pots.

In a way, it's *kind* of cool. It's a bit of a time capsule of my life; it's my own private Eve Museum.

But over time it has gone from being the Very Messy Room to the Storage Room to the Throw-In-Whatever-We-Can't-Decide-What-to-Do-With Room to the For-Pete's-Sake-Don't-Open-*That*-Door! Room. Every year, I make a New Year's resolution to fix it, clean it up, turn it back into a room that our family can actually use…but to no avail.

It's a problem. It's an embarrassment. It's a waste.

Are there worse problems to have than an embarrassing upstairs room? Well, sure. For one thing I could have *two* embarrassing rooms. Or I could have a whole *house* that looks like this.

I could do it, too. I don't like to brag or anything—but I really am *exceptionally* gifted when it comes to the "Stuff" department. If I had a title, it might be "Her Royal Highness, the Queen of Crap." I could look snootily down from high atop my pile of ancient magazines, holding a scepter of dried bridesmaid bouquets, bedecked with a crown made entirely of those extra button packs that helpfully accompany sweater purchases, proclaiming "*Save it!*" in an emphatic yet regal tone.

Practically as far back as I can remember, I've been a saver.

My mantra has long been "When in doubt...*don't throw it out!*" I have a firmly entrenched belief that keeping things can make the difference between success and failure, between happiness and regret, between remembering and forgetting.

If you don't believe me, just take a look: somewhere in the Hell Room I have a shoebox full of my telephone records from college, a box full of ties my dad wore to work in the seventies, and enough leftover fabric from homemade Halloween costumes to provide a trousseau for a medium-sized horse. Then there are the inadvertent additions to the room, left for me primarily by my cats: the dried, hacked-up hair balls and the occasional rodent fragment. Oh yes, it's all in there, and if I may say so, it isn't pretty.

However, in my defense I must point out that to date I have not reached the truly Olympic levels of saving, like the people you see on TV shows with names like *Crazy-Ass Hoarders* and *Shit Central* in which the host despairingly tries to persuade the homeowner to throw away, say, a toothpick or perhaps a piece of food so old it has begun to evolve consciousness.

What's the real difference between the unlucky folks on reality shows like *Hoarders* and me? If I'm honest, it comes down to only one word: scale. Which begs the question, at what point does an embarrassing quirk cross the line into diagnosable disorder? The idea that I might not be on the side of the line that I *think* I am is an idea that, quite frankly, scares me. It messes with my sense of self—of who I think I am. I'll give you a for instance.

A few years ago we had an energy assessment done of our house—our old, creaky, efficient-as-a-rusty-sieve Vermont farmhouse, which I adore beyond all reason. It began with the home energy auditor taking a series of infrared photographs of our house. The heat-sensitive imagery revealed all the areas where heat was escaping in alarming bright blue swaths—around windowsills, across ceilings, and in random places where the insulation had fallen down, been eaten by critters, or never been installed in the first place. According to the assessment—and I'm paraphrasing here—we might as well have been living in a large block of Swiss cheese.

But that wasn't what really bothered me. What *really* bothered me was that this very nice man had to enter *every room of our house*. Even the overflowing laundry room. Even the costume- and game-choked kids' playroom and, my God, yes, *even* the Hell Room. And I had to pretend to be okay with that.

It was really quite humiliating to lead this poor guy through the Hell Room—which I hide from even my own mother—over and around the huge piles of outgrown toddler clothing, falling over mountains of papers and clear violations of the health code, among other things. ("Ma'am, is that a dead mouse?" "We prefer the term *nonfunctional vermin*.") In response to my abject apologies and after exhaling a bit in the doorway, he had cheerfully responded, "Oh, I've seen worse!"

It was a kind thing to say, seeing as how I was pretty sure he hadn't. Suddenly I was seeing myself through his eyes: here was this nice, normal-seeming lady who had a surprising—maybe even just a little bit *repulsive*—secret. And ohhhhh, I did not like it. Not one little bit.

There's nothing like complete and total mortification to motivate one toward change. I didn't want to be this person, this person with a tell-tale heart beating behind the upstairs door, terrified that the arrival of the next electrician or plumber or high-ranking elected official might once again reveal my secret. Certainly it was one thing to have a messy garage or an overflowing attic; lots of people have those. However, *this*, I scolded myself, this was really borderline behavior. Fringe-y behavior. I needed to get it together. And I solemnly resolved, once and for all, that I would.

That was eight years ago.

———

A few years ago I wrote a book about my family—myself, my husband, and our two young daughters—living for a year without eating any added sugar.[1] As it turns out, when you write a book, one of the questions people want most to ask you is what you are going to write about *next*. It seems like a funny question to me—along the lines of asking your kids, while trick-or-treating, what they'd like to be for Halloween *next* year. Like, really? You want to talk about this *now*?

But nevertheless, I knew. I wanted to write about clutter. At this answer, inevitably people would give me a funny look, as if they were pretty sure they had heard me wrong. What train of thought could possibly have brought me from the topic of *sugar* to…*clutter*?

I wasn't sure myself at first, but as it turns out, the problems of too much sugar and too much clutter do have some important things in common. First, they are both relatively modern problems. Second, they both present problems of *abundance*. It is not sugar *or* things per se but the ability to have too *much* sugar, too *many* things, too easily that can get one into trouble.

The fact that we are fortunate to have *these* concerns, as

---

1. Eve O. Schaub, *Year of No Sugar* (Naperville, IL: Sourcebooks, 2014).

opposed to, say, dengue fever, does not change the fact that people do suffer from them. I'm not just talking about not being able to fit into your favorite swimsuit (courtesy sugar) or not being able to find the electric bill when it's overdue (thanks to clutter) but genuine affliction. As I discovered, excess sugar consumption is correlated to every major modern health epidemic you can think of. And as anyone who has seen an episode of *Hoarders* can attest, the problem of too much stuff—left unchecked—can cause intense psychological distress, isolation, and unsafe and unsanitary living conditions. People can, and do, die from clutter.

Much like sugar, clutter is gaining an ever more notorious reputation these days. In short order, we've discovered that hoarding is *everywhere*. Whereas only a few decades ago we had no mutually agreed-upon word for the person down the street with the overloaded front porch and the permanently closed window shades, nowadays our understanding of the disorder has progressed to the point where we even subcategorize: there are *animal* hoarders, *book* hoarders, *food* hoarders. Myriad self-help organizations have sprung up: Messies Anonymous, Clutterers Anonymous, Overcoming Hoarding Together, and so on. In the *New Yorker* article "Let It Go"[2] author Joan Acocella asked the unsettling question: "Are we becoming a nation of hoarders?"

I don't know. But I do know that I really don't want to be a card-carrying member of Too Much Crap Anon. I want my room back, but more than that, I want the sense of control over my belongings—and the life I live with them—back.

---

2. Joan Acocella, "Let It Go," *New Yorker,* December 15, 2014, http://www.newyorker.com/magazine/2014/12/15/let-go.

I don't enjoy walking around my house feeling pretty good, only to need something from upstairs and suddenly remember with dread—oh *yeah*. The Hell Room. The Achilles Heel Room. Ugh.

I have a fond daydream of a day when, like normal, uncluttered folks, I can bring people through my house without hesitation, without secrecy, and without closed doors. More than that, I envision a day when I can confidently stride into every room of my house and find my children's birth certificates or my high school yearbook or a needle and thread whenever the need presents itself without breaking out into hives.

But a more compelling argument might be made that if I don't deal with this Stuff—this Stuff that's supposedly so valuable and important that I can't bear to part with any of it—that *all* of it will be lost. Right? Because if not me, who's going to go through it? My kids? My husband? My cat?

More likely it would all end up, at some point down the road, just going into a Dumpster: the good, the bad, and the ugly. Or parceled out to those mysterious boxes of randomness that you see at auctions and tag sales that potential buyers rifle through. Away will go all several decades of greeting cards (yay!), but so also will go the watercolor by my great-grandmother (gasp!). If I keep *everything*, who's going to know or who's going to say what's really important? If it all gets thrown away someday anyway, then what the heck was the point?

So here's what I think: after years and years and *years* of keeping and keeping—and resolving to clean out and never really managing to do much more than temporarily shift the mess around—after a lifetime of being a compulsive keeper for fear of missing out on some meaningful *something*—it has begun to dawn on me that I'm the chain-smoker who is forever swearing she'll quit *next* year. Really.

And that simply will not do. My house, and with it my sense of self, has arrived in triage, and it's time to make a decision: will the patient live? Can we perform a successful clutter-ectomy?

My plan is to deconstruct the Hell Room—every last bit of it. I will go through all the worry-about-it-later boxes and worry about it now. I will make decisions about objects large and small. I will pitch, plunder, recycle, and sell. I will give up on things. I will even—against all my better judgment—be *realistic*.

———

Knowing me and my eight-year-old resolutions, I'll probably need a timeline. How about a year? If, after one whole planetary trip around the sun, I haven't managed to wrestle this room back into habitable form, maybe I will just have to accept the fact that I am an irredeemable cluttermonger, doomed to have everything while being able to find, use, and enjoy nothing.

Here's my ray of hope: I'm really, *really* ready for change. I'm tired of fighting small, inconclusive battles. I want to win the war. Once and for all. Reclaim the room; reclaim myself.

I can do this, right? I mean, it's only *Stuff*.

CHAPTER ONE

WELCOME TO HELL

"And you may ask yourself
Well... How did I get here?"
　　　—Talking Heads, "Once in a Lifetime" (1981)

R eady? Set? Here I go! I open the Hell Room door.
　　I am confronted with an absolute sea of things. As if frozen in a moment of oceanic tumult, the amassed objects form waves of Stuff, poised at various heights about the room. There is, apparently, no floor.

I immediately despair. Shutting the door again seems like an extremely attractive—and downright sensible— proposition, now that I think about it.

Then I rally. It's no more Mrs. Nice Guy.

I do *not* shut the door. Instead, I attack the first thing I see: very likely a giant pile of paper. A random sampling of paper might contain, among other things: a pile of never-tried recipes, a letter of acceptance to a graduate program I didn't attend, instructions on how to make paper (ironic!), and a sheet from my vegetarian days titled "How to Win an Argument with a Meat Eater."

Deep breath.

A Playbill signed by Donny Osmond. Printed-out emails from 2003. A red plastic barrette I wore in elementary school. Student-published poetry collections from college. A poster from a talk the photographer Lee Friedlander gave at Cornell in 1991. None of which, by the way, I am willing to consider parting with.

After about two or three hours I stand back and feel pretty good—look at what I've accomplished! A whole...well, at least *half* of that egregious pile is now transformed into...three new piles. I manage to recycle exactly five pieces of paper.

I promise myself I'll make more of a dent next time, and I shut the door. Days go by. Weeks go by, during which more papers are covertly shoved into the room, erasing any evidence of progress.

Argh.

I think to myself, for the millionth time: *How did it ever get this bad?*

This isn't the kind of situation that develops overnight, of course. I've been a keeper for an awfully long time, practically as long as I can remember. I was a lucky kid with a big room to myself, so I had hiding places: in the closet, in the back of the drawer, under the bed. There was always *somewhere* to put things.

When I became an adult, got married, and moved into our house in the country, I loved it, not least because it had lots and lots of fantastic new hiding places. The attic. The basement. The garage. Closets. And an entire enormous room on the second floor that had no predestined purpose whatsoever.

It seemed perfect, and for a long time it was. Throughout the house I stashed away boxes of things from all periods of my life: from childhood, from teenagehood, from summer camp, from college and grad school. I had it all. And then there was the fact that I was now more or less in charge of not just my own Stuff but also the Stuff of my growing family, and I was always accumulating more—but that was fine. It was a big house.

Despite all this, for years that big room upstairs remained somewhat usable—for a while as a computer room, as a craft room for the kids, as a room where my husband sewed camera straps that he designed and sold. It was fine as long as you ignored the mess that always seemed to be lurking on the *other* side of the room. And then, somewhere along the way—after I moved the computer to a different room, after the kids started making their crafts downstairs, after Steve stopped making camera straps—there was a moment when we lost even a semblance of control. Most of the time, no one had any real reason to go in there, and so the door got shut and stayed shut. That is, until some more things cropped up that I didn't know what to do with. In this case I'd open the door, make a new pile, and shut it again.

After living in this house for the past eighteen years, I have finally run out of hiding places.

Not that I haven't managed to be in a pretty good state of denial about it. "After all," I think, "my stuff doesn't take over the whole *house!*" (although at times it does seep into other rooms...) and "After all, I don't keep actual *trash!*" (although I think both my mother and mother-in-law might disagree with me on this point...)

"And after all, there's nothing *unclean* about it!"

Well, that's not entirely true, either.

Ahem. You see, for many years we had this cat. Perhaps

you know where I'm going with this. He had a *wee* problem, shall we say. Literally. Bladder stability was not his forte.

Of course, we tried everything: more attention, less attention, behavior therapy, blood work, hormone sprays, anti-anxiety medication, multiple litter boxes. Not only did none of it work, but as he aged the problem got worse. I was desperate. If I could've found a feline hypnotherapist I would've been beating down his or her door with fistfuls of my money, most of which at that point was going toward rug cleaner and paper towels.

And I bet you can guess his most favorite place to pee. That's right! He considered the Hell Room his own private executive washroom.

Of course, I kept the door shut. He still managed to get in. I imagined him, late at night, wearing tiny safecracker gloves and perhaps a cat-size pair of night-vision goggles, pawing gently at the corner of the door.

Although this cat went to meet his furry maker some time ago, if I'm ever feeling nostalgic, the not-so-good news is that I can always go *smell* him. Years later, whiffs of his scent linger delicately on in the crevices and the carpeting of the Hell Room. And because there's so much *Stuff* in there, the idea of removing the carpet has always seemed a little bit like proposing to move the Empire State Building three feet to the left: it's just *not* going to happen.

On top of *that* cleanliness issue, there's also the fact that in an old house in the country we have made the acquaintance of a whole spectrum of tiny uninvited guests: mice, bats, spiders, even a vole once (I had to look that one up), and biblical swarms of ladybugs that surface every time the weather gets dramatically warmer…they all love our house with a passion that is undeniable, and they love the Hell Room best of all. Of course, the tiny visitors don't call it the Hell Room. I'm pretty sure they call it the Room with a Million Terrific Hiding Places.

Once, several years ago, I was looking around for something and moved a piece of furniture only to behold behind it a fuzzy little ball of...what? I looked closer, which is always a bad idea, and jumped back with a screech. Of course, it was a dead mouse. A dead mouse that had been there long enough that it looked a little—what?—petrified.

So I did what any normal person would do in a similar circumstance. I immediately, that very minute, sat down and wrote a story about it. I wrote and wrote until I was pleased with the dead mouse story. And then I used a piece of cardboard to lift and slide the little mouse corpse into a small white box—the kind you use for jewelry. After all, I reasoned, I had just written a *story* about him! It felt like something worse than abandonment to get rid of him now...we were linked! Connected through the sacred ritual of storytelling. And anyway, what if this story ended up, you know, *famous*? What if my dead mouse story ended up being my "The Lottery"? Wouldn't it be incredibly neat to still have the original thing that inspired it?

Yes, this is the way I think.

So you can see the situation is bad. Not only do I have a room that is clogged with clutter and less than sanitary with pee and other evidence of small visitors coming and going, I have at least one dead rodent that I have kept in there *on purpose*. I realize that the dead-mouse-in-a-box represents a crossover between the things I keep intentionally and the things that are accidental. It's easy for me to see how this line of thinking can easily go too far, to the point where I'm keeping dog shit in jars and thinking it's fabulous.

And yet—if a crazy keeper is who I am, then *stopping* being that makes me what? Someone else? Filled with regret? Or, heaven forbid...*ordinary*? I mean, I have to admit I *like* me. I even have a perverse love for the Eve who saves things most people throw away. I feel caught in a catch-22: I can't seem to live with the Hell Room but am deeply ambivalent about living without it. If we all have our own personal albatross, the Hell Room is mine.

Recently I stopped to think about how weird that trope is: hanging a dead, stinky bird about someone's neck...on *purpose*. Where did this bizarre idea ever come from? When I looked it up, I discovered that it came from Samuel Taylor Coleridge's *The Rime of the Ancient Mariner*, one of those famous, boring poems that I'm sure I had to read in high school. I was reminded that the sailor who tells the epic tale ends up wearing the dead albatross like a cross around his neck as punishment for killing the bird.[3] In the course of the poem, the bird's significance shifts: at first the albatross is a sign of good luck, but when it dies, it brings very bad luck indeed.

So it goes with my roomful of belongings. Most of the objects in there have at one point or another brought me something positive: happiness, joy, satisfaction, or simply a connection to various memories. Collectively, however, they morph into something entirely different—something heavy

---

3. Depending on whom you ask, the dead birdie necklace can be taken either literally or metaphorically... I find the literal interpretation much more intriguing.

and obstructing and unclean and mortifying. They become that dead, stinky bird on a rope. I picture in my mind's eye a giant amalgam—all my crazy objects welded together in a huge, horrific Frankensphere, larger than my entire body many times over and tied to a great, big chain hung about my neck.

When it finally fell from *his* neck, do you suppose the ancient mariner picked up that dead albatross and thought, "Well, perhaps I'll write a poem about it, and then I'll be so glad I kept this"?

No. I know that no matter how much good luck they brought you in the past, you have to let albatrosses go. Even if that means they'll go sit in the landfill and no one will ever appreciate or understand them. This includes all dead waterfowl, rodent fragments, and anything at all with pee on it.

But the decisions are bound to get more complicated than that. The charge is ever so much more complicated than simply cleaning up: it's learning how to change in the way I look at things while still remaining *me*.

(Can I keep the mouse, though? I'm thinking of naming him Samuel.)

Ready? Set? Here I go.

CHAPTER TWO

WE BEGIN

"Just what makes that little old ant
Think he'll move that rubber tree plant?"
—Frank Sinatra, "High Hopes" (1959)

The day we officially began work on the Hell Room was the beginning of February vacation for my younger daughter, Ilsa. That fact either made it a wonderfully opportune or completely disastrous moment to begin. I should point out that Ilsa is ten and, if anything, mildly bewildered by my clutter-busting efforts.

As far as Ilsa is concerned, the world exists so that she can collect it. She never gets rid of anything, including old candy wrappers, parking lot rocks, and, most recently, a particularly repugnant pile of mouse fur and bones that came home from a school science project. If Ilsa tells you she wants to "save the world," I would take her *very* literally.

One day, when I was exclaiming about some mess or other in the house, she tried to explain her viewpoint to me.

"Momma, that's the *reality*," Ilsa said sagely. "There's always going to be a lot of stuff. The house is *full* of stuff."

And she was right, of course. Big dreams aside, I had no plans over the course of the next year to morph into a candidate for the next episode of *Tiny Houses* or become one of those people who fit all their belongings into a children's shoebox so they can fulfill their lifelong dream of canoeing around the world. No, Ilsa was right. There *was* always going to be a lot of Stuff.

No, the change I had in mind was a lot less drastic than simply pulling a Dumpster up to the window and getting out a snow shovel. And in that sense it was also a lot harder too: in one way or other I was going to have to confront every one of the things I had deemed worth keeping—or, at least, not worth the distress of deciding about—and reevaluate it. Over and over again. Although I have yet to figure out what drives my compulsion to save, I know this much: it is the thought of making a bad decision, one that I will some day regret, that keeps me up at night.

So even though Ilsa and I are quite possibly two peas in a pod on this issue, and her trying to help me might be likened to rubber cement trying to help glue be less sticky, nevertheless, we were going in. Today was the day, and here we both were. I had little choice but to enlist her help. Today, I had decided, was different than the past. Today I wasn't going to make middling progress only to have it instantly disappear while my back was turned. Today, I thought, would be different, simply because *I said it was*. I had no plan, no strategy, beyond that thought in my mind: *just begin*.

Because I desperately didn't want to feel discouraged, I decided to begin by tackling the part of the room I imagined would be the easiest, lowest-hanging fruit of all: a space that once upon a time had functioned as the kids'"art area." Somehow this area had ended up being used little but trashed a lot. And the more trashed it got, the less the kids wanted to use it, until eventually we came to the point at which the kids would rappel in to grab some popsicle sticks or colored pencils and then dash off to another part of the house to actually *use* them.

It is worth mentioning at this point, in case you haven't guessed it, that I can rationalize a lot. *A lot.* I am right up there with Walter Mitty when it comes to imagining amazing, fantastic new lives for all the sad, broken, useless things I end up holding on to. However, I knew that even *I* would have trouble rationalizing keeping dried-out magic markers missing their caps, glue sticks with no more glue, and paintbrushes permanently petrified with pigment…so in the interest of pure momentum, this is where we would begin. Perhaps predictably, Ilsa decided she'd really prefer to *make* a painting on the easel with some soppy sponge markers rather than help me "organize" (whatever *that* meant). We agreed, on the condition that she just couldn't "make more mess" in the process. Ha ha! As if that were actually possible.

And so, without fanfare, we opened the dreaded door and began pushing and shoving our way in. Once upon a time there had been actual paths through the mess, so re-excavating those trails was by necessity the first order of business. I resisted the overwhelming urge to go find a machete, instead swooping junk with both hands to one side or the other to establish a little goat path. After only a few minutes we were able to arrive at the middle of the large room and the erstwhile art area. Ilsa commenced painting while I grabbed garbage bags and wove around like a drunken high-wire act, throwing away or recycling a small mountain of half-used art supplies: paint containers missing lids, partially denuded sticker sheets, and scrawled-on, cut up paper. Among the preliminary casualties were several sheets of adhesive letters I've been carting around from place to place since I was Ilsa's age, a half-finished purple duct tape skirt, a hefty pile of *Town Reports* (for some reason our town's proposed annual budgets for the past dozen or so years had migrated to the children's art area), and several random blocks of wood.

At this point I had broken out into a sweat. My tiny little two-foot-square area looked better-ish but was still crammed with all the art supplies that were perfectly good. And beyond that…I looked around at the daunting landscape of random papers and clothing and objects and tried very hard not to be completely discouraged. I told myself this is how it starts, one stupid thing at a time. One tiny decision at a time. At the end of about two hours I had thrown away two large bags of garbage. It *was* heartening to have a path now, to see actual carpeting in places again, even if it was littered with dead bugs and the occasional splotch of dried paint.

Ilsa, meanwhile, had somehow amid the cyclonic mess managed to finish two rather soggy masterpieces and gone on to rediscover a knotted quilt project she had left half-done years ago. She then stopped me from throwing out some fabric her sister had been attempting to fashion into slippers, what—four, five years ago, maybe?

"She's going to *want* those!" Ilsa protested. "She hasn't *finished* them!"

It was okay. I had to pick my battles. Also, I was desperately in need of reinforcements.

It was time to include Greta.

Whereas Ilsa is still young enough that I can simply inform her of something the family is doing and it does not really, truly occur to her to object, I wasn't at all sure how my older daughter Greta would react to news of the new "project." After all, I suppose she could be forgiven for being a bit skeptical about her mom's brilliant ideas when the last one involved giving up the world's most beloved food additive for the year. Ahem. Add to this the fact that she was entering her fifteenth year on this earth and consequently could be allowed the intermittent sigh, the occasional "whatever," and the tendency to gravitate toward her room, her girlfriends, and the latest installment in *The Hunger Games* saga. So far, so good, though; no screaming fights or lengthy arguments on the topic of what constitutes appropriate attire for the occasion of stepping outside the house (both of which played a remarkably large role in my teenage years). No, nothing too scarring to my psyche yet beyond the creeping eventual realization that she is growing up and away from me.

As she should.

Sniff.

But, I wondered, when the idea of the Hell Room project was broached, would the wanton contrariness of teenagehood raise its ugly head? Would she think it was *lame*? (Or was that not the appropriate dismissive word anymore? What if she used the new word and I had no idea what it meant?) Would she—and this was important—bring up my promise never to put my family through another yearlong project again? So, one afternoon as we drove home from school I broached the subject: would she consider being an ally in my war on the Hell Room? I braced for her response. Would she freak? Be disinterested? Would actual eye rolling be involved? You can understand my trepidation: what teenager gets excited about being asked to help *clean*? And *organize*? *Wow*! Fun stuff, Mom! Why don't we just schedule a nice relaxing root canal while we're at it?

I was in luck, though, because Greta loves a good project. *And* she can organize and sort, file and label like nobody's business. One look at her bedroom might suggest otherwise— with most clothes never quite making the decision as to whether they prefer the hamper or hanging in the closet and opting instead for the ambiguous safety of the floor—but as we drove along Greta explained to me that the Hell Room was different. She didn't see this as the drudgery of cleaning but rather an exciting challenge. To hear her tell it, it seemed like an adventure into the unknown—who knows what buried treasure we might find? It was as if a switch had been flicked: she became instantly animated and began peppering me with a million questions.

It reminds me of when I was a kid, much closer to Ilsa's age than to Greta's, and how I had felt about our basement. At that time the basement seemed to me a kind of magical place, mysterious and kind of scary. I was afraid of going down there at night, and if I did have to go get an empty box or retrieve some clothes from the dryer I was always half-certain some slimy creature would reach out and grab my leg before I could race back up the stairs to my parents and safety.

The laundry room in the basement was a big, overly lit space with a linoleum floor and white concrete walls; the washing machine and dryer took up one wall of the room, and the rest of it ended up as default "extra" space and there-fore was filled with an odd assortment of things. When it wasn't scary nighttime, I loved to poke around and find things in there: glass jars full of leftover nails, an old doll carriage, boxes of dusty, ancient-looking books. All perfectly ordinary but new to me, which made them kind of fascinating. But the very best part was this closed red door that I saw on the far wall. I had never seen it opened. Where did it go?

I thought about this mystery as I was in bed falling asleep—and I dreamed that behind that red door was a whole wing of the house I had never seen, with rooms and rooms full of objects that were actually ours but we never knew were there. Or that it opened, Alice-in-Wonderland-like, on to another world parallel to our own. And because of that red door, we could escape to another world anytime we liked.

One day, I couldn't resist. I went to take a peek.

Sadly, as it turned out, it *wasn't* a door to another house or another world. It wasn't, in fact, a door to anywhere: it was a *spare* door, propped up against the wall.

At first I was disappointed. After some thought, though, I realized I could still keep that dream inside my head—and enjoy the thought of it whenever I wanted. Maybe someday I'd happen upon an undiscovered Egyptian tomb or a real buried pirate's treasure, but in the meantime I had the *idea* of the hidden discovery, waiting to be made, and for the moment that was pretty good.

So, is *that* what Greta got from me? I wondered, as she started reeling off ideas for the room—the thrill of discovery, even in the mundane? It occurred to me that while Ilsa had inherited my love for collecting, saving, and treasuring objects, Greta had clearly inherited my love for transformation and for finding the adventure in the ordinary. And what could be more ordinary than a room filled with stuff?

I can only imagine that the uncluttering gods were smiling down on us as we made the drive home from school, Greta throwing out ideas all the way. Could we finally take out that stinky, stained old carpet? Ooh! What about the window seat? Could we re-cover it in something a little less, you know, *boring*? Were the built-in shelves coming out? How about painting the floor *green*?

I had my ally.

———

Now that the troops were secured, I felt the need for some sort of strategy. This could be tough because in my long history of keeping things I had amassed a fair-sized collection of anti-clutter reading material, none of which I had ever found remotely effective or inspiring. I had read dozens of articles in magazines with enticing before-and-after photo spreads and exclamation point–filled titles, all to no avail. And then I heard about a fabulous new organizing book, so I purchased it. When I went to read it I was…pretty sure it was…around here…somewhere…

Oh dear.

Japanese cleaning expert Marie Kondo took the organizing world by storm with a wildly successful, *New York Times* bestselling guidebook for the neatness-challenged, and what do *I* do? I buy it and *immediately lose it*. Like a virgin in a volcano, *The Life-Changing Magic of Tidying Up* had been sacrificed to the gods of the vast, gaping maw that, apparently, was my house. I mean, I know that people, *normal* people *without* Hell Rooms, lose things all the time in their houses. But to lose this particular book at this particular moment? It felt like more than disorganization; it felt like a bad omen.

At least I had read a review of the book, which had detailed a few of the author's principles for organizing. The phrase that resonated with me the most was the question she said would-be declutterers should ask themselves when looking at virtually any object under consideration for the old heave-ho. For Kondo-ites, it had become something of a catch phrase.

"*Does it spark joy?*"

It's a question of wonderful simplicity. In fact, ever since I had read the review that question had been resonating in my brain as I went about my day—and when I looked at things I would think to myself often, randomly, "Yes, but does it *spark joy?*"

Of course, I do need things in my life that don't "spark joy"—snow tires, for example. Or the ear thermometer. But when you start to view your personal world though this lens, the number of items that fit this description may surprise you. For example, I realized that my cleaning rags "spark joy" because I made them from a well-loved, but worn-out, set of flannel sheets. When I look at them—*every* time—I feel a teeny, tiny, yet perceptible glimmer of what might just be joy. It's part I'm-still-loving-these-sheets and part satisfaction that I've been able to find a new life for them, conserving and reusing what we've got rather than using up a few more trees' worth of paper towels.

So I may have lost my instruction book, for the time being, but I had a new mantra, which I fervently hoped would help me break out of the Stuff vortex I currently found myself in.

Next, I needed to think about my motivation: What would the Hell Room be, post-exorcism? I mean, you know, besides *not embarrassing*. If this were a romantic comedy, I suppose now would be time for the montage of me with my interior decorator best friend transforming the room into an over-the-top closet complete with chandelier made of Godiva chocolate and Prada handbags. Or surprising my husband with a "man cave" featuring a beer fountain and framed paintings of nachos.

But I think if we are lucky enough to have an "anything" room at our disposal, it should really be something that resonates with one's personality on a fundamental level. I like shoes and chocolate as much as the next girl, but they aren't exactly the building blocks of my personality.

What *is* something pretty fundamental to me is the idea of *making things*. Ever since I can remember I've always loved to make stuff—I loved the sheer act of taking something and, with a little effort, transforming it into something else. It's why I loved baking as a kid as well as art class. In fact, I'm fairly confident that I drove my parents a little crazy with my penchant for always wanting to be *making* something. *Mom!* Teach me to knit! *Dad!* Take me to the hobby shop to buy felt and glitter! Does anyone mind if I cut up this skirt and draw on it? Anybody care if I use/repurpose/destroy this shoebox/baking powder tin/lace tablecloth?

More often than not, my aspirations went far beyond my abilities. One year I found a magazine article about how to make a new bar of soap out of saved old bits of soap—those tiny little slivers that are so small nobody wants to be bothered with trying to lather them anymore. *This was great!* I thought. *Using things that people would otherwise discard in order to make something new!* It was right up my alley, *and* it was free. For months I saved up all the little ends of soap in a box. One day, when I finally had enough, I followed the article's directions and tried to melt them all together in a pot on the stove. They didn't melt as much as they were supposed to, but I managed to get them to kind of stick together, so the end result was a ball of different-colored melted smush with the occasional hair sticking out. I wrapped up this horror and proudly presented it to Mom for Mother's Day.

I invite you to picture the look on my mother's face when she opened up my Frankenstein soap. After only a moment's hesitation, she declared that she *loved* it. That soap quickly disappeared, never to be seen again. This sort of thing happened a lot.

So the idea of transforming the Hell Room into a sort of craft den held great appeal for me. But admittedly, devoting an entire huge room in our house just for little old me and my hobbies might have struck me as just a tad selfish, if not for the fact that I have two daughters who have inherited my passion for making stuff and then some. Now *I* am the one rescuing their knitting, wondering how late the felt and glitter store will be open, considering requests to use the glue gun or the chainsaw. Although it's sometimes exhausting having two such energetic, creative beings under my jurisdiction, I wouldn't have it any other way.

So, when *I* imagine our newly made-over, nonessential room, I picture a room filled with all our many tools and materials for making things—my sewing machine, my 387 pairs of knitting needles, all the girls' origami papers and pipe cleaners. Also—and this is key—actual *space* in which to sit down and make something.

At this juncture, I do feel duty-bound to point out that being a creative person is at least one of the reasons I *have* a Hell Room in the first place. Just in case you don't have a person afflicted with a creative mind in your life, I'll explain why: you see potential in pretty much *everything*. Let's put on this pair of creative rose-colored glasses, and you'll see what I mean. Garbage isn't garbage anymore. Fabric bits and paper scraps suddenly look interesting, rusted car parts seem intriguing, old, dried-up lipstick containers seem downright useful. Remember those little nubs of soap I terrorized my mother with? Honestly, you have to take the creative glasses off every once in a while or risk becoming the kind of person who spends decades making a colossal sculpture in the garage out of old tinfoil and Styrofoam peanuts.

Obviously, this characteristic was bad enough when it was just me, but now that there are *three* of us making things out of other things, it is exponentially worse. There's always *some*one who could use any given object—the twist tie from the bread bag! The lint from the screen in the dryer! The pebble that got stuck in my shoe!—in an art project. Or craft thingamajig. Or something.

As in: "That old sneaker would make a *great* Santa Maria in my Columbus diorama!"

And: "I could use these rusty picture hooks to make a beautiful necklace!"

Be forewarned: art college will only make this phenomenon far, far worse. After getting degrees certifying myself as an Official Creative Person, for years I existed in a kind of weird identity limbo, never quite knowing what I was *really* going to be when I "grew up" and consequently never willing to close off any possible options. Would I end up being an installation artist who lives at a hip Tribeca loft in a tent sewn together out of every birthday card I've ever received? Or perhaps I would be the reclusive creator who makes delicate origami sculptures out of the exclamation point–filled notes we passed in sixth grade. Maybe I would be like assemblage artist Joseph Cornell and make haunting shadow boxes out of rusty flour scoops and old Scrabble tiles. The Hell Room was my enabler in these fantasies, always whispering in my ear: *Who knows? It's possible! Don't rule it out!*

Consequently it has been a deep relief to finally realize where it is I am going, and, though I adore art like a long-lost sister, to acknowledge that, no, I will never become the visual artist I studied to be in college. Upon making that realization, not that long ago I succeeded in parting with a box of fascinating and expensive "future collage materials" I had accumulated, such as old three-tined forks and antique hand brooms, to an artist friend who really *did* make collages and shadow boxes. I tried *very* hard not to look back.

I still did, of course. Regret may be my middle name. Nevertheless, I knew, for my own good, that the time had come to get better at this sort of thing—a *lot* better.

Lucky for me, Greta and Ilsa were—to one degree or another—*in*. In case I faltered along the way, I now had my own personal Greek chorus on hand to call me on it. Simply by their presence, their collusion, and their investment in the final outcome (a room for our projects!) I was counting on them to keep me honest, to give me propulsion, to feed the fire of change. Left to my own devices, I'd been feeding the gravity of an endless black hole, never quite crossing over but feeling the pull to the dark side, which was keeping everything.

And I knew that was not a place I wanted to go. I had seen firsthand what keeping everything *really* looked like.

CHAPTER THREE

THE HOARDER

"You can't have everything. Where would you put it?"
—Steven Wright

O ne morning the previous fall I had gotten a text message from my friend Annette: "Gary died. Last chance to see house. You in?"

And just like that I was on a field trip to experience a house unlike any I had ever seen.

In fact, Annette and I had been talking about visiting Gary[4] for months. The best massage therapists, as those of you who are lucky enough to have one like Annette will know, multitask as a sort of confessor-slash-psychiatrist-slash-advice columnist. Every time I went to get a massage from her for the "keyboard neck" I get from my horrible typing posture, the subject would come up again: I would talk about clutter and Stuff and my difficulty parting with so much as an expired Tic Tac and my fascination with shows like *Hoarders*.

---

4. Okay, you're right. That isn't his real name.

Annette would say, "Well, if you are *really* interested in hoarding, you've got to go see Gary's house," but I had felt nervous about it, and I had been stalling.

I mean, yeah, I was fascinated, and sure, if the description was accurate, Gary's house would make my Hell Room look like the tea parlor at Windsor Castle, but I still felt a little...*funny* about being a clutter tourist. Was it...*okay?* I didn't know Gary. If we went when he was home, would he be...angry? And if we went when he *wasn't* home, would that be...right? I had so much ambivalence about the matter that I probably never would've made it over there. But then, as with so many things, an unexpected shift in the dynamic changed everything. Gary had gone to that great big pile of Stuff in the sky, and therefore it was today or never. And so, over the river and through the woods to the hoarder's house we would go.

Pulling into the short dirt driveway, I was surprised to realize that the house, from the outside, was quite unremarkable. The yard looked downright *neat* by country standards. The shaggy but maintained grass yard was empty save for a large pile of logs off to one side. I wondered, *Could this really be the place I had heard such remarkable stories about?*

Once we parked, however, and came around the corner, it was clear that we were in the right place. The mudroom porch around back was not so much crowded as it was *blockaded*, stuffed right up to hip level with an enormous pile of random objects. Standing sentry just before it stood an overstuffed blue La-Z-Boy right on the grass. Altogether, it didn't look like the entryway to a house as much as it resembled an especially cozy corner of the local landfill. Beyond, I could just glimpse the crazy topography of objects that we had come to see. It went on in every direction inside the house like sand in the desert. It looked like nothing I had ever seen before. It was daunting.

I was there with both Annette and her husband Stan, which was good because Stan was an expert—in both Gary and the navigation of his house. Friends from church, Stan had helped Gary move out a few months prior when "Miss M" (his ex-wife, with whom he had lived) had died. Subsequently, Stan had helped him move back *in* after he was kicked out of a friend's house for almost burning it down. Twice.

It was Stan who had excavated the three belongings Gary had brought with him during that short stint away: a mattress, a table, and a chair. It really *couldn't* have been more; it took Stan five and a half hours to extricate the table alone from its habitation in the entryway because not even a single sheet of newspaper could be discarded—or even *moved*—without Gary's careful examination.

"There could be articles—about *me*—in them," Gary had explained, carefully picking crumpled bits of newsprint up from the floor, from the piles.

Stan had been sympathetic and patient; he was kind of amazed with Gary and his monstrous accumulation. He didn't find it off-putting or horrifying but somewhat fascinating. I found it fascinating too, at least in theory. I wasn't sure how I'd feel when we got inside.

And now Stan would be our tour guide. He recommended Annette and I don the dust masks we had brought. Realizing that I would've been better off in rock-climbing gear rather than the denim skirt and flats I had on, I took Stan's hand to steady me as we climbed up and over the initial two-foot-high hump of detritus. And we were in.

It was dim, and because the electricity had been shut off

years ago, it wasn't going to get any brighter. As my eyes adjusted, the room spread out before me in all directions. An expansive living room had once existed here, probably once quite lovely in a rustic way, encircling a two-sided flagstone fireplace. I imagined the days, decades ago, when this had been—I was told—a cozy ski lodge for perhaps eight or ten guests. A warm fire would've blazed in that hearth, the large picture windows affording views of the famous New England snow.

Its current state, however, was another matter altogether. Stuff was—to put it politely—*every-freaking-where*. Piles and mounds and stacks and hills and heaps and loads and oh-my-God-everywhere *Stuff*. Piled waist high and ten feet deep in every direction were old clothes, game boards, books, empty containers, milk glass vases, dusty album covers, badminton racquets, oil paintings. I saw evidence of an electric organ under a blanket and an unused tag sale sign and a box of 8-track tapes and a roll of wrapping paper and radios from several different eras. It was hard for the brain to register what any one thing in particular was because it was all amassed like a geologic formation, solidly and with no apparent logic. This wasn't a house at all…it was a landscape of crap.

Fortunately for us there was a trail through these woods. From the spot where the three of us stood huddled by the entryway, two paths split off in a "Y," each one just wide enough to allow a person to pass. The way was mostly clear, although as we went along, the occasional set of horizontal chair legs or a large ice chest would have to be climbed over in order to continue on our way. Old newspapers covered the pathway like paving stones.

I breathed into my dust mask and had the odd sensation

that we were scuba diving in a shipwreck. Stepping in slow motion, we followed the newspaper trail around the fireplace, rounding the corner to the far side of the living room where we encountered the entryway to the kitchen or, rather, what had once *been* the kitchen. Peering in, one could find proof of that previous existence in the legions of ancient jars and containers that filled every horizontal surface. A battalion of salad dressing bottles and mayonnaise and pickle jars stood at attention, all with labels whose fonts and colors identified them as at least ten years old. I wondered just how much of a field day a biologist could have in there, cataloguing different states of extreme food decay, just before I looked up to marvel at the explosive hole in the ceiling where the upstairs pipes had one day frozen and burst, never to be repaired.

Stan explained that Miss M had suspected the plumber of stealing from her piles of belongings, and so, rather than deal with such supposedly unsavory characters, she and Gary had left the water turned off. They would pee into jars for the rest of their lives.

We soldiered on. There was a tiny room next to the kitchen that was so crammed it was pretty much barricaded, but Stan managed to climb his way over to the closet to ascertain that it was, as Gary had described, filled two levels deep with Miss M's fancy evening dresses, now ruined souvenirs of another life, dusty and moth eaten.

Crossing back across the living room we entered the wing that jutted off to one side of the house where the inn's guests had once stayed. Off the long hallway shot perhaps eight single bedrooms, dormitory-style, numbers still glued to the door frames. I goggled at the layers of history, the archae-ology of this place. Except an excavation here would likely require not tiny brushes and dental picks but a pick axe and a decontamination suit.

The going got tougher as the path became further clogged. Half of the lodgers' hallway width was entirely blocked with piles of objects, and underfoot the path became more rugged. Instead of walking on newsprint we were now treading on uneven piles of clothing and sheets wadded up with what most people would call trash: empty bottles, half-filled jars, and pieces of food cartons. Stan explained that for the last three years Miss M had been bedridden and living in this wing. Gary had cared for her—feeding her from jars and cans. (Of course, no plumbing or electricity meant no stove and no refrigerator. Stan described how Gary would open a jar, of mayonnaise, say, use it once, and then put it down. Never to be refrigerated, indeed, possibly never to be touched again.)

For her part, Miss M threw jars and containers—of food, pee, and God knows what else—out the one window that was within her arm's reach from the bed. Stan described the resulting pile beneath her window that, until recently removed, had pointed like a garbage arrow to Miss M's location.

At this point, it was all starting to *get* to Annette. Unlike Stan, Annette's reaction to the scene was almost exclusively horror and repulsion. She hung back, as Stan and I pressed on through the hallway, sticking our heads into each room.

Stan kept marveling at the things he recognized in the midst of the chaos, kept talking about what one might find that was salvageable and interesting...perhaps even valuable. Rumor had it that, in addition to Miss M's once-impressive eveningwear collection, there was a box of diamond rings somewhere in her bedroom. If indeed they were there, would anyone ever find them? When the doctor came to pronounce Miss M dead, he'd had to prostrate himself across a two-foot-high pile of stuff just to be able to reach in and take her pulse.

I, meanwhile, stopped to marvel at the lack of evidence of mice and other vermin. Where was all the mouse poop? The bits of shredded fabric and stashed-away clots of corn and seeds? Since moving to the country I'd come to understand that small rodents are magicians. No matter what I did, they managed to find their way into the carefully taped boxes in my attic, shoes in the back of the closet, the drawer under the stove. If that happened in even the cleanest, most organized parts of my house, then why hadn't this place been transformed into a vermin carnival? Stan pointed out that they probably had whole networks of tunnels *underneath* the piles—the thought of which gave me momentary shivers. I pictured an entire subterranean rodent metropolis, complete with micro-batch coffee roasters and Internet cafés.

We made our way, gingerly, back through the hallway. Annette was clearly unnerved, but she was hanging in there. She rejoined us back in the living room as we made the final foray up the stairs to the one-time innkeeper's residence, which, as it happened, was also the place where Gary had been found dead in a chair only four days earlier.

The stairs, actually, were clean. Surprisingly so. A few vases, some paper, but mostly clear. I was nervous that there'd be some...*smell* up there. I thought about my dear friend's brother, who had been found dead after two full weeks in a closed apartment. In Ohio. In August. Almost nothing was salvageable, but the cleaners had brought her a tiny box of papers and videotapes, which were redolent with the smell of...well, *death*. It was that smell that always lurks somewhere beneath the scent of the fresh flowers and breath mints at funeral homes. You *know* it if you've smelled it. *That* smell.

So I was acutely aware that this might, at some point, get really unpleasant as we climbed the small stair. I was really hoping not to throw up, for example. This was on my mind firstly because throwing up is quite unpleasant, but secondly because it struck me as disrespectful to throw up in the house of a dead man I had never met, and lastly because that would somehow, in my mind, bring me into a much more intimate relationship with this environment than I cared to imagine. I mean, up until this point I had seen myself as something akin to a scuba diver swimming through a shipwreck, or an astronaut wrapped in my own separate atmospheric bubble. But the fact was that I *wasn't* wearing a space suit. I *wasn't* separate. I was right here in this poor dead man's house, ogling his most personal belongings and taking iPhone pictures like a tourist at a freak show.

Once again it occurred to me to wonder: was this...*wrong*? Like, morally reprehensible? Were we effectively sightseeing on someone's deathbed? I wasn't sure, right at that moment, how I felt about all that.

All I knew was this was my opportunity, and I had to press on. I *wanted* to press on. Why? What was so fascinating about Gary and Miss M's house anyway? Piles of someone else's crap? Was it the marveling that someone could actually live this way? Was it imagining the time-lapse photos one might have taken over the years as it started out manageable and got worse and worse and *worse*... And why were Stan and I so fascinated while Annette was so repulsed?

It occurred to me to wonder if I was trying to scare myself. After all, here was a cautionary tale in full living color, better than any reality show by far. In my imagination the deep voice of the house seemed to intone out of the very walls themselves: *have trouble parting with things, do you?* Dramatic pause.

So.

Did.

Gary.

It was less catastrophic up here than on the first floor, which wasn't to say it was *good*, but a lot more of the floor was visible. In fact, save for a bookcase lined with a full set of dusty encyclopedias, the entire hallway was actually fairly clear. Clustered around the small central hallway were four tiny bedrooms and a weird divided bathroom with two doorways. Looking around, I realized that this was the first time we had seen actual *furniture* in the house—although presumably the bedrooms downstairs had mattresses in them at the very least, but if they were there they had been so completely covered as to be rendered invisible. Up here, a bed with actual head and footboards was visible in one room. Furniture of indeterminate use was stacked up every which way in others.

Stan, who wasn't wearing a dust mask, thought one of the rooms smelled worse than the other three, and he surmised that must have been where Gary had been discovered. Luckily, with my mask on and the metal bar pushed down to conform to the shape of my nose, it turned out I wasn't smelling much of anything.

Up till now I had maintained my illusion of separateness by touching nothing in the house save for occasionally leaning my palm on a wall to steady myself while stepping along uneven pathways made up of piles of clothing and sheets. (Stan had, conversely, picked up items here and there and gotten a mysterious goo on his hands that he was choosing not to think too hard about.) But now I broke the fourth wall: I reached out and turned the knob of a hallway door, revealing a small closet inside. An ironing board and a stepladder leaned against the back wall—nothing else.

Nothing.

I almost laughed out loud. It was so normal looking—so completely ordinary. And so spare. Like a closet from a Shaker village. Once upon a time this house had been very different than it was now—here was the evidence.

I wondered, as one must inevitably do when confronted with the extremes of human behavior, what is it that has to happen to a person's brain circuitry to make one behave in such a self-destructive manner—collecting and keeping and amassing until one practically buries oneself alive. Just as something about hoarding denies death—if I just keep everything I can't die!—there is something else about hoarding that courts death, invites it. I felt it that day as we made our way through the house: an overwhelming sense of foreboding.

Remember that wall of stuff we had to pole-vault over in order to enter at the mudroom door? Stan said that was *new.*

"What did you do now, Gary?" Stan had said out loud when we arrived and saw it.

I wondered if Gary had, in fact, *known* he was dying. Earlier in the week, on the very day he died, he had been told he had to leave once and for all. The house had belonged to Miss M, and she had decidedly *not* left it to him. He was effectively squatting in his own home: just him and all four million of his and Miss M's belongings, from the racks of evening gowns to the iced tea bottles full of pee. It was clear to everyone he would have to go, but where?

And so, like a wounded animal, he had piled his belongings

in front of the door—as if pulling into place the capstone of a tomb. He had plodded to the furthest, most remote part of the house. And, curled up in a chair with his belongings swirling protectively around him, he died.

I wondered, not for the first time, about the dividing line between enthusiastic collecting and hoarding, between Gary and me. At what point does the death creep in? When does the natural order reverse itself and the owners are run by the habitation instead of the other way around? At what point do all the substances become a cringe-inducing goo? At what point do the ghosts of Vincent Price and Edgar Allan Poe start lurking in the door frames, smirking?

After we had navigated our way back through and out of the house, Annette was greatly relieved. She had an official case of the creeps and wanted to take a shower as soon as possible to make her skin stop crawling. Stan, meanwhile, after guiding us out, went back in to try to find a few snapshots of Gary for the upcoming memorial service.

To me the task seemed a little like trying to locate a contact lens in Times Square, but I half wanted to go back in with him anyway just to see what he would find. I didn't. Probably that was good because once he started actually disturbing objects in Miss M's bedroom and handing some of them out the window, the smell almost made Annette lose her breakfast.

As we climbed back into the minivan to go, Annette was still emitting exclamations of horror. I was quiet. Pulling out of the dirt driveway I absentmindedly put the dust mask in my purse. After all, it was my souvenir of this experience.

Of course I wanted to keep it.

CHAPTER FOUR

PROBLEM? WHAT PROBLEM?

"Don't throw your trash in my backyard,
my backyard, my backyard
Don't throw your trash in my backyard,
my backyard's full."

—campfire song

True confession time: there's something I left out of that story about visiting Gary and Miss M's house. After Annette and I had emerged but before we climbed into her minivan and left, the pastor from their church showed up asking Stan if he could find any mementos in the house for use at Gary's memorial service.

Anxious to demonstrate that I was not some slack-jawed voyeur, I explained that I was a writer and this was a subject matter I identified with.

"Oh, so you're a hoarder?" she asked, pleasantly.

I stopped. It was as if I had been slapped. Then I regained my composure.

"Well…*no*! I mean, well—not on *this* scale…" I gestured vaguely toward the house.

I paused and tried again.

"I have a *room*. In my house. That looks like this." I gestured again toward the house. "A *big* room."

We chatted some more, but my mind was elsewhere. I was still back on "Oh, so you're a *hoarder*?"

The word had startled me. It *bothered* me. Hoarder was such a *dirty* word, especially given what we had just experienced in Gary and Miss M's house. It brought to mind images of filth...and decay and...what? There was something deviant about the term. For those of us with, oh, let's call them object permanence issues, there's a huge mental leap between "I have clutter!" (Ha ha! Don't we all?) and "I'm a hoarder!" (Eeew! Gross!)

After all, when I told Annette I wanted to explore my Stuff problem, she had thought immediately of this house. For the first time it occurred to me to wonder: did my Hell Room *really* put me in the same category as folks like Gary and Miss M? Was the pastor right?

Despite my best efforts, the woman's words continued to stick in my mind for the remainder of the day, like a raspberry seed in my teeth. My jacket still smelled mildly of mildew, and there was a large tear in my jean skirt where I had stretched it too far climbing over the mountains of objects.

That isn't me! I thought defensively. How could anyone look at me and think I could be like *that*?

And all at once it hit me: the lady doth protest too much, methinks.

It was a moment of clarity. I didn't like it, of course, but there was a certain sense of relief.

Hi. My name is Eve. And I am a hoarder.

It's taken me a while to get to this point. I've known for some time, primarily because my therapist tells me so, that I'm obsessive-compulsive. Sadly, it's not the kind of obsessive-compulsive disorder that makes you notice tiny details of a crime scene so you can solve it before anyone else but the kind where you *can't stop* having certain thoughts. Weird thoughts, awful thoughts, irrational thoughts—we all have them, of course, but OCD people like me *can't let go of them*. There's something in our brain chemistry—like a clogged drain pipe—that holds on to these thoughts when it ought to let them go. So there these bad thoughts are, circling and circling the brain, endlessly.

When the drain is clogged in your sink, of course you can't use it, can't put new water into it, because something else is in the way. So it is with OCD. Because you're fixated on some bad idea your brain should've thrown away two hours ago, you can't move forward. You get stuck.

And you torture yourself. That's the other fun part! When I say "torture," I'm not talking about physical torture, but sadness. Misery. Depression. Hopelessness. Stress. A feeling of being overwhelmed by life and an inability to cope with any of it. Paralysis.

In my case, it often took the form of lying on the couch feeling too sad to get up. This was what my smart brain had done to me, all for want of a better thought drainer. So you can see the parallel, right? Suffering from the inability to discard unnecessary thoughts is not unlike the inability to discard unnecessary Stuff. I am nothing if not consistent.

So what did I do? Well, I had years and years and *years* of therapy with a wonderful psychiatrist, who I grew to trust. The very first day I entered her office she raised the possibility of coupling medication with talk therapy, and before she could even get to the end of her sentence I was shaking my head vigorously. Nope. I was *not* going to join Prozac Nation and go through life on a happy little fake butterfly cloud made of rainbow fairy dust—no, no, *no*. So, instead, we talked. And talked. And talked. And it helped. I got better. I got off the couch and got married, bought a house, had children. I functioned. And we kept talking. Every year or so she would broach the subject of medication with me again, and every year or so I would shake my head vigorously. Sure, I still suffered from bouts of depression and tortured myself with bad thoughts. Certainly, I had weird little ticks that no one else noticed—but who did that harm but me? Maybe I was being stubborn, but at least I wasn't harming anyone but myself. Right?

Then one day, at about age five, my daughter Greta looked up at me and said, "Look, Mommy! I'm being like *you*!" And what was this fabulous trait of mine she was emulating in order to be like me? She was *inspecting her vitamin*.

I was horrified. This was one of my nonsensical ritualistic behaviors that *I* thought no one else could see: every morning I'd turn my vitamin over and check it for…what? To make sure it was *really my vitamin*. See what I mean? This is behavior that makes no sense, and I *knew* that, intellectually, but as long as I went along with the program, I knew my brain would relax and let me go about my day. What if I failed to check that vitamin? Then I'd spend half the morning preoccupied, worried I had—somehow—taken *something else*. Maybe I'd have a reaction to it—or even get very ill. In fact, I'd start to feel ill just thinking about it. I'd have to lie down. You see? It was easier just to flip my vitamin over real quick before popping it in my mouth. Who would notice?

Turns out *Greta* had noticed. And if she had noticed this tiny detail, what else had she picked up? Did she notice that I always put my right shoe on before my left? That I never used the green plate? That I always had to carefully position the butter knife just so? And those were the things I *realized* I was doing. What other bizarre behaviors was I teaching her that I wasn't even fully *aware* of? It was that day I realized something had to be done. If not for my sake, for hers.

But I didn't. I had gotten past the "It will make me a different person!" argument against taking medication (since it was suddenly clear to me that this might not be such a bad thing, actually), but after I had peeled back that layer of the onion, there was another one right behind it: I was afraid. Desperately. Afraid of side effects. Afraid it would make me sick. I pictured my hair falling out in clumps. I pictured myself hallucinating wildly. I pictured myself violently ill, and these images circled my non-draining brain endlessly until the only way I could get any respite was to shelve the issue once more in the back storage closet of my mind. Phew.

It would have to take a crisis, of course. And that's what happened the year we took a trip to Sedona, Arizona, for the kids' February break. Actually it was Greta's February break since Ilsa had only recently entered the world and was about a year old. We had rented a single-story house in the suburban sprawl that creeps outward from the picturesque town center, framed on every side by impressive red sandstone formations.

It was gorgeous there, and everyone was relaxed and having a nice time going on hikes and eating Mexican-style food. I was too—until one day in the kitchen I had one of those thoughts I mentioned before: the kind of stupid, awful thoughts you have that your brain rightly discards immediately, like: I could drive my car into this telephone pole! Not because you want to or ever would, but just because your brain is aware that it is physically possible. Dumb thought, right? A down-the-drain thought.

Except the drain is clogged. In this case, I envisioned Ilsa being hurt. By me. And once I saw it, I couldn't stop seeing it. It didn't go down the drain the way it was supposed to. And I panicked. I imagined myself hurting Ilsa—my beautiful, adorable baby girl—over and over again. I didn't *want* to hurt her—any more than I wanted to drive my car into a telephone pole—but there the image was, in my brain, and there it stayed. I began to fear that I *would*—somehow—hurt her. Perhaps I would sleepwalk? I was utterly petrified.[5]

Locked in the bathroom, I had a panic attack over it. My breathing went shallow, and I felt feverish. I had become afraid of…myself.

That was the moment I decided: I would try the medication. And this time I really did. Steve likes to poke fun at the stupendous amount of stubbornness that has to be involved for a person to ignore a doctor's express medical advice for, oh, say, a little over ten years, but I got there.

Today, I am a different person. I take an infinitesimal daily dose of what's called a selective serotonin reuptake inhibitor (translation: Roto-Rooter for my brain). My husband will be the first one to point out the differences between Eve and ever-so-slightly-medicated Eve.

"First, you're more relaxed," he'll point out. "And you let

---

5. Now, before anyone tiptoes off to dial Child Protective Services, let me point out that having "unwanted thoughts" about harming yourself or others is a well-documented symptom of both obsessive-compulsive disorder *and* postpartum depression. Unfortunately, this is a thing.

things go easier. Before, you used to get...stuck. And you're happier. But you can be more...*scattered* too."

"Scattered enough to want me to go back to unmedicated Eve?"

"Oh, *no*! No."

And after all that worry, *are* there side effects? Sure. Every once in a while I get this antsy, uncomfortable feeling in my legs (called restless leg syndrome. Yes! It sounds made up, but it does exist!), especially if I'm sitting for hours on a long car or plane trip. It isn't pleasant, but all things considered, I think I'm making an excellent trade: funky legs once a fortnight in exchange for a better life? Done!

And, yes, I'm a modified me. I used to worry that I would no longer be what I like to consider my creative, interesting self...that medication would sand off my edges and make me dull. Instead, what I found is that it released me from shackles that I wasn't even fully aware I was wearing, preoccupations that were keeping me from doing the things I had always dreamed of. Like...being an author. So I wrote a book. And I took up snowboarding. And learned to weave. And traveled to Italy...by myself.

It's amazing the things you can find to do with yourself when you aren't busy checking your vitamins.

Just because I'm now lightly medicated, however, doesn't mean I'm not still a little wacko. The obsessive tendencies are still there, but they're much, much quieter—it's as if the medication puts a great big pillow over that loudspeaker in my brain. I still always put my right shoe on first. I still wash my hands a fair amount more than most people I know. And you'll recall this funny thing I have in my house called the Hell Room.

So maybe I'm not one of the hoarder specimens you see

on the reality shows who have to sleep in the bathtub because there's no where else in the house left to go. But I can *see* it. I *feel* the thought pattern that points to that horizon, like an undertow. I look at a house like that of Gary and Miss M, and there is a part of me that *understands*.

Whereas my psychiatrist had diagnosed me with OCD, no one had ever diagnosed me as a hoarder. It is only in the past few years that such a conclusion would even have been possible because up until very recently hoarding was considered only a *symptom* of OCD, not a separate diagnosable condition. And while there is definitely a correlation—between 18 and 42 percent of obsessive-compulsives have hoarding issues—the problem is that not all hoarders have obsessive-compulsive disorder. Thus, the most recent *Diagnostic and Statistical Manual of Mental Disorders (DSM-5)*,[6] lists hoarding disorder as its own separate, diagnosable condition for the first time in medical history.

The coexistence of two possibly—but not necessarily—related disorders in one person is called a comorbidity. Fun, right? I am morbid in more ways than one.

Or am I? In the aftermath of visiting Gary and Miss M's house, I felt I had made a breakthrough. In this light, lots of things started to make sense that never had before. *This* is why I have so much trouble getting rid of my plastic yellow raincoat from when I was ten! *This* is why I have a room in my house that looks like the Noah's Ark of Crap and why cleaning it up seems so monumentally impossible to me. I am a hoarder.

---

6. Published by the American Psychiatric Association, the *DSM* is a kind of bible for the mental health profession. *DSM-5*, the edition we're talking about here, was released in 2013.

Ah.

*And yet…*I was far from reality show worthy. The very fact that I kept my "issue" so well hidden meant it wasn't completely out of control, which seemed to contradict my self-diagnosis. Weren't hoarders by definition people for whom their saving was so out of control that it was interfering with their lives?

In search of an answer, I paid a visit to several psychiatric websites that offer questions to use when assessing a potential hoarding problem. I've compiled them here into my own garbled version. So! Who's up for a quick quiz?

Are You a Hoarder? The Quiz!

1. Are you unable to discard (or recycle, sell, give away) things that most other people would get rid of?

    Does a dead mouse in a box count?

2. To what extent does clutter make it difficult to use the rooms and surfaces in your home?

    That depends a whooooole lot on which room you're talking about.

3. How often do you buy items or acquire free things that you do not need or have enough space for?

    Excuse me, could we please define the phrase "do not need"?

4. To what extent do your hoarding, saving, acquisition, and clutter affect your social, work, or everyday functioning?

Do you consider being able to find the *Annie* Playbill that Sarah Jessica Parker signed for me when I was ten "everyday functioning"?

5. How much does your clutter interfere with school, work, or your social or family life?

That depends in large part on whether the door is open or closed.

6. How much distress does clutter cause you?

Who, me? I'm fine! In fact, I hear bathtub-sleeping is all the rage in Iceland. Good for the sinuses.

Okay, in all seriousness, not that much distress. I mean, do I stay up late at night unable to sleep, tormented by graphic images of back taxes that aren't chronologically filed? The piles of sewing fabric lying unfolded? The legions of uncapped glitter pens that will likely not live to see another piece of construction paper? No.

Truthfully, I could go weeks, *months* even, without so much as cracking the door to the dreaded Hell Room.

I prefer to, really. It is almost as if that one part of the house could simply fall off like a scab and none of the four of us in our family would even notice until one of us needed some sock yarn or somebody's school portrait from kindergarten.

I have to say, with all due respect to the mental health professionals, who I'm sure are a terrific and very smart group of people who never have trouble discarding things most other people would get rid of, questions of this sort seem kind of…unhelpful. I don't think any of the factors cited—having enough space, affecting daily functioning, causing distress—are definitive indicators of hoarding disorder.

Would a hoarder ever really think he or she did "not have enough space" for something? Or be able to recognize when "keeping" was affecting "everyday functioning"? Isn't it all relative anyway because some people have enough space to keep their collections of stuff from interfering with their life and living spaces while others do not? By that logic, people with small houses would be more likely to be hoarders, even if they had saved less stuff than people in big houses.

And what about that last question: "How much distress does clutter cause you?" I've read many accounts asserting that often hoarders are not "caused distress" by their keeping at all. Quite the contrary: many hoarders describe the great comfort being surrounded by their belongings brings them. This is confirmed by hoarding reality shows that almost always show an outside force bringing about the intervention: threat of divorce, of condemning the house, of children being removed or estranged. The fact is that hoarding causes *other* people distress. Speaking for myself, I can attest to the fact that what distresses me most about the Hell Room is when *I try to clean it up.*

And this makes sense. There must be very positive feelings associated with saving and keeping in order for a person to go on doing it, especially over the protestations of others. Although I don't take comfort in the company of my piles of Stuff the way many hoarders reportedly do, I know that keeping things fulfills for me at least one very specific need: it alleviates the discomfort of indecision and the fear of making a mistake I will regret (what if I want/need/wish I had kept *this* someday?)

Of course, I can't deny that the existence of my Hell Room does cause me distress, or else I wouldn't be trying to clean it up in the first place, right? However, this distress takes very specific forms: the form of embarrassment (hello, energy assessment guy), frustration (I can't find the decorative hole punch, dammit), destructiveness (*please* tell me I did not just step on our wedding album), and yuckiness (you can't clean up a hairball you can't find).

Sometimes trying to pin down hoarding or diagnose it in any categorical way seems like an exercise in futility. It reminds me of that famous line from Supreme Court Justice Potter Stewart about not being able to define obscenity: "…but I know it when I see it."

I also think we get tripped up by the black-and-white terminology in place here. After all, doesn't it stand to reason that in between "normal" and "full-blown hoarder" we might find myriad gradations of in-between folks like me? If I hadn't thought about this before, once Greta and Ilsa and I began this project in earnest, the issue was on my mind a lot.

Suddenly we—they—all of us—would have to be allowed

to *talk* about the Hell Room—in public. Overnight, the cat was out of the proverbial bag, and my "little problem" was no longer a mortifying secret I could keep behind a locked door but instead fair game for polite conversation. Suddenly, the Hell Room officially *existed*. Friends and relatives might ask what we had done over the weekend, and someone would have to say, "We spent the weekend throwing away crap from the Hell Room!" which, of course, invited more questions. Despite my squeamishness on the subject, I figured this must be a positive development because I had progressed from admitting my problem to myself to admitting it to the world.

But it wasn't always that easy. Much to my amazement, people would argue the point. "Oh, but you don't *really* have a problem...not like *that!*" These were usually people who knew me pretty well, had visited my house, knew I wasn't going to be featured in *House Beautiful* anytime soon, but still couldn't quite bring themselves to view me in the same light as people who save their own toenails in pickle jars.

I felt strangely frustrated by this resistance, this well-intentioned denial. I was trying to *come out* here, people! I thought, *Oh yeah?* I had half a mind to take them upstairs and show them, if I wasn't fairly certain they might need resuscitation.

But they had a point because, as already noted, I *wasn't* reality show worthy—probably not even on community access cable. I was much too good at keeping my secret under wraps; it *hadn't* taken over my life, my husband *wasn't* threatening to leave me over it, the Board of Health *wasn't* sending over little men in hazmat suits. I felt the need for a new word—a term that would describe my particular in-between situation. What *was* I anyway?

I googled the word *hoarder* to find some clues. I supposed I could go with *pack rat*. After all, everyone knows what that is, and it's definitely of a lesser severity than hoarder...but did I really have to be a rodent? I could go with *magpie*, if not for the fact that they've gotten an unsavory reputation as the shoplifters of the bird world. What about *syllogomaniac*? Or *disposophobic*? These are fancy synonyms for hoarder and super fun to say at parties. ("Hi! This is my wife, Eve. She's disposophobic!") but probably too opaque. People might misunderstand and start asking me to operate on their spleen or something.

Maybe the person halfway between ordinary clutterer and high-level hoarder ought to be a...cloarder? That sounded like you'd gotten something stuck in your throat.

Cluttermonger?

Person of Stuff? Thing engineer? Object artist? Item amasser?

Domestic belonging preservationist?

Hmmm. I was still thinking on that one. Next, while we were on the subject of creating a new classification, I wondered, what were the parameters? Where does "normal" segue into non-normal, and at what point does one transition into full-blown hoarder from there?

So I'd like to humbly propose some alternatives to the assessment quiz: first, determining if you have a problem, with apologies to Jeff Foxworthy:

You *Might* Have a Problem with Stuff If...

- you've ever kept something because of its sheer improbable horribleness.
- you own anything that once was part of someone's body. (Whatever it is, yes, that counts.)

- you currently own an object you've retrieved from the trash can/recycling bin/giveaway box *more than three times.*
- you have ever found yourself uttering the words "Yes, but the thing is that *I know where everything is.*"
- something being "perfectly good" is, in your mind, logical justification for keeping it, including used murder weapons.
- you've ever found yourself on recycling day arguing, "But it's a really *good* box."
- you own anything, anything at all, that can be considered "old food."
- you've ever wondered if your high school trigonometry notes might, perhaps, form the basis of a fascinating action-adventure novel that would likely be picked up by a Hollywood scriptwriter and become a blockbuster that would eventually lead to you attending the Academy Awards in a stunning fuchsia dress. Or, alternately, make nice Christmas wrap.

Okay! If any of the above sound like you, it's time to get a little more specific. Remember those "love meter" machines from old arcades that for a quarter would "measure your sex appeal" on a scale ranging from "hot stuff!" to "clammy"? Well, why not a *Stuff*-o-meter? I think using a sliding scale like this to identify those shades of gray is potentially more useful than a yes-or-no quiz. Or, at the very least, destined to be a big hit at bowling alley parties.

———

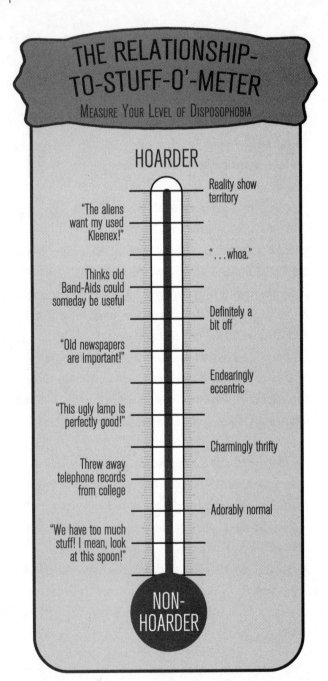

When I put my coin in the slot, I feel pretty certain the glowing lights land somewhere closer to "hoarder" than "non-hoarder." "Definitely a bit off" seemed about right to me. I had no word for this—this thing I am that is neither black nor white, neither here nor there. *Hoarder* seemed about as close as I could get, and I feel a need to own that term as part of my own personal twelve-step program.

But, in the interest of accuracy, I was still feeling compelled to qualify the term: I'm an *amateur* hoarder, a hoarder *in the making*. A clutterer. A clutter addict. I'm addicted to Stuff.

If our forebears were hunter-gatherers, perhaps I could be a "clutter-gatherer." Ha! I kind of liked that one. It was clear enough and neither too obscure nor too euphemistic. It would do for now.

I was as delighted with my new self-designated category as if I had given up trying to find my generic size at the clothing store and made my own dress instead. *Clutter-gatherer* seemed just the right amount of good and bad, all rolled up into one. Nevertheless, it was still a problem, a habituation, a compulsion, and one that, if I may say so, I come by honestly. Perhaps you've heard the theory that addiction runs in families?

CHAPTER FIVE

CLUTTERED BLOOD

"I don't need any of this! I don't need this stuff! And I don't need you! I don't need anything! Except this. This ashtray. That's the only thing I need is this... Just this ashtray. And this paddle game. The ashtray and the paddle game. And that's all I need!"
— Steve Martin as Navin R. Johnson,
The Jerk (1979)

If I was going to conquer the Hell Room—*and* make sure I didn't just recreate it all over again—it would make sense to try to understand why it happened in the first place...but that's no small order. After reading up on the subject, I'd come to the conclusion that what causes hoarding seems to be right up there with the great mysteries of the universe, like where Styrofoam comes from and why celebrities can't give their kids real people names.

It's interesting that the problem of too much Stuff is such a mysterious and recent phenomenon. After all, people have owned stuff ever since first appearing on the caveman circuit, doing cool things with their opposable thumbs and big brains. Once, while traveling, I got to visit the museum holding "Ötzi," the oldest known European mummy, and what struck me about it—what I loved—was that the mummy was discovered *with his stuff.* Yup. Ötzi may have been prehistoric, but he still carried a backpack.

But you can bet your bearskin sandals that Ötzi didn't know anyone who had a hoarding problem. Nope—for a long, long time, having *not enough* Stuff was the problem du jour; having *too much* Stuff wasn't a problem for pretty much anybody.

It would take about five thousand or so more years, give or take, until just around the middle of the last century, for that particular development to come about. What took so long? Perhaps—and I'm theorizing wildly here, which I always find valuable—throughout human history there may have been an evolutionary advantage conferred upon those who were born with a certain propensity to keep things around or reluctance to discard, a "just in case" gene, if you will. And as we all know, evolution has the annoying tendency to work at the speed of molasses in space.

But even an evolutionarily evolved predisposition toward keeping things wouldn't be enough all by itself to bring about the birth of the Too Much Stuff phenomenon—because for most of human history there simply wasn't enough stuff to go around yet. Enter the Industrial Revolution, which meant goods being produced more cheaply and more quickly than ever before. This, in turn, gave birth to the modern concept of *garbage.* I suppose hoarding couldn't exist without garbage: until you have in place a cultural agreement of discarding and planned obsolescence, you can't have a person who goes against that norm and "unreasonably" keeps.

And voilà! The fates have conspired to create a condition that is apparently brand new in human history. The good news is, if my Pulitzer-worthy theory about where clutterers and hoarders like me come from (evolutionary predisposition plus cheap, disposable goods-based economy) is correct, then fixing my problem should be relatively simple: all I have to do is change the basis of the global economy. And/or change my genetic makeup.

Hmm. That could take a while. Well, at least I'm in good company. Despite the fact that the problem of hoarding as we know it has only been around for a few short decades, all indicators point to the fact that the problem of Too Much Stuff is running rampant. The off-site storage locker industry didn't even exist a few short decades ago; today, one in ten households rents a storage unit. Gross revenues for the self-storage industry now hover in the neighborhood of *$30 billion per year*. Heck, there are whole countries that could run on less than what we spend on "extra storage."

Not surprisingly, like Athena from the head of Zeus, an entire profession has likewise burst forth wholly formed from our brave new world of Too Much Stuff: that of the professional organizer. You can now study organizing, become certified, and join the National Association of Professional Organizers. In 2005, CNN included professional organizers on a list of hot new professions earning six figures. That's like *podiatrist* income, people, all for trying to help us deal with our mountains of stuff.

According to the APA's estimates, anywhere between 2 and 5 percent of the population currently qualifies as hoarders. So, how many people *is* that? Well, the unerring wisdom of the Internet informs me that the current U.S. population is about

314 million. And the unerring wisdom of my calculator tells me that means between 6,280,000 and 15,700,000; there are between *6 and 15 million hoarders* in our country alone. Mind you, it could be more. In a recent article on firefighting and hoarding, firefighters told their interviewer they see "'hoarding conditions' in about *25 percent* of homes they enter."[7]

Author Scott Herring puts the official numbers into perspective: "…as many hoarders may exist in America as citizens in Vermont, New Hampshire, Connecticut, Rhode Island, West Virginia, Maine, Kentucky, and Montana combined."[8]

Wow. Who knew? The United States is…hoarding hoarders.

———

Beyond simple logic, I have another really good reason to suspect there is something genetic about Too Much Stuff: the fact that being a clutter-gatherer is a trait I share in common with several of my blood relatives. Although when I was growing up we never had a Hell Room (perish the thought!), after my parents divorced during my teenage years, life became messier for everyone, in more ways than one.

My mother, for example, is very like me: she *likes* things neat and tidy. When she and my dad were together, I realize in retrospect, she was the one who kept things at a very even keel. Although the top of my dad's desk in the basement was always a bit of a disaster, everything else was always

---

7. Olga Khazan, "Hoarding Is Making Firefighting Harder," *The Atlantic*, August 28, 2015.
8. Scott Herring, *The Hoarders: Material Deviance in Modern American Culture* (Chicago: University of Chicago Press, 2014), 1.

under control. Whenever worst came to worst and she was feeling overwhelmed, Mom would simply close the door to the offending room (usually mine). After she and my father divorced, she moved in with her boyfriend John, who, interestingly enough, is *also* a Too-Much-Stuff person.

John is the kind of guy who will move the broken lamp three inches to the left in order to replace it with a lamp that works. He has been known to keep rinsed-out fast-food containers that have distinguishing features that might make them "collectible." When John's mother passed away several years ago, John proceeded to move the *entire contents* of her apartment into the basement of my mother's house—including things like bags of flour and boxes of crackers.

Suffice it to say that Mom has her hands full. These days she manages to keep it contained—mostly—through a variety of strategies: the shell game, the closed doors, and the occasional room that has to be navigated on tiptoe. But you'd never know it if you were a casual visitor on the first floor of the house. Sound familiar?

Meanwhile, from virtually the day my mother moved out, my father's house—the same house we had grown up in that had always been neat, tidy, and organized—was an unmitigated disaster. I remember finding this very confusing as a teenager. What had happened to Dad? Why was his house always a crazy mess? Although he has moved several times between then and now, the Dad Continuum is a constant: whole areas of his house are inaccessible, crammed with papers, dog dishes, stacks of old magazines, receipts, old cassettes. Paths have to be carved to get from one door to another—piles are shoved aside but not dealt with. The room my father calls his office—the one with the desk and the computer—perennially has the look of a room in which a file cabinet has just exploded.

While Dad's house always felt like an inexplicable mess, when we were still living at home it seemed he was in a category by himself—an anomaly. But once my brother Ben grew up and moved out, a pattern began to emerge: every time I visited Ben I was amazed to find him living in what I can only describe as a state of magnificent disarray—as if he had taken clutter to the level of an art form. At first I chalked up strange habitations to "college life" or "rowdy roommates," but when he had graduated college and eventually gotten his own apartment it became clear that this was not someone else, and neither was it a passing phase. On a given visit I would marvel at a fifteen-year-old program from his high school graduation sitting on a side table, looking as fresh and pristine as if someone had attended the event yesterday. Next to it might be piles of exquisite randomness: ancient Yankees tickets. Broken shards of pottery. Plastic figurines, playing cards, dirty dishes so old they'd qualify for an archeological expedition. Stacks of books, stacks of DVDs, stacks of stacks. Occasionally, a room in the apartment would have absolutely no room for humans—the stacks ruled. Then again, once in a while a room would be completely empty—including of furniture—as if, in an attempt to clean up, someone got carried away and simply kept going till nothing was left.

Are you sensing a familial theme here? My mother and I play the closed-door game, and my father and brother both struggle with clutter demons on a larger, harder-to-hide scale.

I have to admit, though, that I never *really* put it all together until we paid a visit to my father's brother. My uncle Jim lives on the other side of the country from us, in California, so we get glimpses of visits with him only once every decade or so. My memory of his place from visiting when I was a kid is vivid: a modest but airy, modern condo with skylights and plaster busts of naked-lady artworks, the occasional coffee table book, and a wonderful old player piano. Out back there's a small walled garden that to my New Englander eyes looked like a cross between the garden of Eden and a tropical rain forest, complete with obscenely lush foliage that creeped and bloomed and cascaded—colors we never saw back at home in nature. Actual fruits—*that were not apples*—grew here! A tiny raised pond held two fat, exotic tropical fish that sparkled in the seemingly endless sunlight.

Fast-forward to my next visit a good twenty years later, on the occasion of Uncle Jim's sixty-fifth birthday. This time, though, he was strangely reluctant to let us in his house—insisting the family eat out, meet at the hotel, and so on. But no family gathering works very well without a home base, so at last he relented. I was aghast—no, not aghast...*astounded*. Jim's neat and tidy condo had transformed to the picture of what a house in Southern California would look like if my brother had lived in it for a few years. Or my dad. Or was composed entirely of the contents of my Hell Room, for that matter.

Random things were *everywhere*. The beloved player piano was broken, strewn with a parade of bizarre art supplies, bits of broken mirror, paint, newspaper. No surface escaped the pile-o-rama: papers, plastic cups, bits of things you might mistake for trash. The naked-lady busts and coffee table books were still there, but you could hardly find them behind the stuff stuff STUFF that towered and loomed and echoed every-where you looked. The lush garden that had so impressed me as a kid had become a desperate jungle—with old pots and broken statuary, bags of dirt, and unchecked vines climbing the walls, the tree, the walkway. The tropical fish had gotten busy in the pond, creating creepy pale offspring that looked unsettlingly inbred.

And my uncle Jim's office? The room with the computer? Looked remarkably like a room in which a file cabinet had just exploded.

Just. Like. Dad's.

What, I wondered, *what* was going on? It was then that the connection suddenly clicked. It all made some weird kind of *sense*—like the stories of identical twins who are separated at birth and both grow up to drink Tab and marry a blond woman named Susan.

Me, my dad, my brother, my uncle Jim? Surely it couldn't be merely a *coincidence*. (And although Mom's boyfriend isn't part of that biological chain, someone could probably do an interesting thesis paper on the fact that my mom keeps ending up with messy men she tries to make neat.)

So, from where I sit, the evidence for the DNA argument looks not only compelling but painfully obvious. Other people must have come to this same conclusion because researchers for years have searched to pinpoint actual clutter DNA…but thus far all in vain. In fact, from what I've been able to gather through a series of Internet searches and my extensive, non-existent medical background, clutterers and hoarders like me exist primarily to confound neurobiologists. The headlines describing newly released studies read like a weird guy on a park bench arguing with himself: "Hoarding Linked to Obsessive-Compulsive Disorder! Unless It's Not!" "Hoarders Brains Are Different! Except They Are Exactly the Same!"

So, we're a bit of a mystery. Like the heads of Easter Island or crop circles, we clutter-hoarders are just kind of annoyingly *there*, and although there are some pretty good theories, no one knows exactly why. Aliens? Fluoridated water? No answer seems entirely satisfying.

Not to mention that it seems like I'm back at square one in terms of trying to unlock and solve my problem. And it occurs to me to worry a bit about Greta and Ilsa too—possibly the most troubling of my unanswered questions is: someday down the road, will they struggle with Stuff the way I do? Will it be occasionally troubling (like mine) or more all-consuming (like my dad's)? And most importantly, is there anything I can do to prevent it?

Short of changing the world or biology, it would seem that my only path forward is to rely on plain old stubbornness, which, not to brag or anything, you'll recall I have a bit of a knack for. If I knock my head against this problem enough times, can I get a different way of thinking to eventually fall out?

It's worth a shot. As for Greta and Ilsa, I think the best thing I can do for them is to start them early.

Like now.

CHAPTER SIX

WE CONTINUE TO BEGIN

"One way to organize your thoughts is to tidy up, even if it's in places where it makes no sense at all."

—Ursus Wehrli

First of all, I want to be clear I had absolutely no idea what I had unleashed.

Sure, I had been counting on the girls for a certain degree of momentum. However, if previously I had come to think of the upstairs room as "my" project...if I thought I was in "control" of this upstairs room and all its contents...I was about to be disabused of any such notions. Greta woke up on the Sunday morning after we first spoke about it and immediately asked if we could get started on the room today. Now.

In fact, Greta had already started a journal, drawn a map of the room, and started making elaborate lists. As I blearily made my way through my first cup of coffee, she enthusiastically showed me her schematic of the room with new locations for all the different storage and functions: sewing desk, "fiber corner," art and crafts area, couch, and coffee table. She had made a lengthy inventory of what we would need to do, get rid of, and acquire. We had a clear day ahead of us with no activities or plans to interfere. She practically dragged me from the breakfast dishes up the stairs to begin.

Ilsa, meanwhile, sat on the couch and pouted. She did *not* want to clean or organize or, really, be any part of this odd endeavor. She wanted to play Apples to Apples or, quite possibly, Clue. But Greta was an unstoppable force, so we finally convinced Ilsa to join us upstairs if only to keep us company while we worked.

Somehow, in the intervening time since I had cleaned in the room with Ilsa not all that long ago, the floor had begun to vanish again. Wait! What about all that great progress we had made? But it was true. In that short time objects not only had migrated onto the floor but had begun to congregate outside the door as well, blocking even our way *in*. Had I actually done this? Was I sleep-hoarding? Uncertainly, Greta and I started to work, one by one shoving aside the objects that barred our path. Within minutes we had cleared the doorway out, again, and, feeling heartened, we picked up some speed and inched forward into the room.

Ilsa took this opportunity to sit on the floor directly in front of the doorway with her coloring book, surrounded by bins of crayons, markers, and colored pencils. Strategically, it was perhaps the best possible positioning from which she might block our progress. Nonetheless, Greta and I kept going. Immediately we identified our key sorting categories: stuff we wanted to keep, stuff we could give to the charity shop, stuff that could be recycled, stuff that simply had to be pitched, and stuff that belonged to Daddy and would have to be sorted by him later. We started shuttling things to the small room just outside the Hell Room door and distributing accordingly.

Ah, the mysterious Hallway Room. Our weird little space in between the hallway at the top of the stairs and the Hell Room. It's neither quite large enough to be a real "room," nor small enough to be considered merely a hallway. Consequently, I've always called it the Hallway Room, which I admit is not a term most people have in their residential vocabulary. Most of the time, the Hallway Room ends up being an unfortunate extension of the Hell Room, housing still more piles of crap whenever I couldn't bear to actually open the Hell Room door. But now I was trying to run that dynamic backward, like that scene from Superman, where Christopher Reeve flies around the world to make time go in reverse. To the lay observer it looked the same, but nevertheless, I knew that a quintessential shift had occurred. Importantly, instead of piles awaiting entry, we now had piles awaiting removal. It was kind of like visiting an ocean beach at different times of the day and thinking nothing much had changed because it looked just the same. You'd have to stick around a while to understand that, in fact, it was changing all the time, and to determine the salient fact of whether the tide was coming in or going out.

Not ten minutes later, however, we hit an impasse. I returned from placing an old box of my husband's negatives in the Hallway Room to find Ilsa and Greta arguing fiercely over what appeared to be a small rag.

Greta: "Mom, *make her throw it away!*"

Ilsa: "*Nooooo!*"

Greta showed me the item in question: a small cloth rectangle, about the size of a large handkerchief. I immediately recognized it as a "burp cloth" from back in the days when needing to have materials immediately on hand for wiping up baby spit had been a regular part of my day. Ever attempting to repurpose (reuse! recycle!), I had moved these bits of cloth to the art area for use as paint rags in the ensuing era of sponge markers and plastic smocks.

Now, however, they were clearly beyond redemption. We found more of them throughout the day, in various locations, but always the same: wadded up, smudged, and stiff with bright paint colors.

"*Well*," I said, holding the item in question aloft by its corner while eyeing it suspiciously, "what shall we do with it?"

Simultaneously the girls cried out:

"*Keep* it!" (Ilsa)

"*Pitch* it!" (Greta)

Oh good. Well, this was going to be easy.

"I want to cut it up and make it into a purse," Ilsa explained logically.

"The object, Ilsa, is to get *rid* of stuff," Greta admonished.

Disheartening though it was to be stymied so soon into the project, I couldn't help but smile. It was like listening to the two sides of my own brain arguing out loud. It was a conversation I was so familiar with, but now for the first time it was being acted out for me, like actors reading a script.

Not wanting to be sidetracked, we put the divisive object to one side and kept going.

And so it went: Greta color-coding the thread spools, Ilsa working on her Cinderella coloring book and providing a running social commentary. ("What do you think about this color for her hair?... I don't know *what* the stepmother is wearing... Why do you think *no one* recognizes Cinderella at the ball? I mean, *no one*?")

At some point Steve showed up and started calling foul: he wanted an official end zone declared in the Hallway Room, beyond which point no piles should dare to venture. He then hastily departed the scene, all but visibly twitching.

Chicken.

Greta and I forged on: wading once more through the oceans of art supplies. Previous efforts had separated the wheat from the chaff—the usable from the used up—but now we were organizing what was left, and of course there was plenty left. We separated the supplies (buttons, beads, pipe cleaners, popsicle sticks) from the paints (gouache, acrylic, watercolor) from the tools (brushes, markers, rubber stamps), each making its way to its own labeled shelf or plastic bin in the new "art corner." It occurred to me that we had more than enough to supply a medium-sized summer camp.

Before too long, an actual walkway encircling the room had emerged. But Greta had bigger plans: she asked if we could extricate a large area rug and pitch that as well. Another hand-me-down from the nursery, I had repurposed it as a sort of drop cloth under the kids' painting area way back when. Now, however, it was a sorry sight—covered with blotches of paint and dead bugs, I realized Greta was right—this should be the first large item to go.

She and I hoisted the nasty thing onto our shoulders, briskly bypassed a protesting Ilsa, and descended the two flights of stairs to the basement, leaving a trail of crunchy insect shells in our wake. This was followed shortly thereafter by a cheap plastic bookshelf so undistinguished that even Ilsa was willing to let it go.

When we returned to the room, the large cleared space seemed magical: look what we had managed! We had worked for more than four hours, and my hands were visibly grimy. I had a gigantic bag of garbage, a full box for the charity shop, a full bag of recyclables—not to mention several boxes of "for Steve to go through" stacked up in the Hallway Room—to show for it. Look at that path! Look at that open, rectangular space! Look at the progress we'd made!

But then, suddenly, I began to worry: what if our progress was, you know...*too* good? What if this project just *wasn't that big a deal after all?* Had I blown the room out of proportion in my head, planning months of cleaning when in fact a good three or four days would suffice? It would be so...so *anticlimactic.*

While I stood there surveying what we had accomplished, trying to decide whether to be heartened or dismayed by our progress, Steve came up to see and immediately gave me the answer.

"*Wow,*" he said. "This is going to take *a while.*"

———

A little while after that, Greta came down with a nasty head cold, which progressed to the point that we gave her some medicine and tucked her in bed with no intention of disturbing her sleep for school the next day. In the morning, after I had let her sleep in several hours, I went in to wake her up and, in her groggy, throaty voice, her first question was: "Am I staying home from school today?" and the second was "*Can we work on the room?*"

An agreement was struck. We could work for a total of two hours on the Room if she promised to rest after that. Following a breakfast of tea and toast, Greta put her hands on my shoulders and literally steered me like a car toward the upstairs room.

"No distractions! No diversions!" she chirped cheerfully.

So, it occurred to me to wonder, at what point did my fifteen-year-old daughter turn into my governess?

Immediately we set to work, and because Ilsa was at school, we made headway even faster. The path we had forged formed a misshaped oval about the room. As we began to work, the path ebbed and flowed, widening, narrowing again, becoming blocked and then opening up once again, like an evolving shoreline.

We pulled together so many scattered scraps of cloth from fourteen years of sewing Halloween costumes that the large wicker basket we had designated for them no longer closed at all.

We shuttled battalions of paintings I made in college from one side of the room to the other, and Greta made the startling realization that not only did they have *nude models* in art school, but *sometimes* they were *male* nude models. Gasp!

We discovered a forgotten wooden bookshelf in the closet and wrestled it out into the room to hold all those little bins of art supplies. Greta got out the label maker and went bananas labeling everything that wasn't nailed down.

After she was finished, she was exultant, despite her sore throat and pajamas.

"Look at *that*!" she said triumphantly. "That looks *great*!" And it really did. Sure, we still had miles to go, but the brand-new art corner was as neat and organized as Howard Hughes's cuff-link collection.

"I feel very *in charge* now, do you know what I mean?" she asked me. I did. Why is it so soothing to walk past an array of well-organized objects? And why is it so particularly satisfying if you are the one who has done the organizing?

I was especially impressed with one development. At one

point I had stealthily placed in the trash bag an old unfinished art project of Greta's—a metal container to which she had glued some decorative beads years before—but right before taking the bag to the garage, I guiltily fished it out. I took it back upstairs to Greta—after all, she was being so great. What if she saw it and went "Awwwww!"? I just couldn't throw it away if it turned out to be terribly important to her, even if I knew she'd never, ever finish the thing.

"Awwwww!" she said when I produced it.

Crap.

And then: "But that's okay. You can pitch it."

What? Really?

And then the *same* thing happened the next time, when I held up the woodcarving kit she had so desperately wanted for her—what?—eighth birthday maybe? Delighted, she had opened the package at the table, still strewn with cake crumbs and balled-up party napkins, and begun to whittle. Within about thirty seconds she had sliced her index finger wide open. Somehow, after that, woodcarving never held the same appeal for her, and the kit had remained untouched ever since.

"Awwwww!" she said when I held that up too. "No…that's okay. You can get rid of it."

Wow! I was beyond impressed with her ability to appreciate the memory an object conjures while almost in the same breath letting that object go.

So here's what I wanted to know: how does she *do* that?

————————

And so it went. Weeks went by when life got in the way and we'd forget about the Hell Room for a while. Often Greta would ask me when we could get back to it, and I found myself in the strange position of telling her that no, we couldn't go clean today because she had to finish her homework or go to play practice or, as often as not, I couldn't quite face it just at that particular moment. I never forgot about the room, but Greta was the one who never stopped advocating for it.

One day she said something to me, and I gave her such a funny look that she laughingly wrote it on a Post-it and left it on my desk for emphasis. This is what it said:

"Listen, we have a job to do, and if it wasn't for me I don't think you would make it!"

She was right, of course.

Then one day spring gave way to summer, and school was out: we had a little more free time on our hands.

"*So*," Greta said to Ilsa one day as we picked her up from her day camp, with the air of a person who is telling you something of particular significance. "We moved a *filing cabinet* today."

Ilsa, however, wasn't biting. She had been at science camp all day where they had done cool things like make slime in different colors to bring home in little plastic bags (Yaaaaay! Can we keep it forever, Mom?). She was sitting in the backseat wrapped up in her thoughts about the Ziploc bag of goo while I quietly prayed it would not develop a leak.

"Look at the slime! We made it!" Ilsa said, displaying it proudly.

"*Actually*," Greta emphasized, after getting no discernible reaction from her sister to her earth-shattering news, "we moved *two* filing cabinets."

"You know, at first I really *hated* the color of the slime…" Ilsa began to explain, clearly not listening.

Greta tried a third time. "Ilsa, we moved *two*—"

"Greta! *I'm going to ice a cake with* slime!"

"*Ilsa.* We moved *two filing cabinets* today in the room."

"What room?"

"The Hell Room."

"Oh."

The car was quiet then, as each girl was presumably considering how very strange her sister's priorities were.

───────────

As the project continued in fits and starts, we were living among the resultant now-everywhere piles. Only garbage got the immediate boot; everything else had to sit in its pile patiently awaiting various fates: recycling, charity shop donation, consignment shop, attic storage, pickup by friend who wants this, books for the library sale, and so on. Mostly these piles were in the small, now-crowded Hallway Room that directly precedes the Hell Room, but often the piles crept stealthily farther, down the stairs, and into our actual living spaces, where ignoring them was becoming increasingly difficult. Although mess in my everyday environment bothers me, if I know a particular group of objects is waiting for some particular destiny, I have an uncanny ability to work around it, ignoring it until such point as I can make that destiny happen. After all, what's the option? To put the pile *back* into hiding, so we can start the process all over again?

Steve, unfortunately, does not share this talent. He consequently gets all freaked out when he is trying to do something completely unnecessary like, say, find the bathroom in the middle of the night, and he ends up stubbing his toe on my mid-project piles of old stereo equipment in the middle of the hallway floor.

In fact, my husband's nickname for me is Fire Hazard Lady because of my endearing habit of actually placing objects *in* doorways, hallways, and other means of egress. I try to explain to him that I really do this *on purpose* because the more times I have to step around a particular pile or box, the more motivated I will (theoretically) be to resolve whatever issue the obstacle represents. This is the time-honored principle of "I'm going to trick myself into doing something that I really want to do but for some reason am not doing yet." (Also, there's always the possibility that the obstacle represents something I want some *other* member of my family to do—in which case I am sending an oh-so-subtle message in the form of, say, the broken lawn mower blocking the garage door.)

Sooner or later, something inevitably happens to jolt me out of my procrastination and back to dealing with the piles rather than stepping around them. It isn't always pretty, of course.

For example, one fine summer Monday in the middle of our Hell Room–related pile chaos, I was confronted with the sudden and immediate realization that my *entire* house was a disaster area. All at once, I became hyper-aware of the mess that was all over the place, and it was completely freaking me out.

A substantial portion of the mess was made up of those deeply well-intentioned objects awaiting dispersal to various appropriate agencies. The rest was the result of the fact that in my rush to enjoy the summer weekend with the kids, I had fallen down on my usual rounds of picking up, laundry folding, and table clearing. Between one thing and another the results were downright depressing.

Add to all of this the measly, protein-deficient breakfast I had eaten of mere cereal (which I should know better than to do by now), and it was the perfect storm, really.

In a daze I walked around the house, feeling completely powerless to remedy any of it. I was beyond overwhelmed: I felt a little dizzy and slightly ill. I realized, as I staggered about my living room like a tranquilized water buffalo, that it's at moments like this that I envy my husband.

Perhaps it has not escaped your attention that thus far Steve had been, for the most part, steering clear of the Hell Room. Interestingly, he's very similar to me in some of the ways he deals with Stuff. He too puts up a pretty good front. He too likes to be highly organized in certain areas, while letting others go entirely to heck. In a perfect world, I suppose, the things I cared about would be diametrically opposed to the things he cared about, and then we'd have a spotless, perfect existence in which everyone's socks were ironed, and no one ever argued about how many dirty travel coffee mugs were sitting on the shelf in the garage. Instead, we have a house in which doors get shut, lids get closed, and problems get deferred to another day.

Where Steve and I differ, though, is in our strategies for dealing with Stuff when it has gotten to the point that it absolutely, unquestionably, must be confronted. For as long as I've known him, Steve's strategy for decluttering has been what I like to call the Dumpster Method: ignore, deny, postpone, and then finally, *blammo!*: Out comes the trash can, and everything goes. And I do mean everything.

One time, before we were married, Steve and I gave a box of miscellaneous clothing to Goodwill and received a call shortly thereafter from a good soul who had purchased an old wallet of Steve's and was surprised to find his social security card *still in it*.

That he hadn't bothered to check the wallet for such paltry

things as, oh, I don't know, credit cards, old photos, or good, old-fashioned cash astonished me. *How could he not have checked?* But I can tell you the answer: the value of whatever he might have found inside seemed to be far outweighed by the relief of discarding quickly. You might call it the rip-the-Band-Aid-off approach, except to me it seems that one risks creating a new wound worse than the first.

Except at moments like right now.

Looking around my house that summer day, I realized that a large part of the problem at hand was what my friend Brian calls the Rubik's Cube effect, which is to say there was a series of object orchestrations that had to take place in a particular order: without the first thing happening first, nothing else can happen; everything comes to a standstill. For example, on this particular day I had four packed boxes of old toys to be taken to the attic, which were now in the living room. I needed Steve's help to move these heavy items into the attic, but nothing could be moved into the attic until we cleared a path *to* the attic through the Hallway Room. But the Hallway Room was currently filled to bursting with piles of crap extricated from the Hell Room. And these piles were so many and varied who knew *when* I'd be able to carve that path... Was the library open today to receive book donations? Not until noon. What about the consignment shop? You need to make an appointment. How about that big pile of dry cleaning? Well, that's a half-hour drive... It was starting to feel like a vicious catch-22, as in I *can't* clean up...until I clean up!

After an emergency protein snack of peanut butter and crackers, I lay down and felt miserable for awhile. It's moments like these that are hardest for me when I'm trying to effect some change, that moment when, in the process of trying to make something truly better, one has to make it worse first. Usually much worse.

After a short while I roused myself with the help of my new peanut butter energy. I reeled about like a slightly crazed woman; I had to do *something*.

I went to my small office, the other room just off the Hallway Room, and like a disease that has spread from one part of the body to every other, it too was now a giant ridiculous mess. I couldn't get to the Hell Room, couldn't face the Hallway Room, couldn't lift those heavy boxes into the attic, but I could at least make headway *here*, right? Here, like everywhere else in my house at this moment, it seemed, I found myself surrounded by a maelstrom of papers and unsettlingly random objects. I began throwing things into the trash and the recycling with an energy that bordered on manic.

Of *course* the bills are late, I thought to myself, they're stacked in piles among adorable notes from the kids! Anniversary cards from a month ago! Photographs, magazines, yarn, and notes about lunch money! I'm behind, behind, behind. I sorted mail like my life depended on it. Junk mail…junk mail…Why can't these people just leave me *alone*? The wind blew through the open window, and all my just-organized piles of paper began to flutter and then dance around.

"*Really?*" I asked the wind. "*Really?*"

Clearly, I had *had* it. And perhaps this was good. I was in the market for a breakthrough, I realized. Or a breakdown. Whichever came first.

Trash! Recycle! Out, damned spot! Even things I never would've parted with otherwise were going in my frenzy to accomplish something, anything. Lists of would-be thank-you notes I swore the girls would write months ago, gift cards

I would never use that had sat neglected for years, and a small card from some flowers my husband had given me that said "With all my love!" all went unceremoniously into the trash.

"With all my love!" I had thought to myself. How could I throw away *that*? How could I not feel that I was, in fact, throwing away, discarding the sentiment itself?

Steve is mystified by this strange confusion I have between the object and the emotion it is meant to represent. He laughs at my idea of the discarded flower note as a rejection of love. I knew he wouldn't mind me letting go of the flower note, one among hundreds of such small notes I've kept from him over the years that all amount to the same thing: an expression of love. *If I throw away this note, will my husband not love me anymore?* I ask myself, only half-facetiously. *Of course not.*

When the dust finally settled, I had a reasonable, clutter-free office space again, at least. Even though I hadn't fixed the Hell Room or addressed the Rubik's Cube situation in the other rooms of the house, I had effected change both in one room and—at least for the moment—in myself.

I felt strange: simultaneously sheepish and victorious. Conflicted. I had won one small skirmish for today, but at what cost? It was so against my nature to act this way, but wasn't that what it was going to take? Wasn't that what I had been wanting, to change? I wondered if behaving this way was betraying some fundamental aspect of who I was. Would I wake up in the morning and, racked with remorse, have to go rooting through the trash in the front yard to retrieve the small card that said "With all my love!"? Or, perhaps just as bad, would I wake up in the morning and no longer feel sentimental about such tiny things?

It felt weird, but then I guess anything new feels weird. Like changing your DNA one molecule at a time.

CHAPTER SEVEN

I HATE EDITH PIAF

"Rule No. 1 is, don't sweat the small stuff. Rule No. 2 is, it's all small stuff."

—Robert S. Eliot

Somewhere in the Hell Room, although I had yet to find it, is my fifth-grade report card. I also have all my other report cards, of course, but the fifth-grade one is special. It was my fifth-grade report card that brought about the first moment I realized with real clarity that not everyone saved things the way I did.

It was during our first big review at graduate art school.[9] I had assembled a small installation with some found objects—a wooden cigar box, a tiny puzzle, a handful of little houses I stole from a Monopoly game. At the last minute I had thrown in my fifth-grade report card for good measure.

---

9. Yes, they have such a thing, and yes, after graduation your lovely framed masters of fine art diploma will come in *extremely* handy pretty much absolutely never.

I thought it was a fairly clever work for a first-year student, and I was ready. I was prepared to talk all about the deep symbolism, the artistic metaphors, the tactile hermeneutics of the yadda yadda whatever. All day long professors filed in in groups with their clipboards and their notes, but I really needn't have bothered because nobody wanted to talk about my installation. Instead, everybody was fascinated with that *report card*.

"*Why* do you still have your fifth-grade report card?" they wanted to know. "That's so crazy! Where did you *find* that?"

What? Like, everyone doesn't still have their fifth-grade report card?

Oh! I suddenly realized. *Not everyone keeps everything they've ever made, read, bought, or been given.* Not everyone still has their three-ring notebook from eighth-grade biology class. Or the dress they wore to their sixth-grade graduation. Not everyone breaks out in hives at the thought of discarding old stuffed animals they never even liked or books they never even read or clothes they never even wore. Not everyone, I now realized, hyperventilates at the thought of throwing out an old oven mitt or suffers post-traumatic stress about the teal polyester bridesmaid dress they gave away—complete with dyed-to-match shoes and teal lace fingerless gloves— which they *never* liked, *even* when teal lace fingerless gloves were considered fashionable.

But *I* do.

Let me tell you another story. Later on, after Steve and I had met and become an item, our good friend Cara was engaged to be married. Only something was…off. One day she told me that she had been feeling just weird. Antsy. She needed to *do* something.

So here is what she did: she gathered up all her old, former-boyfriend mementos—photos, dried flowers, love notes, and letters—looking at and perusing each one before putting them into a little pile. Then she *burned* them.

I was dumbstruck by this story. I can only imagine the agape, moronic look I must have given her after she related it to me. This was pretty much the complete inverse of how I related to the world. The world, in particular one's private, most personal world, was for gathering and keeping! Not for destroying. All those boyfriends—all those memories and experiences—had been reduced to a pile of ash, never to return again. I could not have been more horrified if she had told me she had burned her own childhood.

Cara was very pleased with the act, though. It seemed that something about it had calmed her nerves about the whole "until death do you part" business that lay ahead of her. She was, in a way, saying good-bye to her former life in order to make room for a new one. One could make the argument that it was a beautiful gesture—symbolic and ritualistic.

Beautiful symbolic gesture or not, there was no way I was following Cara's lead. At this same time Steve and I were also newly engaged, and *I* still had the decorated Easter eggshell my crush had given me in fourth grade, the sweatband my tenth-grade boyfriend had given me, and every love letter and note I ever got. I even kept the really *bad* memories: photos of the boys who had stomped my heart into a million pieces, souvenirs of nights I ought to want to forget. Why did I want *those* faces smiling up at me from my piles of snapshots? But—how can I explain?—to get rid of them felt *wrong*, like redacting whole paragraphs from a story so that it no longer made sense.

You might be forgiven for wondering what the big deal was. So you get rid of the wrong object—what's the worst thing that could happen? I'll tell you. As a graduate student at this time I was living in a one-bedroom apartment and finding that my keeping tendencies—although surprisingly helpful with my art projects—were starting to catch up with me in other ways. Which is to say, I was running out of room. All my childhood, pre-college belongings were still back at my mother's house, so I was "only" coping with about eight years of saving at this point. My new fiancé was spending pretty much all his spare time at my place, and I started to see my cramped apartment through his eyes. He was dumbstruck by how much I had managed to shoehorn into the hall closet and a bit stunned, as a fellow photographer, that I had kept not only all my finished, matted art prints but also *all* my work prints, *all* my contact sheets, and *all* my negatives.[10]

I had every *book* I'd ever been required to buy too, from every college and grad school class. In that pre-Internet, pre-everything-at-your-fingertips era, it seemed patently ridiculous to me to have spent all this time, money, and energy acquiring knowledge only to go sell most of it back to the bookstore, as most everyone else I knew did. Why rely on one's fallible brain to recall everything one had learned in Nuclear Physics 101 or the Films of Spike Lee? Who knew where I would be ten, maybe twenty years from now, at a

---

10. I'm pleased to note that I at least was able to discard my photography "test strips"—the little scraps of paper one progressively exposes in a step-down fashion in order to locate the proper exposure range. This is kind of like being proud of yourself for throwing out the banana peel when you're done eating the banana, but I'll take it.

dinner party perhaps, when suddenly Spike Lee turns to me and asks if I can recall the formula for the half-life of a radio-isotope. Because I had kept my textbooks I'd be able to smile and reply confidently, "I don't recall, but I'll look it up when I get home and get back to you!"

As a consequence, my poor little apartment, furnished with overstuffed, hard-springed furniture I had purchased at the Salvation Army, was busting at the seams. Keeping things—filling closets, stacking bookshelves—had seemed so natural and easy and fun. I was becoming an adult! Look! I had *things*: a coffee table and candlesticks and bookshelves filled with academic-sounding titles like *Tibetan Hand Puppetry and Its Significance*.

But. Now things just weren't fitting anymore. The coat closet door wasn't staying shut. I was beginning to have trouble accessing things that I *knew* were there—where's that darned paintbrush/waffle iron/cat?[11]

So I tried. It was, at this point, quite a foreign concept to me—imagine getting rid of *instead of* simply keeping! It would be the first of many, many future attempts to deaccession items from my ever-growing collection. I packed up a few bags and boxes of only the most useless and illogical things I owned to donate to the local charity shop. A small handful of clothing that was clearly horrible on me. Some things I never used: a lawn chair, a plastic boot dryer. And—dug out of the

---

11. Maybe I was trying a bit too hard to compensate for this chaos. One day I came home from classes and realized couldn't find my cat anywhere. In my tiny, one-bedroom apartment, this was cause for deep concern—there just weren't that many places he could *be*. Finally, I pulled open one of my dresser drawers and out he popped, like a jack-in-the-box. Apparently he had settled down for a nap among my winter sweaters, and I had shut the drawer without even noticing him there.

bottom of the coat closet, which was the only place it would fit—an aluminum popcorn popper.

I had always kind of loved the popcorn popper. It had belonged to my parents originally and was this big, sixties-era appliance shaped a little like a tallish UFO with a lid. It had giant metal coils and a somewhat alarming, two-pronged electric cord that had been outmoded several decades ago. This big, honking thing served one purpose and one purpose only—to pop popcorn. I had never managed to use the thing properly; in fact, it's entirely possible that I had never used it at all, intimidated as I was by the prospect of burning down my entire apartment building. But I had fond memories of my dad making us popcorn in it when we were kids—when a device that exclusively made white, fluffy popcorn out of hard little seeds seemed like a truly magical thing.

I distinctly recall thinking to myself, as a kid, "*someday* I'll have one of those. In fact, someday, when I grow up, Dad will give me *that* popcorn popper, and I'll use it and think of all the times we had popcorn together."

I was a lucky kid to have a memory like that. Good stuff. Simple stuff, right?

But. Fast-forward to now, and here I was, getting rid of that very popcorn popper that I had practically vowed to my young self to keep forever and hand down to my great-grandchildren. Into the box it went. And then out again. And then back in. Finally, I had a very stern talk with myself, and, in a bout of frustration with my apartment and myself, I quickly drove over to the Salvation Army and dropped it off, trying not to look back as I drove off.

But. Remember my honorary middle name? Regret.

Oh, how I regretted that ridiculous appliance. I felt almost, but not quite, ill over it. How could I *do* that? After wanting that popcorn popper as a kid! And now it was gone *forever*, never to return. Even if I managed to find another one just like it, it would never be the same because it wouldn't be the very one my father had used when I was a kid, the very one he had used when we had come in from a crisp October day jumping in piles of leaves outside to make us that magical, fluffy popcorn.

Now, I knew, even then, that this was patently ridiculous. Mourning the loss of an appliance! Moreover, one I had never even used. Did I mention that it was dented? I got angry with myself. And then I felt sad some more. This, unfortunately, is what I do. I could reason with myself all I wanted—I never used it. It was probably dangerous! It took up too much room! I can make popcorn in a regular pot! I don't even like popcorn all that much! There are worse problems in the world than regretting the loss of a dented goddamned popcorn maker!—I still can't stop the preoccupation with the idea that I have *lost* something, and with that comes regret.

While Edith Piaf became famous singing "Je Ne Regrette Rien," perhaps *my* theme song could be "I Regret *Everything*." When I save, I regret the loss of a clear, pretty, functional environment. But when I let go, I regret the loss of each and every memory, no matter how insignificant or unpleasant, because it is still some little bit of my past that I must agree to let go of. When I let go of my past, some little part of me ceases to exist; some memory retreats to the deep, dark recesses of my brain, never to be retrieved, ever again.

And of course it wasn't just the popcorn popper. Another time, I had dropped a box of old clothes off at a charity shop, only to return the following day to sheepishly ask if I could get something back out of the box. There had been a night-gown, I explained, put in the box, um, *by accident.*

The young woman informed me that donated boxes were immediately dumped and sorted and contents shipped out all over the country within hours. I didn't believe her, but I was powerless. I imagined my box sitting in the back room, my nightgown still tucked inside. I had abandoned it. Given away a piece of my *self.* It had been a gift from my mom when I was a teenager, and I had worn it so many times… It was warm and cozy and…again, I felt nearly ill over it; I lost actual *sleep* over it. It no longer mattered that I had never liked it very much and that, over time, I had even grown to hate the ugly old thing. Wrong color. Too many buttons. I knew if I was a saner person I'd have been glad to be rid of it, happy at the room it opened up in my drawer for things I did like.

That day, pleading with the charity worker, strongly considering the possibility of racing her to the back room and breaking down the door to see if my box was still there, was a rock-bottom moment in my cluttering career. I was frustrated and ashamed to be begging for my stupid old nightgown back. If I couldn't get rid of the things I didn't even like, how was there hope for me to have a nice, clean, organized home to live in? How would I ever find anything? This was another moment of clarity: my brain *was* playing tricks on me. I had a problem that other people around me didn't appear to have.

Was it the worst thing in the world to have separation anxiety with my Stuff? Certainly not. In fact, that the problem seemed like a ridiculous one to have made it feel all the worse. I'm an idiot, I told myself. An idiot, with stupid problems that don't matter. People in the world are starving, fleeing oppression, fighting injustice, and what am I doing?

I'm staying up at night *stressing* about a goddamned dented popcorn maker. A used ugly nightgown.

What my friend Cara had been able to do with her old love letters and photos was precisely the opposite of my situation: she was letting go of the old with the idea of making room for the new. Meanwhile I was holding on so tight to things that the circulation was draining from my hands. At what point, I wondered, do we hold on to our past so tight that we risk strangling it to death?

CHAPTER EIGHT

A GOOD PROBLEM
TO HAVE

"Look at this stuff, isn't it neat?
Wouldn't you think my collection's complete?
Wouldn't you think I'm the girl, the girl who has everything?"
—Ariel, *The Little Mermaid* (1989)

The summer of no clutter wore on. Occasionally, I would stop and ask myself, usually with a thoughtful, pensive look on my face, what the hell it was I thought I was doing.

One beautiful Vermont day in particular, I'd dropped the kids off at summer camp and was headed home, listening to the news on public radio. I treasure these little pockets of Mom-only driving time as a unique opportunity to catch up on what's happening in the world beyond my kids' schools, my local supermarket, and my laundry room. On this particular day, if I understood the reporters correctly, what was happening in the world was that everyone was killing everyone else in the most egregious and horrific manner imaginable, and nobody was doing anything about it.

And me, what was *I* doing? I was—wait for it—going

home to *clean out a room*. No—it was worse than that. I was going home to *write about* cleaning out a room.

It wasn't the first time that I had felt some creeping guilt about this entire enterprise. Periodically I would stop whatever it was I was doing to register the thought: the very fact that I *have* a Hell Room—much less the leisure to write an entire book about it—is one heck of a First World problem if I ever heard one. Poor me, right? Me and my big house and too much stuff to put in it.

Which brought me to the question of how earth-shattering this all was anyway. I mean, even if I never, *ever* got my clutter problem under control, I had concluded that it was highly unlikely that my Hell Room would bring on the next ice age or result in a worldwide pizza shortage. Odds are good that I would probably not die a horrible death when a pile of my own belongings toppled over on me. And I have gathered that the weight of the Hell Room was thus far not even close to impairing the structural integrity of my house.

On the potential spectrum of long-standing life problems, having too much stuff is admittedly a pretty awesome problem to have. Sometimes I have the weird daydream that before we're born, each person gets to have a session with God in which we spin a *Wheel of Fortune*–like roulette wheel of potential lives. As categories whiz by I catch glimpses of life's myriad possibilities. Genocide refugee, heroin addict, and brain tumor fly by, followed by Picasso mistress, factory farm chicken, and that guy who could only move his left foot.

Mine? It lands on clutterer. See also: *Too much stuff*.

So, you know, I can live with that.

But sometimes I still feel guilty, like, I should just be quiet about my totally lame problem. *Too much stuff?* I think critically to myself, *Who cares?* Apropos to this point, not so long ago I got an email from my friend Debbi who remarked that she *envied* my "Hell Room":

> "I *wish* I had an extra room that was just waiting for me to get to it. Instead, I have the contents of your 'scary room' fairly evenly distributed throughout my entire house, so no one area is 'safe'... I feel I have control over nothing in my house."

I knew she meant nothing accusatory about it, but it did stop me for a moment. Wait a minute, I thought. Is this project...offensive? Is this akin to me being a debutante and blog-whining about the impossibility of confining my ball gowns to *only three* walk-in closets? And where, may I ask, are the *tiaras* supposed to go? (Yes, we all know where they should go. Never mind.)

On the other hand, listen to what Debbi was saying here: "*I feel I have control over nothing in my house.*" Considering how much time we all spend in our homes, that's a heck of a statement. If you can't control your own house, what *can* you control? If you aren't in control of your house, *who is?*

Mark Zuckerberg? The neighbor's dog? Freemason Scientologists?

I've been downright flabbergasted at how many folks say "*Yes!*" when I tell them that I'm writing about clutter, at which point they then launch into a description of the closet, attic, garage, or storage unit that is their own personal Hell Room. If it isn't their own problem, it's the problem of someone they know and are more than a little concerned about. "Oh boy," they say, "Have I got someone for you to talk to!" They often seem terribly relieved to be able to talk about this "dirty little secret." I've come to realize that the Stuff conundrum is one that people in our culture feel quite keenly, even when it isn't on an epic scale. As in Debbi's description, helplessness is the key emotion I hear in these descriptions, and on some level I'm coming to see it as an issue of empowerment.

How big a leap is it, really, from "I feel like I have control over nothing in my *house*" to "I feel like I have control over nothing in my *life*"? I think we all have a tendency to want to judge a book by its cover and see our habitations as physical representations of the people who live in them, which is a source of much guilt and self-recrimination for us keeper types. I imagine that's part of the rubbernecking appeal of the hoarding reality shows: we don't watch them simply for the opportunity to view a horrific mess, we want to see the *architect* of that horrific mess, who is presumably an example of a person somehow gone horribly wrong as well. Consciously or unconsciously, we can't help but compare ourselves to that person mentally, ticking off the ways we aren't like *that*.

On particularly bad, overcrowded days—days that are packed as full as my upstairs room—I feel this blurring of the categories of house and life keenly. On such days, even though nothing particularly dire may be happening, I nevertheless begin to have a creeping sensation that I'm being strangled by my life. As you can imagine, it's not a particularly nice feeling, but what's interesting is that when it happens I generally find myself trying to rectify the *spiritual* chaos by doing something about the *physical* chaos. This is to say, when I get upset I organize. It's how I freak out.

But how can this be? you may ask. *What about that big fat mess of a room? How could the Hell Room ever come about if its owner has a penchant for organization?* Well, let me explain it this way: just as I love objects, and above all love to keep objects, I also love to organize them. I love to arrange them and sort them and have them line up in a pleasing way or a way that seems to make infinite sense. That's right! I:

- alphabetize my spice drawer.
- reorganize the medicine cabinet for fun.
- consider rearranging the towels in the bathroom closet an ideal rainy day activity.

It has also been suggested that I am just a touch overprotective of my label maker.

So it would seem that the problem isn't so much that I have difficulty *organizing*—which I could do all day long—but rather that I have difficulty *discarding*—which consequently makes the required organizing process so ridiculous and Herculean as to seem near impossible. If I had, say, the resources of a nice, medium-sized institution with all the corresponding climate-controlled storage and archival document cases, I'd be in fantastic shape. Heck, let's throw in a staff, too, while we're at it. Then it really *would* be the Eve Museum.

So, when I feel that my life is spinning out of control, I organize. I do this not only because I find it soothing but because it gives me a sense of regaining control. And the more crazy life feels, the more fervor with which I attack the pocket of disorder that happens into my line of sight.

Take, for example, one day *last* summer.

It was all my own fault, really. Should I have *said* something when my husband scheduled our photographers' get-together party for thirty guests the day *after* our anniversary but the day *before* Father's Day? Probably. Should I have realized how *much* it was going to stink bringing Ilsa home from *her* camp in northeastern Vermont three hours away only to have to turn around and get Greta out the door to that same camp without missing a beat? Perhaps.

It had been like this ever since school let out—last day of school picnic! Quick trip to brother's graduation! Final piano lesson makeups! Begin summer math tutor! Aaaaa! I kept waiting for the calm and relaxing part of summer to begin, only to realize that—whoops!—I hadn't *scheduled* any calm-and-relaxing time into the calendar, so therefore it did not exist. Instead we were running like maniacs from one activity to the next, not wanting to miss a thing. I always envision summer feeling like a scene out of *Huckleberry Finn* when lately it was more closely resembling a hallucinatory run-on sentence from a Jack Kerouac novel.

To make matters worse, when I felt guilty about rushing the girls or having to say "no" or "stop fighting" or "get Mommy a paper bag to breathe into," I would promise them little things to make myself feel better…things that didn't seem like a big deal at the time but then added still more on to my list of "must dos." And the cycle got worse.

For example, *before* it was time to spend the entire day driving Greta to circus camp, I somehow ended up promising that while she was away that week I would:

- buy her a bra for her strapless dress.
- get a new battery for her watch.
- photocopy her math tutor's problems for her.
- pack her bags for our *next* family trip—it's right around the corner!
- buy her a pony.

Except maybe not that last one. I hope.

Now. Did I mention *that same week* I was taking a long-anticipated immersion class in Italian? That it took me a full hour each way to commute to and from said class? That the class began at nine each day and ended at four? I live in Vermont! Stores are open for, like, ten minutes a day here. They roll up the sidewalks at four p.m. for everything but nice restaurants that serve fourteen-dollar appetizers to people from New Jersey. *When,* I wondered somewhat hysterically, *the heck am I supposed to go* bra *shopping?*

In the midst of all this peace and tranquility and before Greta headed to camp, my mom came to visit for two days. We had a nice visit. At least I think we did. I couldn't be sure because I spent the entire time breaking up arguments between the girls about important things like who got the better seat in the car, who got to choose the movie, who got better presents, and who will be the first to drive Mommy out of her ever-loving mind. Also, as mentioned, I was trying to pack Greta, seemingly against her will, while doing forty-seven individual loads of "wash separately, on delicate cycle" laundry.

So there I was, in my packing-induced, bickering-heightened, laundry-laden state of utter nerve-fried exasperation, when I tried to obtain something—what? a fan? a sleeping bag? a medium-sized flamethrower?—from the storage room *without* causing several items to come crashing to the floor and failed miserably. *That's* when it happened. I snapped like a toy from the dollar store. Much like my mind at that moment, the storage room was in chaos…suddenly I *had* to clean that room up. *Now.*

But…*why? Why* clean up something as random as a storage room when you were supposed to be packing? When your mother was visiting? When the kids were fighting and Greta was practicing her impression of a kid who is confident camp clothes know how to pack themselves?

My organizational fit probably had something to do with the fact that the storage room was just at that particular moment starting to remind me eerily of the Hell Room. You can only close so many doors in your life before it starts feeling awfully small. No! I thought desperately, *No!* I couldn't make the kids stop bickering, couldn't make the laundry spin cycle go any faster, couldn't keep all my promises to Greta about all those errands, and certainly at that particular moment couldn't imagine fixing the Hell Room, but at least *I could do THIS.*

Sensing that it was perhaps a good time to give me a wide berth, Ilsa and my mom got out a puzzle. I got to work sorting and stacking and—yes—even throwing away as if my life depended upon it. I threw out several weird cleaning implements with lots of interchangeable parts and inches of dust on them (counter steamer, anyone?), made piles of well-intentioned, used-once gadgets to be given away (farewell, rice cooker!), and generally looked askance at anything that wasn't pulling its weight in shelf space.

When the dust finally cleared, it all worked out okay. Greta made it to camp, *with* clothes. Several puzzles got put together and then disassembled. And I could enter the storage room once more without peril to life and limb. Mom had seen that maniacal gleam in my eye, and we all lived to tell the tale.

In the aftermath, it occurred to me that clutter comes in many forms, not all of them tangible, and that clutter of the physical kind can exacerbate clutter of the mind or of the schedule, and vice versa. Just as we are lucky enough to live in a time when people can *have* more stuff than people have ever had before, we also live in a time when people can *do* more stuff than people have ever done before. I wasn't sure I knew how to solve this—after all, just like our belongings, these are all fabulous things we feel lucky to have: circus camp! Italian immersion class! Photographer party! I was coming to realize the deep and profound importance of *space*. Whether that space is the blissful ability to walk into a room and find something you need easily or the blissful ability to be calm and relaxed. Wasn't some of my problem coming down to a kind of nearsightedness, a blindness to the value of leaving my house *and* my schedule more…open?

It's not a new idea, of course. "Less is more" may not exactly be a news flash, but it's a concept that has eluded me for as long as I can remember. Even when I was a kid growing up, getting rid of things almost *never* seemed like the right thing to do.

I learned this lesson when I was very small, so small that I was still learning Important New Things all the time: tying my shoes! Telling time! How not to have the dog reach up and grab my sandwich off my plate when I wasn't looking! One day, while I was coloring, I suddenly, all at once, figured out how to draw a Mickey Mouse head that actually *looked* like Mickey Mouse—I realized that I had to draw that interior bumpy circle of white (or peachy skin color) that makes up Mickey's face and *separate it* from his head and ears, which are black.

I imagine I was about five years old at this time. To me, the discovery of how to draw a reasonably recognizable Mickey Mouse face seemed just short of successfully creating cold fusion in my kitchen sink. I was fascinated with this discovery in the same way that I was fascinated by the doodle of a birthday cake my grandfather drew on my birthday cards every year—with two ovals connected by straight lines to make it look like it was—in a cartoonish way—three-dimensional. I was fascinated by this idea that you could make things that looked—convincingly—like *other things*.

I may have been only five, but I distinctly recall being quite sure that I would keep this little sketch *forever*. It was, at that moment, my most prized possession in the world, made all the more precious by the fact that I had actually *made* the thing.

A short time later, I was really, really mad about something—who knows what? The injustice of the universe, probably. I stormed into my room, and determined to punish someone in the harshest manner possible, I picked up my beloved Mickey Breakthrough Drawing and *threw it into the trash*. Mom would find it there, of course, and realize (a) what an artistic genius I was and (b) how deeply wrong it was for life to be so unfair that it would cause me to throw away such a masterpiece.

Only that's not what happened. Instead, the garbage disappeared the next day, as it always did, and when I remembered to ask Mom about it, she had no idea what I was talking about.

"Oh honey—if it was in the trash, it's gone now. I'm sorry."

What? How had she failed to realize that Mickey drawing *wasn't* trash?! That it being in the trash was a protest!?

Man. I now realized that life was worse than unfair—it was indifferent. As a five-year-old, this was a deeply unpleasant revelation. No one could bring back my amazing first artistic breakthrough. It was gone forever.

My relationship with the trash would never be the same again. My harmless little wastepaper basket now seemed to have grown teeth: the garbage was now a dangerous place where wonderful things—things with stories, with personal significance—disappear and can never, ever come back.

With *keeping*, on the other hand, as far as I could tell, there was really no downside. The only time I can recall this didn't hold true was in seventh grade when a particularly mean classmate shoved her brown bag of lunch garbage—including a leftover uneaten sandwich—into my backpack for me to find later. Once I found it, I was horrified by the nastiness of this gesture. I had to respond—but how? *Aha!* I knew what I ought to do: I would wait awhile and then *mail her garbage back to her*. So I hid this nasty sandwich in the back of my dresser drawer at home for weeks. Months. Fortunately, the sandwich was peanut butter and not tuna fish. Finally I came to the realization that I was never going to actually see my revenge scheme through, so I threw the lunch bag away— which was a distinct relief.

So between Mickey and the peanut butter sandwich, I grew up with the idea firmly planted in my young mind that keeping everything just short of old food was a pretty good idea.

And so I kept things. Before I was old enough to have my own money, I kept things that came free: hotel soaps, restaurant matchbooks, interesting rocks, and the round pop-off lids from Dannon yogurt containers. I don't recall anyone ever suggesting that there was anything wrong with keeping such things—except my mother, who was dismayed that I needed so many old juice containers and oatmeal boxes for my pretend "grocery store"—but if they had I would have been mystified. In fact, I *was* mystified when at one point my mother proposed selling some of my old toys at a local group tag sale—*why on earth*, I wondered, *would I want to do* that?

Didn't I get to keep everything, pretty much forever? Wasn't that what adults did? After all, the adults I knew seemed to have so much stuff—*houses* full of it!—from so many different parts of their lives. How was I ever going to catch up? If, as a kid, I had opened up a fortune cookie whose message inside said, "Less is more," I probably would've reacted as if the message said, "Night is day" or "Black is white."

I would've said, "Huh. Well, *that* makes no sense!"

But as an adult, of course, I think about things that never would've occurred to kid-me. For instance, I wonder about the ethics of owning things. Ascetics exist in many of the world's religions, a common theme among them being the relinquishing of worldly possessions in favor of spiritual goals. This would seem to indicate that these concepts exist in mutual opposition to one another: the physical world versus the spiritual world—pick one! You can't have both. The Bible famously says it is easier for a camel to go through the eye of a needle than for a rich man to get into heaven. But what about the hoarders? (I know Dante reserved a circle of Hell for them in *The Inferno*, but I'm trying not to take that too personally.)

I wonder: on a very basic, fundamental level does enjoying things *so* much make me, well, a bad *person*?

Even though many people want to chalk the explosion of the Too Much Stuff problem up to bawdy American consumerism run amuck, I don't quite buy that—literally. I may technically be described as "materialistic," but in the most exact and literal sense of the word—my materialism isn't the kind that can be purchased at the neighborhood mall or in one of the seven million catalogs that appear unwanted at my doorstep every year. I don't blame my overabundance of objects on a shopping compulsion or a rabid consumerist impulse or a need to impress with my status-y belongings because none of these themes particularly resonate with me. Sure, like any good middle-class member of our consumer-focused American culture, I've flirted with each of these ideas—tried them on like funny hats at a costume shop—but none of them ever fit.

I've been to the Mall of America, a shopping complex so vast that it accommodates life-size Lego sculptures and a full-size amusement park in the atrium. I've been to outlet malls so expansive they require their own maps and zip codes. I've been to pre-Christmas Black Friday sales so chaotic that boxes of shoes from the store's upper balcony were cascading like falling rocks on dangerous mountain passes, terrorizing the shoppers waiting below to fork over their cash in long, snaking lines.

And you know what? I kind of don't get any of that.

No. I'm talking about just plain loving *things*—objects. When I was young, I remember being quite distressed by the idea that someday I would be dead, primarily because this could result in me being separated from my teddy bear. I had a great hypothetical moral debate about this: what would I do? Should I tell my parents I was to be buried with my teddy bear, just in case? But that seemed a terrible, morbid thing to do with a stuffed animal, whose job in life is to bring joy and comfort to people. And this was a *particularly* wonderful and comforting teddy bear. Was it fair for me to want to keep him all to myself, even in death? I wondered. I struggled with the issue at length on nights when I couldn't get to sleep. I never did reach a satisfying decision on the matter.

Sure, all kids feel strongly about their favorite stuffed animal, even if they don't have the disturbing debate I did. But looking back, I realize I did this about so many things: as a kid I could sit and moon over my collections for *hours*. I'd categorize them according to different criteria (Now I'll organize the matchbooks by *state!*), noticing different trends (I have seven lemon yogurt lids but ten vanillas! What does that *mean?*), admiring instances of symmetry (I have just as many blue pieces of beach glass as green!), and enjoying the sheer objectness of them all. Each object was a teeny-tiny reference point to a moment in my life, big or small—like a million stars in the sky, each one connecting in an invisible line back to me.

In retrospect, I wonder if this is how a hoarder is usually born. Is it a wrong way to think? Does it always begin innocuously enough but end one day with a clogged-up, embarrassing house, karmic punishment for the sin of overvaluing mere things?

So I do worry that I'm too in love with objects. They are, after all, inanimate. Shouldn't I care more, spend more time on, oh, I don't know, say, people? Animals? Ridding the world of those little pills on sweater elbows? As a grown-up my collections have changed, but I still obsess over them, or I did before I had kids and "free time" became a theoretical concept. In particular, I kept a rather obsessive album with Polaroids of all my beloved antiques in a binder complete with receipt and description of where I bought or from whom I had inherited each Yellowware bowl or aluminum ware tray. I could lie and say I made it for insurance purposes or something, but in reality it was just something I felt compelled to *do*. Catalogue. Organize. Obsess. Enjoy!

These days, however, as a mom who can't find time to tie her own shoes half the time, I look at that album and it all strikes me as slightly bonkers: *what was I thinking? Who has time for that madness?* But it's obvious. I was in love. I'm in love with it all.

It's not always about love, of course. For someone else, creeping-keeping-itis might be another issue entirely; for my grandmother, it certainly was.

I didn't know my maternal grandmother very well—I can probably count the number of times I saw her in person on one hand. The few times we visited her when I was a kid were memorable, though. Everything was always the same and always in its place: porcelain Royal Doulton figurines of wispy women in bell-shaped dresses looked out over us from the mantel, a brass cage on the end table held a mechanical bird that sang a song when you wound the knob underneath. Grandma always kept a bowl of hard candies in a little blue glass bowl on the coffee table, which no one ever touched. I knew *I* wasn't to touch *anything*.

She was famous in the family for being fastidious to a fault. As in many families, there was the story about how she had thrown my uncle's entire baseball card collection in the trash with the inevitable punch line that it would surely have been worth a fortune today. With Grandma there was always a sense that if the bed were unmade or the dishes left undone, somehow the *neighbors would know*. This reputation was confirmed by the few times I met her. There was never a time when I visited her that there weren't fresh vacuum tracks on the carpet; everything was always spare, neat as a pin, dust-free, and exactly where it had been the last time I visited to within a nanometer. As a kid it struck me as weird. Her apartment always felt hermetically sealed and a little lifeless, more like a diorama than a home.

The last time I saw her was when I was twenty; it was her ninetieth birthday. Family had flown in from all over to see her, but what I remember most about the entire event was the fact that she became nearly apoplectic when she opened my gift. This was not because I had figured out the most insanely perfect gift for a ninety-year-old (I gave her a decorative candle—hey, I was twenty.) but rather because it was packed in Styrofoam peanuts, some of which were *falling on the floor*. I mean, there might have been eleven peanuts on the floor: this was not Exxon Valdez. But my grandmother's voice went up an octave, and a garbage bag was called to the disturbing scene *immediately*. Geez. She acted as if the floor gestapo might arrive at any moment and put us all to work in a decorative candle factory as punishment. That was my grandmother: scrupulous. Meticulous. Everything in its proper place. Unlike her grand-daughter, weird-saving behavior was just *not* in her makeup.

Or so I thought.

It was lucky I went along with my mother to clean out her apartment when my grandmother passed away at the age of ninety-five, or I might never have known that even *she* had a little hoarding stash of her own. When we opened her bedroom closet, we found something unusual in the deep side shelves where the shoes or purses would ordinarily be. We found food. Cans and cans of it, stacked in neat rows all the way back to the wall: rows and rows of beans, peas, corn. And again, in the upper shelf of the hallway coat closet, where the hats and gloves might ordinarily be: boxes and boxes of crackers, rows and rows of ketchup. Grape jelly. Vinegar.

Don't get me wrong. This wasn't epic-scale food hoard-ing—it was all fairly easily packed up in a handful of boxes and donated to the food pantry. But knowing what I did of my grandmother and her extreme fastidiousness, her the-neighbors-will-know-if-a-pin-is-out-of-place hysteria, it felt as surprising to me as if we had found evidence that she had been distilling moonshine in the bathroom or had been involved in the Iran-Contra affair. It felt like we had happened upon a deep secret. I think if she had been there that day with us, making that discovery in her closet, she would have been a bit embarrassed.

Although I certainly wouldn't have wanted her to be. After a moment I made the not-so-difficult connection: my grandmother was a child of the Depression. Finding that hidden food certainly helped me to see my uncle's baseball card story from a different perspective. It's one thing to bemoan the loss of, essentially, a fat profit margin ("I got this for five cents! Now it's worth $5,000!"); it's quite another to have lived through the pain of real hunger and, no matter how many decades ago it occurred, to have that awful memory never very far from one's mind.

So I guess what we hoard says an awful lot about us and what we're afraid of.

If hoarding is born of fear, then it would be logical to ask myself: what am *I* afraid of?

The answer comes in two parts, which I will title "Nostalgia" and "Potential."

Nostalgia

First and foremost, I am afraid of losing the past.

Logically, my line of thinking usually unfolds like this: in large part, our memories make us who we are. The thing is, I have a terrible memory. Truly. I'd like to take this moment to apologize to every person whose name I've ever forgotten, which is pretty much everybody. Other ridiculous things I have been known upon occasion to forget include my own phone number, zip code, and time zone. It's bad.

Consequently objects have become my crutch of choice, helping me to recall things I never would otherwise. I'm always shocked by the things that objects can bring back into my mind with vivid clarity, which I otherwise am certain would have been forgotten entirely. As if they never even happened.

Without my memories, who am I? If I equate memories and objects, then to discard an object is to lose a piece of myself forever. This is why I keep souvenirs even of negative occurrences in my life, for fear that without them I would forget that event and even any lesson I may have learned from that event. The other day I came across a hastily scrawled page full of phone numbers and notes I took as plans were formulated for an intervention for a family member. A deeply painful and anxiety-ridden time—wouldn't I sooner forget that?

No. When I ran across it, the event had so faded from my memory that the sheet of paper surprised me with its very existence. The urgency of the handwriting, the exact details of a plan that had changed by the hour until it finally happened. I had been in the process of forgetting it—or at least I felt like I had been. Have you seen the movie *Memento*, in which the character has rapidly occurring amnesia and is constantly tattooing notes on his own skin in order to remind himself who he is and what is happening to him? Sometimes I feel like that guy—sending notes to my future self in the form of objects.

I fear that I am dangerously close to saying that somehow, without my objects, I cease to exist; however, I know with my rational mind that this is not true. If I lived in a circumstance that required I own very little—if I was a nomad in the Gobi Desert or lived in a broom closet in Brooklyn—I have no doubt that I would adapt. I would have to. I would survive. I would be me…but I would be a different version of me. Would that version of me be okay? Would it be good enough?

Potential

If this were a late-night advertisement, this would be the part where the announcer enthuses, "But wait, there's more!" Yes, I get two fears for the price of one neurosis. It is the idea of need. I worry that someday I will *need* this thing, and my life, my happiness, will in some way depend upon it. This covers a broad territory. It could be as frivolous as "I must keep this ugly bridesmaid dress because someday someone might have an ugly bridesmaid dress party—and I'll be ready!" and as dire as "I should keep these unused antibiotics in case the world ends and antibiotics are *never made again.*"

Seriously, and I blame Stephen King for this, ever since I read *The Stand* I've suffered from "What if you end up being one of the last people in the world?" syndrome. I don't have the time or the sustained interest to become a *real* doomsday prepper, but when the opportunity presents itself, I have a lot of trouble combatting "what-if-ian-ism." Several years ago, a dear friend of mine mailed me a package containing a year's supply of birth control pills, presumably in the hopes that I would stop procreating.

They had originally been prescribed for her, and she no longer needed them, so I guess she thought of it like sending me a coupon for cheese sticks or something—like, why not? It's worth money, and I know you eat cheese, sooooo… I knew better than to take someone else's medication, though.

But did I throw the pill packs away? No. My logic, and I swear this is what went through my head at the time, went like this: well, I should keep these because in the unlikely event that there is an apocalypse, destroying most of civilization as we know it including most Rite-Aid pharmacies, then I will have birth control backup.

The fact that birth control might be the least of my worries in the event of the end of the world, which would almost certainly involve brain-eating zombies, plagues of locusts, and rampant gluten, apparently did not enter into it.

My mind is certainly entertaining.

Both of these twisted-logic thought patterns strike me as a kind of self-distrust. That my ability to survive in some far-off unlikely hypothetical future hinges on keeping around weird and expired bottles of random medication seems not only like I worry *way* too much but also like I can't simply…relax. Can't I just live today and trust that I will find a way to live through tomorrow and the day after that?

When finally I did find Marie Kondo's book *The Life-Changing Magic of Tidying Up* and began to read it, I realized that I may be onto something here because it seems that this is exactly what she has in abundance that I do not: *extreme confidence*. Trust in herself to make a decision based on her needs today, not tomorrow or next week or when it starts raining frogs. I'm in awe of the power that gives her and a little frightened by it too… I can't help but wonder what happens when you get carried away and throw out your wedding dress—what happens to your extreme confidence *then*? Are you like Icarus, flying too close to the sun on wings made of hubris and wax? Do your wings get all melty like American cheese in the toaster oven?

But I couldn't worry about that right now. I added another mantra to the first one. In addition to Kondo's "Does it spark joy?" I added my own. "Trust yourself."

For my first order of business as a person who is going to trust herself, I decided that taking pleasure in/relying on inanimate objects does *not* make me a bad person. After all, I've never been asked to choose between rescuing a person and rescuing one of my beloved objects—for example, if each were tied to a separate train track and I could only save one from an oncoming locomotive—but if I were, I feel pretty confident I'd choose the person every time, even if it was my beloved teddy bear versus that girl from seventh grade who left her garbage sandwich in my backpack. That has to count for something.

(Parenthetical question: in the above-described scenario, choosing between the mean girl and my teddy bear, am I allowed to *ever*-so-slightly hesitate?)

CHAPTER NINE

WE CONTINUE CONTINUING

"It looks worse."

—Steve

Not to be paranoid or anything, but more than once it felt as if the Hell Room were fighting back. From the beginning, going into the room felt somewhat like I imagine entering a tropical rain forest would feel—claustrophobic and a bit dangerous. One of us would trip and fall into a precarious pile that would then trigger a toppling of other containers and boxes. An ankle would turn on something on the floor, or an elbow would get a nasty scrape on a filing cabinet corner that seemed to appear out of nowhere.

Nevertheless, slowly, methodically, we'd been proceeding with our excavation. Any of my prior feeble attempts at keeping things organized over the preceding years had long since been abandoned, so it took a fair amount of doing just to gain a basic understanding of what we were dealing with. Following our initial floundering efforts, we got a little more systematic about things. The number one order of business became to group like items together before even getting into any more decisions about what to keep and why. I could have used a traffic-directing megaphone: *Attention, family photos! Family photos! Kindly proceed to the giant stack by the north-facing window! Fabric! Calling all fabric! Please throw yourself in the pile by the south window!* Any paper rolled up poster-style went over *here*; framed artwork of all shapes and sizes stacked against the back wall over *there*. A mountain of kids' artwork rose up in the room's center, like a volcano emerging from the sea. And so on.

Goat paths gave way to walkways, meeting up in plazas and piazzas that opened up and closed again, rematerializing somewhere else as we shuffled, vacuumed, sorted, and shuffled some more.

By necessity, the beginning had entailed dealing with lots of big stuff: in addition to throwing out the bookshelf and the paint-covered rug, we brought large things I couldn't bear to part with—like the kids' largely neglected art easel—to the attic. We folded up and stored in the basement the two eight-foot-long tables that had been Steve's old workstation for his camera-strap enterprise. I gleefully shoved a remarkably heavy and much-peed-upon-by-the-now-deceased-cat file cabinet out the far window to come down with a satisfying *crash* in our driveway... At least I could be unsentimental about rusty, smelly old file cabinets, if nothing else.

A gargantuan blob of black metal and plastic had formed in the Hallway Room, which was coming to be known as the "Ask Daddy" pile. At its largest, it measured in at perhaps two feet high and eight feet long and resembled a prop cabinet for Ansel Adams's worst nightmare: cable releases, empty equipment boxes, old filter sets, elastic cords, camera bags, lens pouches, and plastic, technical-looking doodads that had accumulated over the prior two decades of Steve using cameras and bending them to his will with adjustments and modifications. Piled together in and among these higgledy-piggledy treasures were camera magazines, old promotional materials, show reviews, press releases, lots of cryptic, scribbled notes featuring order numbers, phone numbers, and calculation numbers, none of which made any sense whatsoever to me—like shorthand from Mars. But far and away the biggest culprit was an enormous amalgamation of photographic negatives: loose negatives, plastic-sleeved negatives, panoramic negatives, color and black-and-white negatives, snapshots, architectural interiors, artworks and...and... It took my breath away to behold the enormous I-have-no-idea-what-to-do-with-this-ness of it all.

I kept asking Steve when we could, you know, take a moment and address the hall pile together, at which point he would say loudly, "What? I can't hear you! I think we have a bad connection!" Then he would get up from the dining room table and race to his studio.

But the good news was that now the easier things, the larger things, had at this point been dealt with and the category piles were established. I realized we had reached a pivotal moment: we had as much open *floor* space as *occupied-with-stuff* floor space... It was roughly fifty-fifty. Ta-da!

It was still a god-awful mess, mind you, but compared to where we had started, it felt like an absolute transformation. Look: there was floor! You could walk! Random piles had been converted to themed piles! No more paint splatters on the carpet and dead ladybugs on every horizontal surface! The girls and I each kept remarking in an admiring way at "how much like a real room" it was starting to look, which struck me as funny, as if we were complimenting a dog wearing a hat on how much like a real person he looked. But it was true—we were terribly proud of the sense of "room-ness" the former Hell was evincing.

Now it was time to begin the slog I was dreading most of all: sweating our way through the *small* stuff, which, quite overwhelmingly, was composed of *paper*. The paper seemed to me to present by far the most daunting task of the entire enterprise and one I had been avoiding with extreme vigilance. Old birthday cards, math workbooks, ticket stubs, piles of ancient tax returns all glommed together to form the To Be Avoided at All Costs island chain.

One large culprit: years ago my husband and I ran an art gallery. Consequently, a major ingredient of the paper salad with which I was currently confronted was a wide variety of papers to do with that long-lost enterprise. I was relieved to come across entire file folders filled with detailed correspondence with artists I didn't even remember we had carried. Amazingly, I had printed out *every single* email message that had been sent and filed them all away—obviously I thought posterity would be deeply excited to know whether Philippe De l'Artist would be shipping his artwork via UPS or FedEx Ground.

Things I Can't Get Rid Of without Listing Here

Occasionally I need to perform some sort of magical, symbolic act before I can get rid of a particular object. Taking a picture sometimes helps. So I figured maybe it would help if I write some particularly stubborn items down here so we can all agree on how ridiculous this is.

- *Plexiglass cup personalized with my name and a snowman.* I have no idea where this came from. When you have an unusual name like *Eve* and don't know where your personalized cup came from, that's just creepy.
- *My grandmother's cheap, brown plastic thread spool case.* Trust me, this is not how *anyone* would want to be remembered.
- *My old yellow raincoat from when I was a kid.* Before you say "aw!" let me point out that it is some weird kind of vinyl that over time has become tacky to the touch. If I were to wear it during the summer I'd come home looking like one of those hang-from-the-ceiling fly strips. Also, my mother wrote *EVE OGDEN* on the inside in black Sharpie, and it shows through, so if I were ever to wear this again I'd have the benefit of: (a) looking like I'd just escaped from a home for dementia patients or (b) being easily recognized, from behind, by anyone who knew me before I was married and is dyslexic.
- *Greta's "School Skate" laminated ID card from five years ago, with* no *picture.* Seriously, I need help.

So, of course, the ancient emails could go straight into recycling, right? But, clearly, I had to actually *look* at every single sheet of paper, just to be sure one of them wasn't accidentally an original copy of the Declaration of Independence or something. As I did this, however, I could feel something beginning to creep in around the corners of my brain, the beginnings of a conversation between one part of myself and the other: *sure* I could get rid of this! Or…could I? Was there any conceivable way I might wish I had kept these notes back and forth? I mean, it really was a *little* bit interesting—all this correspondence—and, you know, once this information was *gone*, it would be gone *forever*, never to be gotten back. So, I'd better think this through.

Now look: here was an exchange with an artist who I got annoyed at for dropping off the face of the earth, only to have him at last reply testily that he had been getting a divorce—but look, here's an earlier note sent from his wife. Hmmm. Do you think they were having problems because his artwork wasn't selling? There's a story in here somewhere.

I mean, what if, and stay with me here, what if I wanted to write a *novel*…about an art gallery? Wouldn't this sort of be just what I would need? And actually wasn't that *kind of* a good idea? Maybe, *just in case*, I should set aside a box of all the artists' correspondence…

See? See? This is what my brain does to me. Every. Single. Time. I'm so busy trying not to exclude possibility, not to close off imaginary roads somewhere down the line, that I can forget what I'm trying to accomplish *right now*.

So I actually had to have the following conversation with myself: "Eve?" (pause) "Exactly *how* likely is it that you will someday write a novel that takes place in an art gallery?" On a scale of one to ten, ten being most likely, I gave that possibility at best a two, which is to say: extremely unlikely although not completely impossible.

And then I had to ask myself, possibly in the voice of an exceedingly patient kindergarten teacher: am I currently working on a project that actually *exists*? Perhaps the project of cleaning up this room and proving to myself that I can have control over my objects?

Right! That's right! I'm writing about *that*, and as we all know a bird in the hand is worth two in the bush and fourteen in the Hell Room. Having effectively talked myself off the ledge once again, I continued going through the papers, but my resolve was shattered. I abandoned the task and went off in search of another job less fraught with ambivalence— for example, throwing out moldy vegetables.

———————

For a change of pace, one day Greta was the one who got sidetracked. While I emptied out a large box of old, abandoned knitting projects, she got mired in what is surely the lightning quicksand of the Hell Room landscape: the family photographs.

To the right of the doorway and in the middle of the room, we have a full nine-foot window bench, with built-in shelves below and cushions above. It was utterly overwhelmed by our family's combined life's history of photographs and snapshots. They are at least partially organized by chronology, and Greta immediately became entranced by a box containing the snapshots of her as a newborn and then continued exploring further back in history. Because they've been so hard to access, she's never seen any of these photographs before. As I plowed through random piles of papers, her interjections floated across the room to me.

"*Wow*—I slept a *lot!*" (Greta the newborn)

"You look *terrible* here!" (How do I explain the paradox that new babies sleep a lot and yet new parents sleep hardly at all?)

"Okay, I'm going to assume this is your *boyfriend*." (Quick! Scan every memory of every boyfriend I've ever had and try to guess which one she's talking about from the tone of her voice.)

"*Mom*! I don't know what *that* even *is*!" (A book of collages from art school featuring such lascivious subject matter as shirtless college boys, baby dolls, and nude models.)

"Whoa! He was hot!" (You are not allowed to say that about your uncle, Greta.)

She came upon the photo-collage album we had made for Steve's father when he was dying from cancer. She came upon a photo of my parents at what looked like an Under the Sea–themed prom dated 1962. She came upon my collection of little cow figurines.

She came upon a small box of patches I had earned as a kid for passing various levels of ice skating and swimming competence. (Not achievement, mind you. *Competence*.) None of these were candidates for getting rid of, of course, but we were having fun.

It occurred to me that it was as if we were both—the two of us—walking around inside my brain. It was all there: happy things, sad things, surprises, confusion. At times it seemed as if we were exploring the history of a completely different person. And then I thought that, perhaps, *this* is what I had been saving all this Stuff for—not for posterity, but for…now. For this moment. I had retold a story of myself that I had forgotten all about—shared it, enjoyed it with Greta. What more was required of these things? Could it be, I wondered, that their job was done?

Theoretically speaking, of course.

The effort to tame the Hell Room was, for me, proving to be quite the emotional roller coaster. One day I'd be riding high and feeling confident, the next I'd find myself wandering the outskirts of despair, giving way to waves of frustration. Part of the problem is the fact that I am, admittedly, a terrible multi-tasker. Horrible. (On the upside, I am a *fantastic* mono-tasker, but sadly, there's not much call for that around my house.)

And the unraveling of the Hell Room—surprise!—necessitated all kinds of multitasking: not just sorting, piling, and rudimentary first aid but *distribution*. I couldn't bear the thought of anything going to a landfill that could possibly be of any use to someone somewhere. And that was a problem because getting things to the people who could appreciate them took time, orchestration.

This was an issue, incidentally, untouched on by Marie Kondo. She talked an awful lot about throwing things away, but could I really live with myself if I solved my problems by dumping them into the landfill?

Among the things we were finding that I could get rid of, many of them were "perfectly good" items ready to be used by someone somewhere. For example, I happened upon five boxes of plain white pocket folders—should I throw *them* into the trash? Despite myself I managed to compile boxes of unloved books, boxes of outgrown clothes, boxes of unlistened-to CDs and unwatched old DVDs and video cassettes… None of these things were broken or unusable—they were just extra to *me*.

Not long after the fun sidetracked day with Greta, I had one of these especially exasperated moments, brought on by a mixture of ill-advised multitasking. Greta, as it turned out, needed an unexpected ride to Grandma's, which would take me a good hour round-trip, and I was stressed about getting some time to write in.

But hey, I figured, why not take advantage of this opportunity? As long as I was going to Manchester, I might as well throw some things in my car to donate to the charity shop. These days I hardly seemed to leave the house without something to get rid of somewhere along the way.

So I quickly filled an *enormous* moving box with an assortment of misfit belongings, including a Mitt Romney bobblehead that "poops" candy (I swear) and a variety of small plastic "organizing bins" (*ha!*). Right before putting the box in the car, I implemented a strategy I devised years ago: once the box was packed, I allowed myself one or two items to take *back out* of the box—my own personal sacrifice to the gods of clutter.

I was anxious—as I always am—about getting rid of the things that were in the box despite the fact I was angry at them. All of them had been sitting stubbornly in the Hallway Room for weeks, blocking up the passageway, tripping up my steps, and clouding my vision. Every single time I passed them I'd looked down at the items and think to myself—"Yup! *Those* can go—next trip to the charity shop. *No* problem!" Still, after packing up the box, I hesitated. Mentally, I went over everything I had just packed in the box, reviewing what had gone inside it just minutes before, giving myself one last chance to change my mind about any of it. I was in a hurry, and that made me more nervous than usual that I would make a mistake.

But I had extracted my two items. On this occasion, it was a hat box that I was feeling sentimental about, despite the fact that I neither wore nor still own the hat, and the world's ugliest eighties-era purse, in pristine condition because I had never used it. I have now tried to get rid of this purse approximately twenty-seven times; slowly the purse is migrating to the category of "things I must keep precisely because they are so preposterous." Usually that ritual worked and allowed me to stop the cycle of reviewing it in my head over and over or, worse, riffling through the box in the charity shop parking lot, which always made me feel more than a little bit demented.

So there I was, Greta traipsing around behind me as if connected to me by a string, wearing a wide-eyed, exasperated "can we *go* yet?" expression. As I attempted to wrestle this ridiculous box of ridiculous things into my ridiculous car, I ended up feeling slightly—I don't know—ridiculous. In a stroke of genius I decided to remedy this situation by *also* wrestling the super-saturated, utterly overflowing basket of recyclable paper I'd accumulated while cleaning out Hell Room file cabinets into the recyclables container in the basement. Two minutes! It would only take two minutes, and then my anxiety would recede. I'd feel so much better. Like that strange day I had frantically cleaned out the storage room, I was trying to rectify my spiritual chaos by calming the physical chaos.

Sadly, however, the physical world was not on board with my plan. The recycling container, as it turned out, wasn't in the basement after all. It was still by the road from pickup the other day. So I headed out to collect it and discovered it wasn't out by the road, either—it was in a ditch by the side of the road.

Somewhere in the midst of all this fun, Steve must've overheard me swearing under my breath as I tromped exasperatedly up and down the stairs and lugged around my boxes and overflowing bins. He called out to me from his armchair in the living room, "What are you *doing*?"

"What am I *ever* doing?" I replied in a tone of voice that managed to be both testy and despondent. "*Moving crap around!* That's my *job* in life! Moving crap from one place to another! *Hooray!*"

So when I finally got myself into the car with Greta in tow and Ilsa going along for the ride, I was in that state of complete ill humor that one feels when things just aren't going the way you had hoped despite all your good intentions. One begins to wonder if, perhaps, the universe is harboring a secret grudge against your plans.

That's when I heard Ilsa snuffling in the back—she was clearly upset, and I asked her what was wrong. But I knew what was wrong; she had been given the choice by her father to go with him to the studio for the next hour or come with me to drop off Greta. As is characteristic for Ilsa, she had been so indecisive that we had had to decide for her, lest the seasons change before she made up her mind.

"It's just…*decisions*. I just can't *make* them." She snuffled from the backseat.

"I know, they're hard, right?" I said back, my empathetic-inner-mommy-self winning out over my frustrated-clutter-magnet-self.

"Why not?" Greta asked Ilsa innocently.

"I *hate* them, Greta—*I hate them*."

"Okay," Greta said gamely, deciding to demonstrate to her how easy decisions could be. "Pink or black?"

"Pink," Ilsa answered, then stopped herself. "No! Black!"

"Strawberry or vanilla?"

"*Greta!*" At this point Ilsa's voice was equal parts anguish, laughter, and despair. "*Don't make me kill you!*"

And I realized that Ilsa's anguish, laughter, and despair were also mine: although our indecision is over different things—I have no trouble choosing what I want to eat at a restaurant, whereas if we gave Ilsa an entire week she quite possibly still could not answer this question. But it comes from the same place, is rooted in the same deep-seated insecurity: I will make the wrong decision. I will fail. I will get rid of the wrong thing. I will rue the day I chose strawberry.

And, not coincidentally, that's exactly what we're doing every time we venture into the Hell Room: we're making decision after decision after *decision*. No wonder I'm jumping down everyone's throats, I thought. The whole reason the Hell Room came into being was my desire to *avoid* making decisions—to keep? Not to keep? Oh, *heck*—just put it over there, and I'll think about it tomorrow. And ever since we had begun this project months ago, I'd been haunted by the ghosts of unmade decisions past.

I was retraining myself to make those decisions now rather than put them off, or ripping off the Band-Aid quickly by chucking it all in a Dumpster. Nope, this was ripping off the Band-Aid in sloth fashion: one hair at a time. It was painful and, to make matters worse, if I was ever going to get anywhere in the course of one measly year, necessarily involved that atrophied multitasking muscle too, whether I liked it or not.

What was it I told Ilsa whenever she agonized over what to order for dinner or which T-shirt to wear? "It's okay. Go with your gut. There's no wrong decision here."

Huh. What do you know? That sounded like shorthand for "Trust yourself."

———

"Mom?" Greta asked me one afternoon in the Hell Room after happening upon an old-looking wooden box. "*Mom!*

What *is* this?" She opened the box to reveal a shiny set of monogrammed silver-plate flatware nestled into soft little velvet indentations.

"That? Oh, this was Grandma's silver, I mean, Great-Grandma's silver. We've never used it."

Greta gave me a look of abject disbelief. She paused, contemplating.

Then, in the most accusatory tone possible, she said, "*WHY HAVE WE NEVER USED THIS?*"

I shrugged. "Why? Umm. I don't know. It has to be hand-washed...?"

Greta gave me a very direct and serious look.

"*Mom.* I want you to leave me this. In. Your. Will."

I was so used to being the person who admonished other people about holding on to things that I was surprised. Greta was calling me on another, related score: *using* things. And she had me there. Because if I've learned anything at all from my clutter-filled ways, it's that saving things is often the direct opposite of using things. This is partly because when you save, you just can't find all the things you might use, but also because using things often means someday using them *up.* Things get broken. Things get threadbare. Things stop working and fall apart.

Of course, this is why comic book collectors don't actually read their valuable comic books, sometimes buying a second "reading" copy to ensure the pristine condition of their first copy. It's what my friend Miles discovered when she sat down with her kids to read an ancient, inherited copy of *Little Lord Fauntleroy,* so brittle the paper began to fall out and disintegrate upon page turning. She was incredulous—a book you can't read? What's the point in that?

Why *own* this set of silver plate, Greta was asking, if we aren't going to use and enjoy it?

We all anthologize our lives to one extent or another: photo albums, yearbooks, collections of old letters, or saving one's wedding dress…these are all the activities of a curator rather than a user. Although Marie Kondo disapproves, I'm not about to stop collecting my own life. It has been a source of pleasure for me ever since I can remember; it helps define me. However, I do think Greta has touched importantly on another key that's been eluding me.

Which has brought me to a third mantra to add to my collection: "Keep less. Use more."

———

Between all the random and bizarre items we were uncovering, the girls were discovering all kinds of things about their mom. Thus far, we were up to roughly five Hell Room–related Mom revelations:

1. Mom was a *total* hippie! Or punk. It's kind of unclear. Remind me why rubber bracelets aren't ugly again?
2. There is photographic evidence that, before becoming Mom, she had *boyfriends*! (Does Daddy know about this?)
3. She painted *naked men* in college! (Does Daddy know about *this*?)
4. She has beautiful heirlooms up there that she *doesn't even use*!
5. She keeps some things just because they're so weird. Which is *so* weird.

And while we're on the subject, let's add another to the list: Mom was an occasional juvenile delinquent.

"Mom? Where did *this* come from?" Greta was eyeing me keenly, and at once I knew there was no getting out of this one.

She was pointing at a small red-and-white metal sign that said, "NO PARKING—RESERVED FOR PRINCIPAL."

Sigh. Okay, okay. So, in my oh-so-wayward youth, I had stolen a parking lot sign. From the principal. Possibly, this is the most mischievous thing I have ever done, the runner-up being that time my friend and I spent an afternoon at the superstore putting plastic pears among the real ones in the produce section. I looked at Greta. This was one of *those* moments. "Did you ever do drugs, Mom?" "Did you have sex before you got married, Mom?" "Have you ever gotten a speeding ticket, Mom?" This was one of those moments when you'd very much like to hit the "pause" button on life and quickly figure out how to reconcile your current life as a parent and your past life as a person who nobody in particular was looking up to.

Would she think badly of me now? Would she be deeply disappointed in me? Would this start her down the road of a lifetime of criminal mischief, and when they brought her before the judge after she was caught painting graffiti on the White House, would she say, "But your honor—*Mom stole from the principal!*"

"Um, yeah. I did take that," I admitted. "From the…school parking lot. A long time ago," I added lamely. "I…shouldn't have."

Greta looked at me blankly.

"Really?"

"Really."

Pause.

Pause.

"I *love* you for that! I *love* that!" She was laughing and beaming from ear to ear. "*Mom* stole a principal's sign! Ha ha ha!"

Oh yes, we were learning all *sorts* of things.

CHAPTER TEN

DO YOU WANT THIS?

"Give it away, give it away, give it away, give it away now."

—Red Hot Chili Peppers,
"Give It Away" (1991)

L ately, it had felt to me like the entirety of the world was *downsizing*. I've never liked that word—*downsize*—because it's one of those annoying corporate euphemisms that has infiltrated our collective vocabulary, as in: I haven't been laid off—I've been downsized! I'm not obnoxious and pushy—I'm proactive! I'm not a cocaine addict—I'm highly stimulus-motivated!

Nevertheless, I don't know what *else* you say when your parents decide it's time to get rid of a whole lot of stuff and move to a smaller place. Unless it's: "Look out!"

I say this because over the course of the last year or so, everywhere Steve and I go it's like the last day of fourth grade all over again and Mrs. Rose is trying to give me a lifetime supply of bent flash cards and half-used math workbooks. (I took them, by the way.)

"Do you want this?" "Would you like this?" "Is this something you might have a use for?" In my particular situation, these are words to dread. Somehow, when it's someone I love, desperately trying to get rid of something, I have enormous trouble saying, "No, thanks!" even if I really, really, *really* don't want it. Partly, of course, this is the result of old habits dying hard. But partly this is me being the problem-solving good girl my personality always seems to default to: wanting to help, remove their separation anxiety, even gain their approval. Yes! *I* can solve your problem! *I'll* take that monstrous, glass, art nouveau cigar ashtray off your hands—*I* will appreciate it and will give it a good home!

As fate would have it, *this* year, of all years, my mom is moving. My dad is moving. *Steve's* mom is moving. Also our friends the Kravitts are moving. If we add all those people up, we're talking somewhere in the neighborhood of three hundred sixty-some lifetime years of accumulating that has to be gone through and winnowed. That officially scares me because I've never learned how to say "no" to the question "Do you want this?"

How easy would it be, I wondered, to just fill my Hell Room right back up in an effort to solve all the Stuff-oriented problems of my friends and family? Way, *way* too easy.

And yet, I couldn't just turn away, plug my ears, and lash myself to the mast like Odysseus because there were bound to be some things I really *did* want: old family photographs, for example, or other artifacts whose existence I might not even know about yet. So me hiding under the sofa to wait it out wasn't an option, either. I'd just have to face the music.

Midway through our year of removing clutter, the siren songs began.

Monica and Marty Kravitt are good friends of ours who have been coming to Vermont as a second home for years. And this year, at long last and after decades of planning and discussion, they were making the Big Move. They were moving to Vermont full-time.

Which was great, except for the fact that it seemed to be killing them. Every time I'd seen either one of them for months now, they looked like they'd just been through the spin cycle of one of those efficient European washing machines. Despite the fact that their other house had already sold and the moving vans had come and gone, they still had far more stuff then their one remaining house could accommodate— not enough had been shed in anticipation of the move. Their rooms, the basement, the garage, the unfinished attic they hoped to renovate into office spaces were all filled with things that had nowhere to go. I kept thinking it had to end soon: at some point it would have to start getting better, wouldn't it?

But not yet. And from the sounds of it, not anytime really soon, either. Even after reluctantly discarding and selling and recycling everything they could bear, they were continuing to tear their hair out at the sheer volume of it all.

Consequently every week or two for the past few months Marty had been showing up on our doorstep with their daughter Alex's old bicycle. Or a giant kite. Or an assortment of snow sleds. Or a perfectly good computer monitor. Or *three* perfectly good computer monitors. Would we have any interest in some wine bottles? No, there's no actual wine in them; they're empty.

I was getting tons of much-needed practice in saying "no," but after a while, I worried it might be hurting our friendship.

They looked so...so *desperate*. Sure, they knew about my project, but from the wide look in their eyes I knew they were so swamped with Stuff that it wasn't fully occurring to them that helping them meant sabotaging my Year of No Clutter. No, the *Titanic* was going down, and here *I* was, crappy friend number one, refusing to throw them a life raft.

It was all the harder because I could completely relate—I knew that feeling of desperation all too well. That was the feeling that made me want to just start pitching things out the window with a pitchfork, yelling, "Who's in charge around here anyway!? Get out! *Get out!*"

So it made sense to me what happened next. Not long after that I was going through some boxes of VHS tapes Marty had dropped off one day with the idea that our girls might like some of them. Sure, there were kid movies in there, which made sense, but at ages ten and fifteen, I doubted the girls were going to be choosing a staticky *Dumbo* over a Hi-Def streaming of *Harry Potter and the Elaborate Magical Plot* anytime soon. So I was transferring most of the tapes to another box for donation to the local library sale when I realized that something *else* was going on.

My first clue? Mixed in among the store-bought titles there were homemade tapes inscribed not just with movie names but also more personal-sounding stuff: "Dressage Clinic with Yvonne" and "Marc and Nathalie's Wedding." *Hmmm*, I thought. But surely, they've gone through these, I reasoned. They must not want them.

And then came a bombshell: "Alex's Fourth Birthday Party." Alex is their daughter. Okaaaaay, I thought. Hold on here. I know I tend to be *way* more sentimental than most people, so I always try to stop and perform a reality check in instances like this. Just because *I* would have kept something like this doesn't mean these were gotten rid of by mistake...right? I knew the last thing poor, beleaguered-looking Marty would appreciate is a box of *anything* boomeranging back his way. Maybe there was a perfectly good explanation. Maybe...maybe they have other copies? Or...or...

And then: "Pommier Family Reunion" (Monica's family). And then: "Alex's *First* Birthday Party."

All right. Assuming they had neither made copies nor suddenly morphed into Mommy and Daddy Dearest, there was *no way* they had intended to give away these tapes. I was sure this had been a mistake.

It felt weird, and oddly gratifying in a way, to be confronted by my worst nightmare: the unintentional giving away of something deeply personal and irreplaceable—except for the important detail that it was happening to *somebody else*.

Also, I found myself in the super-heroic position of being able to rectify this tragic wrong. I left our friends a phone message and then went off to look for an appropriate but tasteful cape and tights combo that would properly convey the persona of my new alter ego: SuperSaver! Savior of all meaningful objects everywhere!

And of course, it *had* been a mistake. In fact, considering the sheer magnitude of the lifetime accumulation they were wading through, if this was their biggest oversight, they were probably doing pretty well. When Marty came by to pick them up, he held the box of ten or so tapes and shook his head at them. Maybe it was disbelief that they could have accidentally given away something so sentimental, but it didn't feel that way to me. Rather, it was as if these objects *just wouldn't cooperate*—they insisted on tormenting him.

"I don't know what we're going to do with *these*," he said hopelessly. "We don't even *have* one of these players anymore. Did we give it to you? No? Well. We don't even have a player for these anymore."

"You could always get them converted to DVD," I ventured hopefully. "There's a place in Rutland that does it."

"I don't know," he was still shaking his head disconsolately. "I don't know *what* Monica will do with these. I don't know if she'll even keep them."

What? Nooooo! I thought. And for a second—a split second—SuperSaver contemplated grabbing the box back. That's right—if no one else would save Alex's fourth birthday party, *I* would!

Briefly, the mental picture of me *watching video tapes of Alex's fourth birthday party* flashed thorough my head. Now, I'd like to point out that Alex is a lovely young lady who I like very, very much. However, I think we can all agree that I—who do not have enough unoccupied time to watch even my own children's home videos—have no business watching home movies of her toddlerhood. Even SuperSaver could appreciate the unvarnished, nonsensical weirdness of this impulse.

Fortunately, I restrained myself. But as Marty drove away, I went back in the house and felt sad. Because, in the grand scheme of things, at that particular moment it felt like whether I saved those few home movies mattered little. Alex's fourth birthday party won't be around forever, just as people who care to sit down and watch that tape won't be around forever.

Although it seems like common sense, nevertheless it's a thought that continues to elude me, probably because I *want* it to elude me. Who wants to think about the time in the not-too-distant future when we will all be dead and gone?

How long does it take until no one will remember us at all? Even the non-clutterers among us try to save certain things, histories, memories—through snapshots, home videos, scrapbooks, souvenirs—but what does it all come to in the end? A box full of memories that no one recalls, an album full of pictures of people who are dead, a panoply of media that have been outmoded and no longer function.

These are the kind of thoughts I find singularly depressing but nevertheless are a good reminder for me, who most of the time tends to behave as if history stops with me. That's right! I intend to live forever, curating the Eve Museum into eternity. It makes sense, therefore, that keeping things can be interpreted as a kind of denial of death, as is often postulated.

Which I suppose means, conversely, that when we get rid of things, we are admitting our own mortality.

Geez.

It's no wonder Marty's been looking so tired.

———

Just like the Kravitts, my mom had begun planning her own big move months ago, so I'd gotten a series of calls from my mother once again featuring the remarkably popular and catchy hit song "Do You Want This?" as she moved methodically through her house putting sticky notes on furniture and boxes. Now, my mother likes her Stuff as much as the rest of us in the family, but I've never known her to sit and *moon* over things the way Dad and I do. She's not the type to keep a moldy book or a broken old toy for sentimental reasons. She sensibly saved me a small box of my cutest baby clothes, made me an album of my nicest childhood photographs, and has been known to utter such unfathomable phrases as "You don't want your old dollhouse, do you?"

You would think she'd know me by now. Yes. I want it. I want everything, Mom. I always do. Yes. Yes. Yes.

Unlike the Kravitts' offerings, to which I had no emotional attachments or memories, I felt helpless in the face of losing forever pieces of furniture that had been in my parents' house since before I was even born and were prominently featured in the background of all those photos my mother had so carefully collected.

Consequently, when my mother's house finally sold, it was time to pay the piper. I couldn't quite remember exactly how many things I had said yes to over those phone calls, but I knew they were not small things: yes, my old dollhouse. Also, a six-foot-long, heavy, very sixties-ish walnut wood buffet.

And, well, a *piano*.

Perfect. I thought. The heaviest, most impractical to move piece of furniture that exists? A piano. Of course I had to have it. Maybe we could throw in an elephant and a collection of lead bars while we were at it?

It all began because my maternal grandmother was a staunch believer in the idea that no well-bred household should be without a piano. It was a sign to all who entered that this was a home of culture and good taste. I find this interesting because my grandmother lived with her parents, even after her marriage, never went to college, and did not drive. She was not, in short, what one might call a "woman of the world," but perhaps that was exactly the point.

At any rate, as a direct consequence of the supposedly transformative power of the piano, as a child my mother was forced to take years of mandatory lessons that she came—perhaps inevitably—to despise. Of course, this was not the "Let's have fun and explore music!" kind of piano lesson that one might enroll a six-year-old in today. Rather, from my mother's description it was more along the lines of "Let's do rigid posture scales until our fingers fall off!" Yaaaaay.

Fast-forward to years later when my parents married and had their first home together. My grandmother—of course—bought *them* a piano, presumably so that the neighbors would be alerted to the fact that they were living in the vicinity of a cultured and refined couple who knew how to serve a decent canapé. I imagine the unintended benefit was that my mother could look at it every day and feel relieved no one was going to make her play the wretched thing.

A few years later, I appeared on the scene. I was cute as a button in my seventies bowl haircut and plaid, bell-bottom pants. And I was curious about that big honking instrument we had in the living room that no one else ever went near. I played around on it—picking out "Mary Had a Little Lamb." I composed the "Different Every Time I Play It" symphony that I made everyone listen to. My brother and I staged elaborate multidisciplinary performances that involved music, modern dance, and extended snack breaks. I figured out a mangled version of "Heart and Soul." I got a little older and tried playing some of the sheet music stored in the piano bench without much success because I knew what I was doing about as much as a frog knows how to perform gallbladder surgery.

I asked for piano lessons. But my mother knew better than to torture her daughter with years of scales. Instead, my mother signed me up for every *other* kind of class available for kids within a forty-mile radius: at one point or another I took tap dance, ballet, gymnastics, pottery, puppet making, horseback riding, painting, softball, karate, Brownies, and even something called "Indian Princesses."

Cultured? Well-rounded? This was my mom's version.

The fact is that, no matter how long your life ends up being, it's still probably going to be too short for all the things you want to do in it. I was luckier than lucky to have a mom willing and able to give me so many different chances to explore. I don't think that there's a frustrated concert pianist hiding in me somewhere; truthfully I'm not even sure I'd enjoy the piano at all. I suspect it's just because the piano was *there* all those years, and as a kid I thought that everything exists for a reason. That if there's a piano in the living room, then, of course, it *belongs* there. It never occurred to me that it might be something entirely else: a symbol of some invisible struggle between my grandmother and my mother about who it was, exactly, my mother was going to be.

So when my parents split up, interestingly, it was my dad who took the long-neglected piano. Then when Dad remarried, his wife brought her *own* piano to the relationship, so Dad loaned ours to some friends for a few years. At this point I was a little sad because I fully expected we'd never see the thing again. But I was in college… What was I going to do? Lug this behemoth through my series of small apartments so I could *not* play it in all of them?

But one day, after Dad and his second wife divorced, the piano really did get returned. And then, this summer, Dad moved to Kansas and the piano went back, like a homing pigeon, to Mom. And then, as Mom prepared to move, what was I to say when she offered me this millstone? How could I say *anything* except, "Yes, I want it"?

On the fine summer day when the moving truck arrived,

however, it is safe to say Steve was *not* pleased with this new plot twist: the Invasion of Large, Obnoxious Furniture from Eve's Childhood. There were words, shall we say. He was frustrated and exasperated with me: how could I have agreed to so much large stuff? For one thing, we already *have* a piano (my grandmother's piano, the one my mother learned to play on), he sensibly pointed out, and no one plays that one, *either*! Yes, yes, he knew these things were from my childhood, but where, *where* was it all going to go? Here you are—he pointed out, irritatingly—in the middle of a getting-rid-of-Stuff project—and *what are you doing*, bringing in *more* stuff? *Really big* stuff, for that matter?

He was right, of course. Life would very likely be easier if I had simply let go. If I had said, "Oh, no, that's okay. Just sell the piano. Donate the buffet. Throw away the dollhouse."[12]

But that simply isn't me. I would have to find another way because even in the midst of shedding and culling and even though it made my existing job that much harder, giving away these things seemed wrong to the very core of my being.

And that's how I can take things in, even as I'm trying to discard. If there was ever any question, I now knew for certain that the Year of No Clutter was not about trying to stop keeping meaningful things. Rather, I was trying to get better at *filtering*: at knowing which things are truly meaningful as opposed to keeping them all and figuring that somehow I'll just sort it all out later.

So, against all odds, we found a place for the dollhouse. A

---

12. For the record, I *almost could not write* those words: "Throw away the dollhouse." Really.

place for the buffet. And, yes, a spot for the piano. At least it wasn't in the Hell Room.

But just in case I was getting a little too self-congratulatory, it was time to face a much bigger challenge than the Kravitts' Stuff or Mom's Stuff or even my Stuff.

It was time to go help Dad.

CHAPTER ELEVEN

LIKE FATHER, LIKE DAUGHTER

"In the midst of chaos, there is also opportunity."
—Sun Tzu, *The Art of War*

Sitting in my dad's dining room is a difficult thing to do. For one thing, there's a smell. For another, there just isn't a lot of *room* anywhere. And I know from past experience that if I were to go downstairs or upstairs, matters are likely to get infinitely worse. In fact, just sitting here is making my skin crawl.

He is talking to me as we sit at the dining room table, and I am nodding, looking out of the corners of my eyes. All I can think about is how I would clean it up. What I would throw out. Although we're both big-time keepers, a large part of what my dad keeps makes no sense to me. Also, he keeps on a far greater scale, which means exponentially greater, ah, cleanliness problems. I can feel my organizing persona start to kick in, chomping at the bit. *I could fix this!*

My eyes roam behind him to a series of mail-sorting organizing shelves, dozens of cubbies stuffed with a crazy assortment of yellow newspaper clippings, recipes, cartoons, appliance manuals, birthday cards, coupons. Every horizontal surface is subject to a pile—so that in order to sit down one must move things both off the chair *and* off the table. Recycling bins, milk crates, and old three-ring binders stuffed in boxes crowd the floor, hemming me in to my seat. On the kitchen island behind me are piles of more papers interspersed with dusty old soup cans holding an assortment of writing implements, broken crayons, and sticky pens. I know that the kitchen drawers will offer up mouse-chewed place mats and ancient soy sauce packages. One year, after I found mouse droppings behind the toaster *and* on the stove, I obsessively washed every pot, plate, and fork both before *and* after using them.

And then there's Amber, the dog. Because of her, there is a wafting perfume of "l'eau d'urine" in the house, but what I really avoid is the basement laundry room, which smells like the place where dog shit was invented. It is summer, and there are fruit flies buzzing and hovering, making me twitch. Dad doesn't even seem to notice.

This has been the state of things every time I've visited my dad for years. It's all I can do not to turn into a Tasmanian devil armed with garbage bags and paper towels. I can't tell if my impulse to clean up is motivated more by altruism, claustrophobia, or being completely ooked out—but I know I can't do it anyway. For one thing, my dad is, like most savers—me included—fiercely protective of his piles, and for another, what would be the point? I know darned well everything will go right back to the way it was once I leave. This visit is different, however: this time I *am* actually supposed to help get things in order because of the imminent move.

My younger sister Brianna and her boyfriend Nasir were

making plans to move to Kansas, and they had asked Dad to move with them. Was I skeptical of Dad's decision to move to a place he's never been and where he knows no one? Sure, but then again, I reasoned, it could be a perfect fit—Brianna and Nasir needed a place to live, and Dad needed someone to live with. As it turned out there really was only one thing standing in the way of this terrific plan: Dad. Or, more specifically, Dad's *house* and the seventy-some years' worth of accumulated belongings, objects, and random crap within. According to Brianna, Nasir, and Dad, they had all been working on the Get Ready to Move project in every spare moment for the past year; months ago Nasir had even stopped working entirely and devoted himself full-time to the endeavor. But as I looked around, I struggled to see what impact that had made, if any.

Which is why I was here now: to help, among other things, with the Dad's House Tag Sale.

Undertaking *anything* to do with my dad and his Stuff was no small matter because, as I have alluded to, my dad is a saver of stuff on a level that far surpasses my petty one-room nonsense. Clearly, I'm an amateur. It's hard to tell if Dad's saving tendencies have gotten worse as he's gotten older or if he's simply had more time to amass stuff, but I suspect it's a combination of both. Looking back over the course of his two marriages, it seems clear that each of his female counterparts had managed to counterbalance his frantic compulsion to keep, but each time Dad regained his bachelorhood, the Problem with Stuff would come roaring back with a vengeance. Once returned to solitary life, it never took very long for his home to come to resemble an Amazonian jungle of Stuff once again.

I arrived the day before the sale. That night I asked Dad about a story my aunt Karen had recently told me when I had brought up the subject of Stuff. She had said that my dad's family had moved twice while he and his two brothers were growing up and that each time my grandfather had made the executive decision to throw all the boys' things away. All of them. It's a memory that she says still has the power to make my uncle Terry sad. "There are things he wishes he still had," Karen told me. "Terry doesn't like to talk about it."

I described this story to Dad: did he remember any of this? He looked thoughtful. Counting back, he calculated that the first move had happened when he was very young—maybe only four years old. But the second move he remembered quite clearly—he had been a teenager, and the move, for him, had not been a welcome one. The subdivision they were leaving was a happy place for Dad—with his school within walking distance and a pond for swimming nearby. "I could get to all my friends' houses on my bike," Dad recalled. "I was a teenager... I missed my friends. And I was really confused. All that growing-up stuff. It was a hard time."

He looked right at me. He had a funny look in his eye. "And maybe...I was missing my stuff, too," he said.

So *did* Dad remember it? Was that the beginning of a life-long backlash? Did that story explain *anything*? There was no telling. That funny look in his eye was as close as I was going to get.

"The stump!?" I cried out in disbelief. "You *still have the stump?*"

As we had been going through the garage in preparation for the sale the next day, Dad had been acting as unofficial tour guide, an interpreter of the weird, wild, and wooly things we were finding along the way. But what had stopped me short was something I needed no interpretation for.

The stump. There it sat—defiantly. Smugly. Oh-so-innocently. As if to say, "Oh, yes! You didn't think I'd go *away*, did you? Just because I tried to *kill your daddy? Hmmmmm?*"

That's right—a tree stump tried to kill my daddy. Back when I was young enough to still think he could do pretty much anything, Dad had been loading pieces of a chopped-down tree he had found into the back of our station wagon for firewood. When he went to pick up the impressive tree stump, however, there was a distinctive snap in his back. It was the beginning of decades of crippling back pain that would affect my dad ever after.

Were we planning to take a family trip? Maybe there was an important business meeting or a play my mom had gotten expensive tickets for months before? Well then! Time for my dad's back to go out. Lying on the floor, grouchy and groaning, unable at times even to crawl his way to the bathroom, these episodes scared the bejesus out of me as a kid. What on earth had happened to my Super Dad?

But I knew: it was all the fault of that damned stump. Astonishingly, he still managed to bring it home that day and *has kept it ever since.* When pressed he always remarks that he thinks it would make "a nice outdoor stool."

Never mind that that stump represents years of agonizing back pain. Never mind that my dad's spine curvature is now so pronounced that he spends his entire day impersonating the local shoelace inspector. Never mind that he would no more sit on a stump outside than he would sleep on a bed of nails.

Despite every bit of common sense against it, there that stump sat. Mocking me.

But, nevertheless, I do understand—in a way. After all, the stump is a marker—a bookmark from Dad's life, like one of the color-coded tabs in the dozens of three-ring binders that haunt his closets and hide under his kitchen island.

When I asked Dad *why*, for example, he kept those binders, many of them from his years and years as the manager for the local kids' soccer team—complete with each team member's contact info, email printouts of schedule changes, and directions to game locations—his eyes were shining. "It's all I have," he explained.

"But you have the memories." I countered.

"But those papers are the *trigger*," he explained. "If I don't have those papers, I'll probably *never think of those memories again*." I wasn't about to admit it, but he was playing my song.

But looking around I could also see the consequences loud and clear: when you try to keep everything, control everything, you end up losing it all, controlling nothing. All the three-ring binders in the world can't stop the advances of nature, the ravages of time.

After years of experience observing my dad and his Stuff, I had begun to develop a theory. My theory went something like this: just as nature abhors a vacuum, nature also abhors a surfeit. Consequently, there's a law that seems to come into effect, which says that once you have a certain critical mass of Stuff under your care, some of it must be returned to the circle of life. And things begin to happen.

The basement floods. "Oh! Were those family photos something you wanted to *keep*?" Nature asks callously, flipping her hair. "Sorry about that!" The mice move in. "Golly gee!

I didn't know you actually *wanted* those clothes. You won't mind a few holes in them, will you?" And the mold arrives. "Are you sure you really *cared about* that box of books? 'Cause they're, you know, *kind of* smelly and all stuck together now."

All these things happened in my dad's house and more, often repeatedly. And just in case the message wasn't getting across, not very long after Dad's second divorce, there was an event more catastrophic than all that had come before: a house fire.

Yes, there's nothing like a good house fire to make your already fraught relationship with Stuff all that much more messed up. So, at that precarious moment my traumatized Dad—newly single, still sharing the care of the two young children of his second marriage as he moved from hotel to rental home to hotel—made an interesting decision. He decided *not to make any decisions at all.* Everything, and I do mean *everything,* salvaged from the fire went into a storage locker on the other side of town. Books, photographs, home movies, furniture, suitcases, artwork, knickknacks, you name it—all in varying states of disrepair and smoke damage were moved en masse to the locker. And there they sat for the next ten years.

I didn't know this then. I only knew this now because, when I arrived to help with the tag sale, I was astounded to find myself wading through boxes and boxes and *boxes,* the contents of which were unusually bizarre and random, even for Dad. Most of their contents had weird, shadowy burn marks and a smell reminiscent of barbecue briquettes. In preparation for both the tag sale and the move, everything had been resurrected from the storage locker and brought back to Dad's garage. Surprise!

At one point Nasir led me to a wooden cabinet filled with

charred, melted audio visual equipment and shrugged at it, helplessly. What do we do with *this*? It was like so many things we were being confronted with—useless, destroyed, and yet Dad was paralyzed by indecision. It was as if he had looked back when fleeing the house fire that day and been turned into a pillar of salt. The DVD player, the cassette player, other mysterious metal rectangles were all stuck—*welded*—to their shelves. Below these a Betamax player—*a Betamax player*—was blackened and sooty. I was incredulous. He had kept burned electronic equipment? *Burned electronic equipment that was outdated in 1983?*

At that moment, I became a woman possessed. I clawed at the sooty pile of technology—pried off the useless media players with my fingers, and one by one Nasir tossed them on top of the "electronics recycling" that already held at least four computer systems that dated from the early Paleolithic period. My hands got black and smelly. I knew rooting through burned electronic equipment with my bare hands probably wasn't a fantastic idea—but I wasn't stopping. I couldn't. Something had to be done.

Within minutes we had the sad, burned-out cabinet in the driveway for the garage sale along with the rest of the sad, burned-out detritus—bins full of charred cookbooks, blackened kids puzzles, framed posters with broken, blackened glass. Creeping mold had taken over many things that the fire had spared, and mouse droppings and nests were everywhere—in the corners of boxes, the bottom of bags. I picked up a glass pitcher and shrieked when my eyes focused on the inert little furry beanbag inside it.

It was a good reminder, actually, of the same line of thought I had when Marty took his videotapes back. It's *all* going bye-bye, eventually. As are we all. And that's where this line of questioning all goes, right? Fear of self-annihilation. Fear that we—our memories—the things that tell us who we are—will all go, just as we too will one day go. Letting go of our Stuff is a little bit like death. If Dad lets go of that evil stump, will he forget that story too someday? Will he just be a guy with a crooked back but no story to go with it?

After all, what do so many people fear most about getting older? Do we fear getting hit by a bus while crossing the street? Are we afraid we will be overcome by a nasty bout of varicose veins or crow's feet, maybe? No—we fear Alzheimer's. The living death. According to recent polls, Alzheimer's is the number-two most feared disease, second only to cancer. I believe this is caught up in our sense of self: the fear that one day we'll forget so much that we'll no longer be sure we ever existed at all. Seen in this light, keeping things is a frantic attempt to hold on by any means necessary.

So yes, I get exasperated with Dad—with his stubbornness, his indecision, his inability to step back and see the forest for the trees. But the more we talk about it, the more I also realize I know *exactly* what he's talking about. So I do the sensitive thing. I offer to chop the stump up into pieces and make a nice campfire.

––––––––

The tag sale, when it arrives, is a surreal experience, as if I am selling off pieces of my life, my family's lives. "How much for this priceless childhood memory?" people ask, pointing to my brother's old toy chest, the family toboggan, a lamp that my parents bought for their first apartment half a century ago. "A dollar," I say. "Fifty cents."

Much more of the garage sale is from Brianna's childhood, not mine. She, for her part, seems downright delighted to let go of objects from her past—the plastic picnic table, stacks of outgrown books and toys, a lamp with fluffy purple feathers that sat on her bedside table for as long as I can remember.

I ask, "Do you want to keep this?" Brianna's response is always the same: "Nah."

I am mystified by this.

I ask her about her old dollhouse, which looks, well, a little the worse for wear. There are stickers on it, and it seems sooty, with garish splashes of paint in odd places. She explains that it too had been in the fire.

"So Dad thought I should paint it," she says with a hint of exasperation. "So I did. I mean, I *tried*."

I know exactly what she means. Sometimes Dad's unrelenting optimism, his inability to let *go* already, can feel a bit like denial. And it can be exhausting.

So, just as I discovered about myself, for my dad too, it all seems to come down to one of two things: nostalgia or potential. Although Dad had managed to keep every remotely nostalgic item from making its way into the sale (and many such items—the soccer binders, the evil stump—wouldn't be very sellable anyway), he was clearly still grappling hard core with the *potential* he was losing in every item that sold.

You read about this in the literature describing hoarders, their tendency to see potential in everything, everywhere. They—we—are effectively crippled by potential. At one point during the garage sale, Dad and I have a lengthy conversation about an unopened, two-decade-old roll of shelf paper, which I want to either sell, throw away, or shoot into space. ("But it's perfectly good!" he protests. "Dad, *they* have *shelf paper in Kansas!*" I argue.) It's like this about practically everything; nothing seems easy. Every single solitary item, from the tallest to the smallest, requires a seventeen-minute argument/conversation, and it is kind of killing me. On top of this, as the sale goes on and we continue to bring things out, Dad starts trying to take things back; at one point he refuses to sell an item to a customer.

"*That's* not supposed to be out here! I'm sorry, that item is not for sale," he says firmly as the customer reluctantly hands the item back over to him.

And then, while going through a pile of old sports equipment, he asks to see one of the baseball bats, one that looks handmade. "Is that one crooked?" he asks as I lift it up for inspection. "Yeah, that was mine when I was a kid—that was my bat."

I look at it, and in that moment the innocuous stick of wood is transformed—I see my dad as a kid, playing stickball with the kids in his development in Illinois. A minute ago I would have sold this for a quarter. Now, I hold on to it tightly.

Offhandedly Dad adds, "You can sell it."

On my way to put it in my car, I show Brianna the bat to make sure she doesn't want it. I tell her incredulously, like the punch line of a joke—"and Dad said to *sell* it!"

"I know," she replied. "He wants to sell all the wrong things."

I pile things in my car—terrible things. They are the ghosts of objects past, things I never even knew I didn't have anymore that have risen from the grave to haunt me: dusty posters from my childhood walls and charred books. A broken pottery handle, a metal serving bowl we used when I was a kid—back when I was little and all four of us lived under one roof and ate at one table. Things I neither want nor can part with. And yet I'm better off than Dad, who is saddled with his cartons of burned books and piles of musty trade magazines.

I came out for this weekend, determined to be here. As evidenced by the baseball bat, Dad's idea of something worth saving and mine could differ wildly, and I wanted to be sure something I cared about didn't go bye-bye. Or go to Kansas, for that matter, since knowing my dad's track record it was highly likely I'd never see it again. I had a vague sense too that I was *looking* for something, something significant. But what was it? The old dead mouse in the glass pitcher? Or the broken, moldy pictures of me and my brother from high school? The Betamax player welded to the cabinet shelf by fire? What was there left for me, really, amid this catastrophe of belongings?

It wasn't until partway through the day that we would come upon it. An ancient-looking suitcase—a trunk, really, big and boxy. It had a long-suffering look about it, dirty and neglected as it was, splattered with paint and mildew spots. Clearly, it had been stacked for years under the many horrors of the garage, yet, it appeared sturdy in the way things were sturdy back when people actually used to think things should last pretty much forever: with brass hinges and corner protectors and a leather-covered handle.

It was so formidable—stately, so clearly of another era—that I knew I wanted it before I even knew *what* it was. And then Dad said, "Oh, that must be my father's old WearEver kit. From when he was a traveling salesman and went door-to-door."

I knew this about my grandfather: he had prided himself

on being a self-made man who had worked his way through college "polishing doorknobs" (really? This was a job?) and later selling aluminum pots and pans door to door, eventually working his way up the company ladder. Dad had told me that his routine had been to show up on the doorstep of a home and offer to cook a meal for the lady of the house so she could see for herself just how wonderful these aluminum pans really were.

It wasn't all that long ago, a few decades maybe, but the story came from culture so completely foreign to us today as to sound almost unbelievable. Let a strange man into your house? And let him cook in your kitchen? It sounded like an episode of *Leave It to Beaver*.

If I thought the old stories were incredible, my eyes about fell out of my head when we opened the trunk. I couldn't look at things fast enough. The first thing I noticed was that the inside of the lid acted as a full-page spread. Pasted inside was a made-to-fit advertisement featuring photographs and ad copy all about the wonderfulness of WearEver aluminum pots and pans. Then I looked at the contents. It was filled to the top with papers, newspaper clippings, programs, tickets, letters, photo albums, none of which I had ever seen before. It was a souvenir box of my parents' lives, in particular the lives they had before my brother and I happened upon the scene: Dad's handwritten letters to Mom in college, ticket stubs from a Brown versus Harvard football game, a theater program from a production of *Hair*, menus from restaurants my parents visited on their honeymoon, an old photo album with tiny black-and-white photos of my father fishing with his father and ice skating on a pond, my mother's high school autograph book with cryptic, private jokes written in swirling cursive by her teenage friends.

I was aghast. I was speechless. This ratty old trunk had survived like a time capsule to tell me a story of my parents that I knew in only the most shadowy outlines. It had survived the floods, the fire, the rodents... I was blown away by the sheer improbability of the fact that I could be sitting here, looking at a piece of paper that itemized what my parents ordered for room service in 1967 (him: eggs and toast, her: pancakes.)

Now I know. Who *cares*, right? Who cares what they ate for breakfast? That's why people *throw away* room service orders. Who, besides crazy me, that is, wants to look at moldy old movie-theater programs for *Thoroughly Modern Millie* and *Funny Girl*? One could make the argument that there was very little here of any real significance; this wasn't King Tut's tomb.

But it was meaningful to me. And possibly to a few other family members, but that would be the full extent of it. Isn't it right and proper to have a curiosity—as do most of us—about where we came from and what came before? To want not only to know about our personal history but *to touch it*?

After offering Brianna a look through the trunk's contents (she selected a handful of colorful old license plates from all the places my dad has lived), I quickly hoist the trunk up to put into my car before anything can happen to it. Behind it is something else. It's...another trunk.

You're kidding me.

It was as if, in that moment from *Raiders of the Lost Ark* when Indiana Jones and his sidekick Sallah find the ark and have lifted it out of its container, Sallah then looked *back* in the container and said, "Oh, look! There's *another* one!"

Upon examination, the second trunk proves to be exactly like the first, in all appearances, down to the brass hinges and the pasted-in paper advertisement in the lid. However, it has different contents: instead of stacks of old papers inside, there are stacks of old home movie reels in protective, tin containers. One says "Mexico" on the side and another simply "1949." These have to be home movies from Dad's childhood, and right now I have no way of knowing if they are salvageable. But the smudged papers in my grandfather's fountain pen make me hope fervently that they are: "Michigan—July 1943 Marian [my grandmother] and I take a weekend holiday…Xmas 1944…1st pictures of David [my dad]," and so on. Another notation explains "Couldn't buy film during war/rationed my supply to get pictures of David." I turn the pages over and see that the notes are written on letterhead from the Aluminum Cooking Utensil Co. with my grandfather cited below it as "Manager, Pittsburgh District."

I am prepared to arm-wrestle Dad for the trunk, yet, just like with the baseball bat, Dad seems oddly, uncharacteristically detached. *He cares more about his old soccer schedules than this?* I marvel, uncomprehending. And yet I say nothing. We both obey the Clutterers' Code: Don't question what others value, as you would have them not question you. With his permission I close it up and tote that one off too.

Despite the fact that this new acquisition is probably in direct violation of my Year of No Clutter, I don't care. I'm too happy to have it. Do I have a use for these things? Do they fit into my life in any rational way? No. But perhaps Marie Kondo might be persuaded to approve anyway because, whatever the reasons, for me they clearly spark joy.

But it's even more than that. Recently I've been getting interested in genealogy and starting to trace my family history. It didn't take long for me to realize that not only do many of us *know* very little of our recent forebears but, as for physical, tangible evidence, we *have* even less. I'm mortified in the knowledge that I don't have a date for the death of my father's mother listed in the family tree. She died when I was a kid, in the seventies, so this is not exactly ancient history.

What's worse, when I looked at *other* people's trees that also include her, no one else has the date of death for her, either. No one. When I ask Dad to tell me about what his mother was like, he falters. He's apologetic, but he doesn't remember much about her. Unlike my grandfather, there aren't lots of family stories about her. She just seems to have faded away.

Notably, it was her mother—my great-grandmother—who, for me, had been reduced down to a single object: the watercolor portrait of a "Gibson girl" that was sent to me by my aunt. *Is that it then?* I think incredulously. *One object equals one life?* What object might *I* might be reduced to only two generations hence? Looking around me now, and the gazillions of things that surround my everyday life, it seems completely inconceivable that such a thing could ever happen. But I've been to estate sales, garage sales, flea markets, all filled with the things that someone once cared about. I know it happens every day.

My mother likes to lament this. "That's the way it is!" she'll say with disdain. "Fifty years after you're dead, and no one remembers you! It's as if you never even existed. No one cares."

But I don't think that's true. I think some people do care. I think many of us are fighting against the ravages of time with all we've got, trying to save, preserve, remember. The cards are stacked against us: we can't save it all. We're working against some serious opponents: nature, time. Nature is no friend to history. She'd just as soon send the *Mona Lisa* downstream in the next flood or let rats nibble on the Magna Carta. We try to choose wisely, which is a really, excruciatingly hard thing to do when you see potential everywhere.

Before I leave the next day to head home, I open up the back of my car, just to look at the two trunks again. I see them there, full of buried treasure, and smile. I got what I came for. This is what I wanted.

I go back in to say good-bye to Dad. I look around the house, chaotic as ever despite the never-ending attempt to pack, despite the surprising amount of stuff we were able to unload over the weekend. Whatever else my dad is, he's a man after my own heart. I'm deeply grateful to him for still having these trunks after all this time, against all odds and despite everything that would argue or fight against it. The fact that most people would've gotten rid of such things long ago is what makes having them so incredible. So amazing. I think to myself—*my dad is crazy.*

And so am I. And then again, so is everyone. We all have our own unique brand of crazy.

And then I drove off. In my car full of clutter. Treasure. History. Whatever.

CHAPTER TWELVE

WHAT WE TALK ABOUT WHEN WE TALK ABOUT CLUTTER

"A place for everything and everything in its place."
—English proverb

S o, what *is* clutter?" Jacob asked. It was early one Friday night, and we were at one of those school functions where the parents are supposed to wander around reading trifold presentations about the history of Spain or something but instead just end up standing around drinking coffee and gabbing all night. Jacob is not only a friend and fellow parent but also a college professor. He has a knack for zeroing in on key points that, until now, everyone else had missed. And by everyone, I mean me.

"For example, what is the difference between clutter and, say, just being messy?"

Wow. Once he had said it, I was annoyed that he had, in the space of about a minute and a half, just identified the one thing I *hadn't* done in all my many months thinking and obsessing about clutter: define it. How can you have a year of no clutter if you can't even identify what clutter *is*?

Up until now I'd been relying on the "I know it when I see it" rationale, but now I saw I was going to have to do better than that.

So I looked it up. Merriam-Webster online gives the following definition for clutter: "A large amount of things that are not arranged in a neat or orderly way: a crowded or disordered collection of things."

Now, that didn't seem quite right to me. How was that any different from "a mess"? No, when we talk about clutter, we aren't just talking about being sloppy or having a mess. To me, a mess implies that there is a way to clean it up—that the items involved all have other places they ought to be, they have places to *go*.

For example, every night my kitchen can be a mess—before I do the dishes, before I put away all the pots and pans and my cookbook and so on. None of this is clutter. These are things I use, and they all have designated places to be put away.

On the other hand, if, hypothetically speaking, we had a stack of CDs purchased back in the days when vinyl stopped being cool—but before it started being cool again—piled in the corner of the living room next to a pile of toddler videos that no one watches anymore thrown together with some random orphan camera equipment and the water bottle with the leaky top, these things are neither being used nor have anywhere in particular to go right now. They are all question marks. At least until the moment when someone comes along and makes a decisive decision about them—to give them away, feed them to a bear, whatever—they are clutter.

To clarify this point, I've created a handy-dandy chart for figuring out what kind of stuff you have.

WHAT IS MY STUFF?

		I do use it on a regular basis	I do NOT use it on a regular basis
I do have a designated place to keep it	I have NOT put it away	☹ "A mess!"	☹ "A mess!"
	I have put it away	"My belongings!" ☺ *Neat!*	"My mementos!" *Neat!* -or- "Just in case!" ☺
I do NOT have a designated place to keep it		"I need a bigger place!"	☺? "Clutter!"

As you can see, you can have unused stuff but still have a place for it to go—and because these unnecessary things aren't impeding the progress of your everyday life, these get to be called nice names like *souvenirs* or *mementos*. On the other hand, you can have stuff you do use but not have a place for it, for which the technical term is *needing a bigger apartment*.

In fact, according to my highly reliable chart, there are only two instances out of a possible six scenarios that qualify as a "mess": when you have things—whether essential or not so much—that have a place to go but for some reason haven't gotten there yet. Beer bottles left out after a party but not yet recycled? A mess. Beer bottles left out after a party that you intend to keep for the beer bottle collection that you keep in a glass cabinet in the living room? Still a mess. But put them in the cabinet and voilà! The mess is transformed to part of your collection. Beer bottles left out after a party that you can't bear to part with that end up sitting along the wall in a cardboard box, making you feel like a bad person? Now *that's* clutter.

As we've discussed before, get a certain critical mass of clutter together in one spot, and you start to inch your way toward hoarding. Have you gotten to the point that you can't walk through your living room anymore because you have so many boxes of sentimental and/or destined-to-be-somehow-repurposed beer bottles in the way? Congratulations, you've graduated. Your clutter has become a hoard.

Of course, this is all wildly unfair. It's all the same stuff, isn't it? All that changes is the *context*. As we go down the chart's right-hand column, the semantics change from mess to memento to clutter regardless of what the object is, dependent entirely upon: (a) whether you have a place to put it and (b) whether it gets there. You can have an enormous mansion and keep everything from eggshells to expired coupons, and as long as you put everything away neatly in its "place," you're not a hoarder. An eccentric collector, perhaps. I think the history of hoarding will bear me out on this theory.

Perhaps, like me, you heard some version of the cautionary tale of the Collyer Brothers when you were a kid. The first widely publicized case of hoarding, the Collyer Brothers lived a solitary existence in a Harlem town house in New York City in the thirties and forties and had largely withdrawn from society. They spent two decades accumulating things and navigating their home via networks of winding tunnels that were booby-trapped for fear of burglars. They lived this way for decades until one brother was crushed to death in one of his own traps; the other brother, who was an invalid, then starved to death.

Charming story, right? And like all really good stories that get handed down from one generation to the next, there was a not-so-hidden moral: *You see?* that story said, wagging its finger at my kid-self, you *see* what happens when you refuse to clean up your room? You get *killed* by it!

Of course, at that time, no one knew quite what to call the phenomenon that investigators had encountered upon entering the house. People were repulsed and entranced by the swirling rumors and newspaper accounts of the packed-to-the-ceiling rooms and reportedly crazy objects that were discovered in the brownstone. A two-headed baby in form-aldehyde! A horse's jawbone! A stuffed alligator! But the vast majority of the stuff was simply an overabundance of extremely ordinary things: fourteen pianos, old newspapers, bowling balls.

As you can see from my chart, I don't think it's the stuff, per se, that makes a hoarder. Most people keep *some* things they don't absolutely need, and many of us keep things that other people might even consider odd, but neither necessarily adds up to hoarding disorder. What I really think it comes down to is this: the failure of the hoarder to choose a func-tional living environment over the continued accumulation of objects.

Because that's what "normal" people do, right? Privilege living space over storage space. The hoarder inverts this tra-ditionally accepted relationship, often living in closet-like spaces in order that the objects may take over.

Consider famed newspaper magnate William Randolph Hearst, who built an entire castle complex to house his collec-tion. Remember that first trip Dad and I took to visit my uncle Jim in California? Well, after seeing him, we drove up the coast to visit Hearst Castle. Now, *this* was a guy who had *stuff*! I recall being mesmerized by the story of this man who had brazenly collected everything that wasn't nailed down everywhere he went. Nothing seemed beyond his voracious appetite for accu-mulating: medieval church ceilings, ancient Roman temple facades, Egyptian statuary. Forget sideshow oddities like the Collyers' horse's jawbone. *Hearst* owned George Washington's waistcoat, Thomas Jefferson's Bible, and a sideboard that had once belonged to Charles Dickens. I had been on many tours of houses-turned-museums in my young life, and the impression I came away with was always the same: everyone at the time had wondered if the owner was crazy, but *look* at all the marvelous things this person collected! Now everyone sees how truly visionary it was to save all these things!

This is how we have agreed, as a society, to view *certain* accumulations of stuff: the ones who are organized are visionary, an indication of brilliance or, failing that, at least of style and panache. Do you think people would come from all over the world to visit Hearst Castle if they called it "Hearst's Hoard"? Don't you think it could easily have been one if there had been no staff to sort it out and keep it organized?

This kind of transformation—migrating from one context, one perception to another—is precisely what took place when Andy Warhol passed away in 1987, and his estate had to be gone through. Stories began to emerge about his voracious collecting, rumors circulated about rooms full of unsorted belongings, still in shopping bags with price tags on. People started using terms like *pack rat* and *obsessive shopper*.

That would never do. Not with Sotheby's handling the estate sale of such a popular and successful artist; too much money was at stake. When the sale came it famously marked the first time the famed house had deigned to auction such low-brow collectibles as Fiestaware or cookie jars. But in preparation for the sale, Sotheby's went through Warhol's town house and cleaned it up for photographing purposes, made it look as if everything had had a place and that the collections were somewhat organized; like items were grouped together nicely and lightly stylized.

In fact, documentary photographs taken before this makeover show the actual chaos of Warhol's home, which was obviously somewhere on the spectrum between clutter and hoarding.[13]

Just to be clear: what Sotheby's did when it sent in the stylists was to transform Warhol's clutter into a *collection* and Warhol himself from a hoarder or a pack rat into a *collector*, simply by the process of arranging his stuff and making it look as if everything had a place it belonged.

This brings me to something that's been bothering me for a while—the strange case of Big and Little Edie Beale. If you're up on your hoarding history, then you know that these two eccentric ladies are oft cited as hoarders, notable because they were formerly of high society and close relations of First Lady Jackie Kennedy. The two are the subject of a popular documentary film by Albert and David Maysles titled *Grey Gardens* released in 1975.

The two women spend the majority of the movie bickering with one another, singing, sunbathing, and feeding their menagerie of cats and raccoons. Mountains of empty food cans pile up in corners of formerly grand rooms. Cats pee on oil paintings. Raccoons fall through holes in the roof. Sitting on their beds, the women huddle over jars of pickles and scoop melted ice cream from the carton.

It's an unsettling film to say the least. I came away from it with more questions than I knew what to do with, but chief

13. Scott Herring, *The Hoarders: Material Deviance in Modern American Culture* (Chicago: University of Chicago Press, 2014), 70–77.

among them: *was* this hoarding? If so, where were the piles? Where were the "goat paths"? Or was their condition more accurately described as an aversion to taking out the trash?

Now that I have my chart, I think I have the answer. The only hoard one encounters in the film is of old cat-food cans piled in corners—this is either trash or recyclables, but either way there's no getting around the fact that there *is* a place for such things to go—the dump—and the ladies have neglected to make that happen. In one famous scene from the film, Little Edie does a quirky dance performance with an American flag in the main hallway by the staircase. The more I thought about it, the more I was struck by was the fact that the stairs are bare, the hallway is unobstructed, a chair sits in the background, empty. *These* are hoarders?

Contrary to general consensus, I'd argue that Big and Little Edie *were not* hoarders. They had simply created a *mess*. A huge, kind of disgusting mess, but a mess nonetheless. Their things have somewhere to go.

This isn't to say that hoarders can't end up with gross circumstances too. As we've seen, when one privileges storage over living space, as I've done in the Hell Room, things happen.

Take Vula, for example. One of the most memorable episodes of the reality show *Hoarders* features her, a hoarder/cat lady whose house was so feces-strewn that, despite the cleanup crew's efforts, by the end of the episode it was condemned. Throughout the entire episode Vula remains in such a state of complete, impenetrable denial that it was impressive to watch. It was to the point where you half-expected her to say, "I'm not even standing here, right now!"

The only time she appeared to flinch was when a man in a decontamination suit held out what looked like a furry piece of orange driftwood for her to see...except it was a dead cat. All told, they found thirty-six cats in her house, thirteen of which were dead. I know—it's so horrifying I can hardly stand it.

Unlike the famed Beale ladies, however, the feces and dead cat situation in her house was a direct result of the fact that she had so much clutter everywhere that she couldn't properly take care of her cats. Consciously or unconsciously, she was making the decision that her Stuff took precedence over the cleanliness of her home *and* the well-being of the cats.

I don't think hoarders prefer squalor. Rather, I'd theorize that when yucky things happen, for some the attachment to objects is so strong that they must exist in denial rather than confront the cause: the clutter. The hoard. An overabundance of objects with no proper place to go.

This is a big revelation for me—and a big relief. It tells me that I don't have to get rid of my weird things in order to stop being an amateur hoarder as long as I have a place for every-thing and everything in its place. There's nothing wrong with keeping things other people deem strange because it's not the things you keep that make you a hoarder. What makes you a hoarder is whether it takes over.

I find this revelation helpful as I look out over the remaining piles of I-Don't-Know in the Hell Room. Just like when I pick out a box and say, "If it doesn't fit in here, then I can't keep it!" I realize I need to see my house like that too. The attic has storage space enough to accommodate my penchant for keeping and col-lecting my own life. But when that seeps into my home and living space? That's when alarms should sound. Support groups clutch-ing empty donation boxes should show up and ring my doorbell; perhaps Marie Kondo could parachute into my living room and tell me once and for all to get rid of Samuel the dead mouse.

However—and this is a big however—if I can manage to keep it at bay, keep my living spaces clear and doors open, then the stuff I *do* keep can be as random as I want. You mean to say if I get rid of some stuff I can still keep my fifth-grade report card? And my hand-carved wooden beaver dressed like a Native American paddling a canoe? And all my other weird stuff? That's big motivation for me right there.

Hell Room, meet Hearst's Castle. I may be getting out of the hoarding business, but I still want to keep my own quirky collectorism. I'm delighted to realize I can keep my own versions of George Washington's waistcoat or the Collyers' stuffed alligator or Andy Warhol's cartoon character wristwatches and toenail clippings. I'm going for that perfect balance that embraces weird but excludes squalor, allows for cabinets of curiosities yet still preserves living space.

I mean, I'm going for normal-ish but not, you know, *boring*.

In light of these newly defined terms, it occurred to me that it might be helpful to think of my house as a giant puzzle. Our family loves puzzles—well, the girls and I love puzzles. Steve loves *not* doing puzzles and does a very good job being not completely annoyed that we are constantly spreading them all across the living room coffee table, leaving cardboard dust crumbs everywhere, staring at the surface of the coffee table for hours at a time as if the three of us have been hypnotized by the God of living room furniture.

And as anyone who loves doing puzzles can tell you, one of the most satisfying aspects of assembling a puzzle is when a puzzle piece slides perfectly into place, and all feels right with the world for a moment. *Click.*

A BRIEF HISTORY OF TOO MUCH STUFF

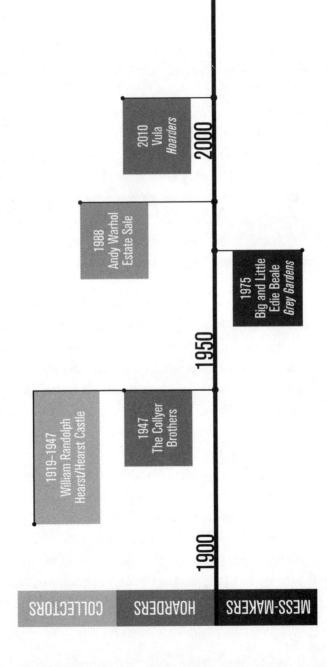

COLLECTORS

HOARDERS

MESS-MAKERS

1900

1919–1947
William Randolph
Hearst/Hearst Castle

1947
The Collyer
Brothers

1950

1975
Big and Little
Edie Beale
Grey Gardens

1988
Andy Warhol
Estate Sale

2010
Vula
Hoarders

2000

That's the way I'd like to feel about my house; that it is a puzzle, perhaps the world's largest and most complicated puzzle, with constantly moving and ever-changing parts. Every day some pieces appear, others disappear, and always, somehow, there seem to be twice the number of pieces as the overall image requires. And the pieces are somewhat fungible—we can decide which ones stay and which go, and, within reason, all will pretty much come out right in the end. But if we get rid of a piece that's essential—say, the refrigerator—there will be a big hole in middle of the finished picture.

I liked this analogy. It came in handy on a subsequent morning when I was cleaning out the contents of the hall coat closet. Upon closer examination, I came to the startling realization that I, somehow, had managed to accumulate three sun hats.

Now, if pressed, I'm might've guessed I had more than one, sure, but *three*? It brought me up cold. *Three?* I thought. *Who needs three sun hats?* Not fancy hats or special occasion hats, but everyday, wear to the beach or the farmer's market sun hats. And I knew the answer: no one. (That is, no one except Cerberus, the three-headed guard dog of Hades, and I had no plans to meet *him* any time soon.) I realized the situation for what it was: I had three puzzle pieces for only one spot on the puzzle. And so I picked out my favorite hat, and the other two went into the donation basket. Done. Easy, actually.

Lucky for me, there were no fond memories or nostalgic vibes emanating from any of the sun hats, or I might have found myself frozen on the spot with indecision, impersonating Han Solo's stance sealed in carbonite. But still—the point was well taken: one puzzle piece per spot, ma'am. No exceptions.

I've been attempting to wrap my mind around another real-ization for some time now—objects are mortal. They have a life and a death much like people do. But this is a tough realization for me. I have long thought that objects, if you took good care of them, should last pretty much forever. I expect clothes to last forever, cars to run forever, even the cheapest glue-bound paperbacks to hold all their pages forever. I tend to take it as a personal affront when they do not do this for me.

"What do you *mean* my car needs new brakes? It only has 259,000 miles on it!" "What do you *mean* these shoes are worn out? I only bought them, like, fourteen years ago!" "How can the phone be dead? I didn't even know it was sick!"

My husband laughs at me. "You think everything should last forever," he says.

"Well it should," I reply.

"But it doesn't."

"But it should."

Perhaps because he is a card-carrying member of the cur-rent century, he laughs when I wear the smock dress that I bought in high school, and at my surprise when I find out VHS tapes and even DVDs and CDs *don't* last forever, or the photos in my childhood album are fading away, even though they haven't been exposed to any light. *How can people sell things that they know will break, fade, and die?* I think to myself incredulously. Isn't that, like, fraud? Or at the very least, false advertising? Apparently in another life I was in a time period where planned obsolescence hadn't been invented yet, and people still used the same hairbrush that had belonged to their great-grandmother or something, and a large part of my brain has yet to relinquish that manner of thought.

This clearly transitions into Hell Room territory. How many dead and dying things have made their way to that upstairs sanctuary simply because I was somewhere between bargaining and denial in the stages of grief?

I have even been tempted to keep things, upon occasion, that wouldn't even have *fit* into the Hell Room. For example, when my first car was on its last legs, I wanted to keep it. Don't ask me how. Yes, I was going to get another car, but for crying out loud! This was my *first* car—it was *sentimental*. It had all my favorite band bumper stickers on the back, and I had met my husband while driving it, and...

But even I realized that this was crazy talk. If I could've, I would've given myself the same look my mom had given me when I told her I thought we should keep Grandma's apartment when she died. That's right! My mom's mother lived in Pittsburgh, to which we now had no earthly connection since Grandma was deceased. But it was a *nice* apartment, with a lovely panoramic view of...Pittsburgh. Yeah. *That* was the look my mom gave me. She sold it.

So one day during the summer of no clutter I was making dinner, and the handle of my pasta pot, which had been jiggly for the past few years, suddenly fell off in my hand. I looked at it, dumbfounded. My mother had bought this pot—nothing special, just a nice, hefty aluminum pot—for me when I went off to college. This means that I had been making food in this particular pot for the last *twenty-seven years*.

I went to Steve, handle in hand. After a short inspection he pronounced that the plastic handle had been glued on, and therefore, could not be safely reattached. Using the pot minus the handle wasn't an option either; it seemed a really good recipe for dumping boiling water down my front.

So? I thought. *I'm just supposed to give up on it?*

Yes, Eve, you are. That's what most people do. They throw stuff away.

I briefly considered my options. It could be…a planter! Or…or…a water bucket for water fights! But I already had enough planters, enough buckets. What I needed was a pasta pot, which this apparently wasn't anymore.

The pot hung around for weeks after that making me feel bad—on the floor, near the stairs, in the Hallway Room… It inched ever closer to the Hell Room. I looked at it and sighed. Twenty-seven years of devoted pasta boiling, spinach wilting, broth simmering…my very first cooking pot that had followed me from apartment to apartment to apartment to house.

Laura Ingalls would have kept it, I thought ruefully. She would've found a use for it—feeding the pigs or watering the horses, or perhaps storing treasures in it under her bed. But I'm not a pioneer girl with fourteen objects to my name, and I don't live in a time when objects are made to be repaired, treasured, handed down for generations. It was time to accept that the pasta pot was dead. One day, with a sigh, I took it, the puzzle piece that no longer fit, and placed it into a plastic bag filled with other garbage, and I put it in the bin in the driveway.

Would it be the popcorn popper all over again? I wondered. The ugly plaid nightgown? I dreaded the thought of how much lost sleep I was in for. But, amazingly, it really wasn't all that hard—no sleep lost, no agonized fretting. *What gives?* I wondered. Had I reasoned myself into a new frame of mind? Had I simply used up my lifetime supply of unnecessary regret? I didn't know. For once I had said good-bye to an old, reliable friend-object, and that—it seemed—was that.

CHAPTER THIRTEEN

STRATEGIES OF STUFF

"We must do whatever it takes to endure and make it through alive."

—Bear Grylls

You may have noticed that there is no shortage of advice out there on the subject of decluttering. Unfortunately, as I've alluded to before, most of it is about as helpful as a heat rash—at least to people like me. Between all the magazine articles, all the books, all the TV segments…there's a lot of feel-good palaver out there that fills air time and sells ads but does very little actual good.

It took me a long time to figure this out, and well into my year of no clutter, I was still formulating my theory on why this was: what was it that was so wrong-headed about most of the advice out there?

A big reason for this is a misunderstanding of the many different stumbling blocks there are to getting and keeping clutter-free. The advice columnist or organization expert on the talk show might address *one* of the existing problems or even two but none of the others. This is kind of like Google starting to give you directions to the picnic spot but cutting out when you're only a third of the way there. Sure, you *feel* like you've made progress—*I'm on my way!*—but, really, you're just lost. You might even be worse off than when you started.

For example, you might be fine with getting rid of things, but not have the vaguest idea how, in the most practical sense, to go about doing it. Or maybe you know just how to go about it, but convincing someone *else* to part with stuff is the major obstacle in your way. Because there are so many different facets of the Stuff problem, they all can merge together to form a tangled mass as daunting as that island of plastic floating around in the Pacific Ocean, which then becomes yet another problem in and of itself: *the problem is so big I can't possibly begin to deal with it!* But maybe it can help if we break the elements down into their components and address our solutions accordingly.

For me, of course, the biggest stumbling block is what I call:

> **The Psychology of Stuff:** Bringing oneself to part with something without being wracked with remorse until death. (This can be nostalgic fear of remorse or fear of giving up future potential, but what it all really comes down to is fear of making a *mistake*.)

Over time, I'd developed little mental mantras that help allay or avoid these fears. Tricks. Mind games. A round of Mother May I? played out in my head. You'll recall: "You are allowed to give away that box of clothes to the Salvation Army, but only if you take out one thing first."

I'd also come up with: "You are allowed to throw away the broken thing that will never get fixed" and "You are allowed to give away the sweater you never really liked if you haven't worn it in at least ten years." More recently I'd tried taking pictures of things on my phone or making lists of them on pads of paper before disposing of them... I'm not suggesting any of these are brilliant or even healthy ways of dealing with Stuff, but only that sometimes they work. In fact, these were acts of desperation. If I thought standing on my head in Times Square while singing "Oh Susanna" at the top of my lungs would make letting go of things a little bit easier, I'd be on the next train to Grand Central with my hat and a harmonica.

If there was any doubt that the Psychology of Stuff was much on my mind lately, I had begun to have vivid dreams on the topic. I dreamed I was trying to check out of a hotel room, but somehow, the corners of the room kept filling up with random belongings for me to sort and discard or save. I dreamed that my cousin Nan suddenly asked if I still had that denim strapless dress I had worn so many years ago. (For the record, this dress does not exist.) I shook my head, sadly.

"No," I'd said in my dream. "I'm pretty sure I'd never wear *that* again."

Here I was, confronted with some mysterious opportunity in the dreamworld to wear this dress—though I can't for the life of me remember what the dream proposed was the perfect occasion to wear a denim strapless dress...a convention for people with horrible fashion sense? A contest for the worst outfit ever? Whatever it was, I would have to make do without the dress. I was sad in my dream to recognize a small, missed opportunity. I had made a misstep and gotten rid of something I now had a use for, and there was nothing I could do about it. But I knew, deep down, it was also, basically, fine.

I experienced many variations on this heart-stopping dream theme: the broken, cow-shaped cutting board! Would I part with it? And so on. I woke up amazed that this was what I now dreamed about instead of flying or sex.

My brain was practicing. It was like I'd discovered a new muscle I'd never used before. What was unreasonably painful and anxiety-producing at first had now become something I could do. Just like with the old pasta pot, I was finding that with practice, I was able to shed some of my undefined sense of panic that came with discarding.

Slowly, I no longer felt *quite* as compelled to check through each and every box beforehand—had I accidentally given away a Ming vase? An undiscovered daguerreotype of Abraham Lincoln? In a tutu? Rational thoughts like these were mysteriously receding like an ocean at low tide.

This bolstered my confidence—maybe I *could* do this— and gave me hope that I could tackle some of the other, often overlooked, issues of Stuff:

> **The Prevention of Stuff:** How to prevent unwanted and/or too many things from coming into your house in the first place.

> **The Persuasion of Stuff:** Convincing someone *else* in your family to part with something. Good luck!

You can see that just as you manage to conquer one obstacle to decluttering ("How can I *bear* to part with my broken harpsichord?"), the next may pop up to confound you anew

("Who on earth is going to *want* my broken harpsichord?") or another when you least expect it (*"Mom!* You can't get rid of the *harpsichord!"* or "Now my grandmother wants to give me *her* broken harpsichord!")

What follows are a few of the more interesting other strategies I've encountered, categorized according to which of the above aspects they address.

Problem: The Prevention of Stuff

How to prevent unwanted and/or too many things from coming into your house in the first place.

Proposed Solution: The Gift Ban Strategy

Gifts can be one of the most challenging sources of clutter. Why? Because presents are an expression of love, and how can you reject an expression of love without rejecting the love itself? Without the giver feeling spurned on some level?

We grappled with a very similar issue during our family's Year of No Sugar because our culture treats sugar in very much the same way we treat presents, which is to say as if there's no downside. Warm cookies aren't somebody's attempt to slowly poison you with undigestable toxins, they're someone's expression of affection for you by giving you something *extra*. Something you didn't already have and that you *don't even need*.

Likewise with presents. In fact, the less you need it, the better a potential present it may be. I mean, given the choice, who would rather be given something they *need* (Sweat socks. Detergent. Pencils. Sensible shoes.) rather than something they *don't* need (Fireworks! Lingerie! Puffy stickers! Manolo Blahniks!)

However, in buying you a present you didn't already have *and* don't desperately need, what are the odds that your parents or your best friend or your great-aunt Mildred might end up getting you something you neither need *nor* want? Now multiply those very good odds by every gift you've ever been given for every holiday and birthday you can recall. Now quick! Find a place for all these unwanted things because to give them away or sell them or attach them to a herd of stampeding buffalo might be construed as a lack of affection for your loved ones.

Nothing could be further from the truth, of course, but try telling that to Great-aunt Mildred when she comes to visit and wonders why you aren't using her sterling silver avocado fork. No, it's all too easy to get confused between the gift and the love it represents.

Despite this, it's important to understand that, just like with sugar, there *is* a downside: there's the fact that an awful lot of us are out here drowning in stuff. To us, Stuff-sufferers, well-intentioned gifts can have the opposite of their intended effect. It reminds me of the cartoons we watched as kids in which Wile E. Coyote is flailing frantically trying to avoid falling into the Grand Canyon when the Road Runner suddenly appears and helpfully hands him an anvil.

Which brings me to my friend Miles. What you need to know about Miles is that she has serious guts, true grit, and, quite frankly, balls of steel. (Figurative ones, but nevertheless.) The reason I know this is because one night I received an email from her titled "Stuff!" that read, in part:

> Hello, friends and family who have given me gifts over the years—
>
> Thank you! I have received from you gifts that are funny (I'm lookin' at you, Cake Wrecks!), useful (Can't live without my apron! And my tray! And my cookbook

stand!), beautiful (luna moth suncatcher), meaningful (Isle of Wight paperweight—also in beautiful category!), comforting (my own hand-knit socks, really?), and so much more.

However...I now officially have a new relationship with material goods...so, despite all the joy I have received as gifts over the years, I would appreciate it if you never, ever buy me a present again.

Got that? *"I would appreciate it if you never, ever buy me a present again."* Wow. She went on:

I don't need Christmas presents, birthday presents, I-went-somewhere-cool presents, or Mother's Day presents. I don't need gift cards or money to buy myself presents. I am just full up with stuff and each individual item may be lovely, but the collective sum has become a burden. I'm sure all of you can relate to some aspect of this!

As I read this, my mind reeled. I was astonished, goggle-eyed. You could *do* this? The only thing I'd ever encountered even remotely close to this idea was when Greta or Ilsa received an invitation to a kid's birthday party with the notation "Please, no gifts!" or the more poetic "Your *presence* is our *present!*" inscribed below the RSVP. Despite the fact that my kids have, in the course of their young lives, accumulated enough toys, dolls, stuffed animals, and general random doodads to entertain a mountaintop village composed entirely of preadolescent girls, I never really felt right putting such a dictum in place. *Can I take that away from them?* I thought to myself. *Is that fair?*

But Miles wasn't speaking for her kids, she was speaking for herself. How will *that* play out? I wondered. At Christmas would she sit there watching everyone else open gift after gift after gift—while she twiddles her thumbs? Would jokes be made to break the tension? Would they give her gifts anyway, and if so, would she refuse to accept them? Was it inevitable that Miles's family members would feel hurt or angry that they've been barred from professing love and affection for her in the form of tangible gifts? In her email she wrote "there are so many ways to celebrate with you other than gifts, so let's focus on that!" But *are* there so many ways? In our culture we are so focused on things that even I—who have given the matter entirely too much thought—still feel pretty much at a loss as to how to celebrate Miles without a corresponding object to stand as evidence.

Which brings me to a confession. One night, several years ago, I was at Miles's home in Ohio, visiting. Her husband was off with their daughter, and we had the place to ourselves for the evening, but for some reason Miles was somewhere else—on an errand? In the shower? I don't recall where she was. But what I do recall was that I found myself idly wandering around her home looking at all her many things. I happened upon some items that had been given to her by other friends—framed photos of them smiling and so on. And that's when I did a very strange thing. I started looking for evidence of *our* friendship among all those belongings. Did I rate? I wondered. Did she have reminders of *our* friendship around her house, too?

I tried to recall the different presents I had given her over the years while scanning the bookshelves and end tables—where was that coffee table book I had sent? Why were there no framed pictures of her and *me* smiling and laughing? Should I have sent her one?

Was Miles forgetting me? Was I not as beloved as her other friends?

Mind you, I'm not proud of this particularly insecure moment. What made me think that Miles needed a prominently displayed doodad as evidence of our friendship? At some point I stopped myself. I tried to imagine Miles at my house doing the very same thing—trying to measure the depth of our friendship based on the number of items placed around the house that had something to do with *her*—and I smiled. Well, *that* was ridiculous!

Come to think of it, I didn't have any smiling pictures of me and *any* of my friends around my house. As for gifts, I knew there was one pillow on the couch Miles had brought me back from her travels…but probably nothing else super-prominent or obvious. Did that mean I didn't value our long friendship, because she didn't have sufficient visible symbolic representation? And if she gave me a gift I didn't care for that I decided not to keep, would that be tantamount to friend-divorce? Of course not. Trying to equate objects with the love I have for my friend was like trying to compare apples and aardvarks: a silly and pointless exercise. I had become Great-Aunt Mildred wondering about the avocado fork.

But back to the Great Gift Experiment. Miles and I have talked countless times over the years about the problem of clutter; our desperation about the volume of Stuff that comes into our lives is one of the things we have very much in common. Yet in all that time, she had never attempted anything quite so drastic as this. What, I wondered, had driven her over the tipping point now? What had changed that caused her to send this message out to people—important friends and family she loves and cares about—who might not understand?

In a word: bedbugs. Yep. And I had thought the time my kids got *lice* was bad; turns out lice is to bedbugs as one sequin is to Liberace's piano. I called her for the lowdown and heard Miles talk about fumigating their home, cooking all of her family's clothes and belongings in the dryer, living out of plastic bags for months on end... I decided that if we ever even *think* we have bedbugs the only sensible thing to do will be to abandon our house like a sinking ship, flinging clothing off, shrieking and shaving our heads as we go.

But this had been a while ago, before the beginning of our Year of No Clutter project. Now that some time had gone by, I called Miles to ask about the results of her gift ban. She said she had not considered the experiment much of a success.

"There are people in my life," Miles explained to me, "that love giving gifts *so much* that the present ban caused them great confusion and distress." They tried desperately to get around the ban: here's a plant! That doesn't count, right? Here's a gift card! You can buy anything you want with it—so that shouldn't count! Here's something edible! So there won't be anything left over!

One beloved friend even went so far as to have her *daughter* hand Miles a gift, as in "Um...don't look at me! It's from *her*! You wouldn't say no to a *kid*, would you?"

But ultimately these folks just gave up and went back to their regular present-buying ways. Which is to say, ultimately, they ignored the present ban.

Today, Miles is philosophical about the matter. "In hindsight, I came to regret having sent the email at all," she says. "Social norms evolve because they are what make people feel comfortable. In trying to make this change I was making my family and friends, who are incredibly well-meaning and who I adore, uncomfortable."

"So today, I gratefully accept what people want to give. And I gratefully accept if people do not want to give. I make an effort to use the gift, but if after that it isn't something that fits into my life then I put it in the box for the Salvation Army."

Wow.

Maybe Miles regrets having sent that email, but I'm awfully glad she did because I found it pretty inspiring. I think what she did was something that many of us Too Much Stuff people at one time or another feel tempted to consider but would never have the nerve to actually do. If nothing else, Miles' experimental gift ban has helped me to stand back and see gifts for what they are, but nothing more. As a result of our philosophical ruminations on this account, whenever an unused gift rears its head in the Hell Room, I no longer hesitate to put it into the rotation for the consignment shop or the donation box. I remind myself that I'm not rejecting anybody's love by doing so. The best part is that I know *someone* out there will just love it, and just thinking about that person coming across it and having it make their day makes me happy.

But I must admit I'm relieved I'm allowed to give Miles gifts again—officially. Having her birthday or Christmas come and go and not ever sending her anything to mark the occasion just felt kind of...*wrong*. I make a point to be thoughtful about it, though, and regardless of the holiday, if I don't find anything that grabs me by the lapels and shrieks *Miles!*, then I don't send her anything until I do.

That's good because I *really* didn't want to have to send her another gift card for an edible plant.

Conclusion

Not everyone can successfully institute a gift ban. But we can let go of gift guilt if we remember that presents are an *expression* of love, not the love itself.

Problem: The Persuasion of Stuff

Convincing *your kids* to part with something.

Proposed Solution: The Sneaky Parent Strategy

I don't know why, but every once in a while I feel nostalgic for my metal Holly Hobbie lunch box. It's funny because I never especially liked it. I mean, I wasn't a Holly Hobbie fan; my mother had picked it out for me. I envied the girls who had *Charlie's Angels* lunch boxes or the characters from *Peanuts*. Or, really, *anything* but Holly Hobbie, who didn't seem to have her own show or comic strip or anything, just an oversized head with a blank expression. You could never see her *eyes* because she was always hiding behind that bonnet! What was *that* all about?

Nevertheless, I wish I still had it. Compared to the space-age, foam-insulated boxes my kids tote to school every day, it would probably strike them as something quaint and historic that ought to be in a museum, perhaps between a Victrola and a nice pair of leech tongs.

My missing old lunch box reminds me of how mystified I used to be when my mother would describe a certain dress she used to own whose outdated style had now come back into fashion: "Oh, I used to have a *beautiful* one of those—it had a low back and straps and pleats and this little trim, and it was this gorgeous color. I *loved* it."

I'd ask her, "Do you still *have* it?"

"Oh *no*," she'd say, shaking her head as if I had suggested a concept that was patently impossible, as if I had asked her if she still had the leftovers from her wedding dinner in our refrigerator. The impression I got was that if you weren't watching very, *very* carefully, clothing was liable to vanish from one's closet as if by magic. To indicate the matter was closed, she would shrug as if to say, "That's just what *happens*."

But not to me, my young self resolved, silently. I was incredulous: how could my mother not have foreseen that someday, *someday* saddle shoes with socks or polyester maxi dresses or macramé handbags would come *back*? And what was with that shrug, anyway, as if she bore no responsibility in the matter? Had *aliens* abducted her clothes? Maybe it was because I was a young teenager, or maybe it was because it was the eighties, or maybe it was because, although I didn't know it yet, my parents were on the verge of divorce, but for whatever reason I had begun to have the feeling that nothing was truly "real" in the world anymore. I lived in a world of parachute pants and strip malls... Everything seemed fake. I had the uneasy feeling that all the good stuff had already happened, and I had missed out. I longed for something I couldn't quite define—something that felt "real." Even if it was just a "real" poodle skirt or a "real" sweater set or even a "real" pair of combat boots from the Army Navy Surplus—I wanted things that belonged to a past—a history.

Of course, it wouldn't be until much, much later—decades later—that I would start to see my mother's side of things, once I began to have children of my own and realize that babies and small children are, in fact, clutter-generating machines. Then I was swimming in a sea of Stuff-i-tude the likes of which I had never seen before. And so I began to have a greater appreciation for the alien-abducted clothing. It was, perhaps, a necessary function of the universe.

You'll have realized it already, of course: that in our house, my mother was often the alien doing the abducting. In fact it was one day not so long ago that I happened upon an article detailing advice for dealing with kids who hang on to old things you wish they wouldn't: a grubby teddy bear that no longer has any distinguishable facial features, a baby doll that suffered an unfortunate haircut, or an embarrassingly ratty blankie. Personally, the idea of parting my child from her security blanket or beloved teddy against her will, no matter how ratty or smelly it might be, turns my stomach. But I was curious if the article had any big picture advice on making letting go any easier, so I read on.

One strategy described was specifically for security blankets. The article explained the idea was to rip the offending blankie in half every time it was washed, so that it gradually became smaller and smaller until it ceased to exist right before the big visit to Blankie Heaven.

And that was when it hit me like a bolt of lightning: *my mother had used this trick on me.* As a young child I had developed an attachment to a soft cotton blanket: it was off-white with a soft pastel plaid pattern running through it and pink sateen binding all around the edge. It had a lovely smell that I can't account for, really unlike anything I had ever smelled before or since but that acted upon my nervous system the way I imagine pink martinis or quaaludes do on others. In my brain this scent meant comfort, safety, and home—maybe it was just the smell of a happy childhood.

So, like many toddlers, I carried it everywhere, rubbed it

against my cheek thoughtfully, wrapped myself up in it, and certainly couldn't possibly be expected to sleep without it. When stressed I would sniff the warm, peaceful smell of my cotton blankie, and everything always seemed much, much better.

I suppose my parents always just assumed that someday I'd tire of it. But I didn't. I slept with my blankie for years. Nursery school, kindergarten, first grade, second grade, third grade... Every so often my mom would pry it from my hands and insist on washing it. I distinctly recall waiting up past my bedtime for my blanket to be done in the dryer before I could be properly tucked into bed. At a certain point, and I don't know exactly when, I began to be aware that my blanket was somehow—inexplicably—*shrinking*.

Yes, it was definitely shrinking. I hadn't been sure before, but now it was definitely much smaller than it had been, and I had extremely dim memories of it existing as a full-size, bed-length blanket... What could be happening? My child brain pondered this conundrum for a while and ultimately gave up. Mom had no idea.

It was another of those things that *just happen*, I supposed. When you're a kid, so many things in the world seem bizarre and mysterious and magically unreasonable that a blanket slowly disappearing of its own accord, as if it were a leftover Entenmann's sheet cake in our fridge, seemed entirely within the realm of possibility. And so I kept getting older, kept sleeping with my blankie. And it kept getting smaller.

It continued its inevitable march toward nonexistence until one day it stopped. My blankie had reached the size of a very large postcard or perhaps a hankie. I accepted that, yes, this must also be the mysterious magic of the world at work. I'm sure my parents were exceedingly frustrated with my inability to let go of my now grayish and fraying little scrap of fabric. At this point it resembled an incredibly soft and well-loved dust rag. I have a vivid memory of going to my first sleepover party in sixth or seventh grade and being terrified my friends would discover my childish secret hidden under my pillow.

But at last I got to the point when I really could sleep without it. Nonetheless, I still treasured that little rag, grateful to it for all those years' worth of warm reassurance. It sat on my nightstand for years and at last moved to a keepsake box in a drawer. On the occasional trip home from college, I might happen across it and pull it out and give it a test sniff just to see if that old happy childhood smell was still there, which of course it always was.

And never once, in all those years, did it ever occur to me that every time she washed it, my mother was down in the basement laundry room, ripping my beloved blankie in half. And returning it to me smaller. And smaller. Until finally the game was up. You can't rip a postcard-sized piece of fabric in half and hope it won't be noticed…even incredibly slow-on-the-uptake me was bound to figure it out.

Here I was, nearly four decades later, and I sat riveted to my chair with the sudden clarity of the realization: *my* mother had done that. My own mother.

Okay, I couldn't resist being melodramatic there, but really, I do get it. As moms, we're all just tap-dancing as fast as we can. In fact, sometimes I wish *I* could get away with being the sneaky parent. But I can't. For one thing, I have it on good authority I have the world's worst poker face. Also, my kids are much more observant than I ever was. Whenever *I* try to surreptitiously get rid of the Whatever before the kids get home, it inevitably blows up in my face.

One of the best examples of this happened midway through the Hell Room year. One morning Greta was sitting at the breakfast table talking about the blue duffle coat she had found a few months before at the local church rummage sale—she was making plans to wear it that day and it would be just perfect, but for some reason she hadn't remembered seeing it lately. Meanwhile, sitting across from her, I made funny faces, like someone was stepping on my foot. Steve thought she should look in the winter storage, but I, in a strangled voice, managed to tell Greta that I had been under the impression that she liked her new *red* coat so much better that I had... I had...

Yes, I had given the blue coat away. Without asking her. In my feeble defense I will only say that it took up a *ton* of space in the coat closet, was incredibly heavy, and hadn't been touched in months. But. I felt *terrible*. I mean really, completely awful. Oh my God, I thought, how would *I* feel if someone just went into the closet and gave something of mine away without asking? And she had been *so* proud the day she bought it, having found that coat for just a few dollars and talking about how it was this terrific bargain and that you could tell from the tags that it was vintage and how they didn't make coats like this anymore... What had I done? Did it have to be the coat she had been so proud of? Something so utterly—I only now realized—irreplaceable?

I was such a remorse-ridden wreck at breakfast that day that Greta ended up consoling *me*. It wasn't like me at all to do such a thing; rather, it was the product of one of those periodic bursts of exasperation I'd fallen victim to with increasing frequency this year. In this state of mind, I am likely to throw out the Hope Diamond should I come across it. In fact, was it a direct result of the Hell Room project? Had I been getting better and better at getting rid of things until finally I got carried away?

Obviously I was terrible at this getting-rid-of-things business. I got rid of all the wrong things. Who was I kidding? Probably, I would never give anything away, ever again.

As if to emphasize the point, and somewhere right around this time I was driving Ilsa to school one day when we heard a strange noise from the hatchback area of the car—strange chirpy, growly noises. It sounded like someone back there was quietly trying to kidnap Beeker from the Muppets. Neither of us could figure out what this could be. Suddenly, all the color drained from my face. Oh. I knew what it was. One day while the kids were in school, I had put in the trunk two boxes of neglected and outgrown toys to give away, and there had been one of those incredibly annoying motorized Zhu Zhu Pets inside. *It was the hamster!* He was talking to us—probably squeaking: "Ilsa! Ilsa! Don't let her give me to Goodwill!"

Slowly it dawned on Ilsa. "Hey wait a minute… That's… *Zhu Zhu!* That's *my hamster toy!*"

I was caught. Ratted out by an electric hamster.

I made my confession to Ilsa—who now looked like she was pretty sure she would never trust her mother ever again. I apologized for the deceit and promised I'd let her go through the contents of both boxes before giving anything away. She would have absolute veto power.

And this is what we did. Gritting my teeth and muttering under my breath all the while, I brought both boxes *back* into the house and put them in the hallway to await Ilsa's inspection. Going through the boxes, Ilsa picked out exactly the very last things I would have kept, including the Zhu Zhu, the motorized blabbermouth. She filled about half a box with things she wanted to keep. Everything else could still go.

I was grateful because based on her previous behavior I had fully expected her to keep *everything*. Then again, a month later, that half-filled box, hamster and all, was still sitting in the hallway, untouched. Hmmmm, I thought. Do you think she'd notice if it disappeared?

Oh, she would.

So you can see that I am practically hopeless in the role of the sneaky parent. The hamster saved me from myself, it seems. Too bad, I thought, that Greta's duffel coat couldn't have done the same.

Or…could it?

Several weeks went by. Then one day, I was bringing some of my things to the upscale women's consignment shop in town, and while the salesperson sifted through the clothes I had brought, I wandered around and looked through the racks. You'll never guess what I found on the rack of coats.

That's right. I stopped stock-still and stared at it for a full minute. There was no mistaking it—it had the big hood, the toggle buttons, the ancient tag sewn inside. And it was bright cobalt blue. It was the blue duffel coat.

Greta's blue duffel coat.

When I came back to myself, I picked up the tag and read: "$135! Retails for $400!"

Shit.

Greta had bought this same coat for $18 in the church basement. Apparently she had been *really* right about what a great bargain she had found. So! Could I possibly feel any worse? Would the universe like some road salt to rub in my wound please?

Obviously, there was no way I could justify paying that much money to get the coat back for her. Greta already had more outerwear than she really needed. I walked out to my car with my hangers, feeling miserable. *One hundred and thirty-five dollars. Ugh.*

As I approached my car, though, my pace slowed.

My brain was talking to itself. *You screwed up*, it said. *You have been given a chance—an almost unbelievable chance to make this right. And you're walking away? Really?*

Well…it *was* 20 percent off day…What was 20 percent of $135? I could go back and ask, at the very least.

I found myself heading back into the shop.

"*Actually*," the salesgirl informed me, "this red 'X' on the price tag here? That means it's 50 percent off."

What? Really? I brightened. So that brought it down to…$67.50.

"You *also* have a credit," she went on. "Do you want to use that?"

What? Yes! Yes, I do. How much is my credit?

I had a little more than fifty dollars in credit. Therefore, the out-of-pocket cost for Greta's blue toggle coat—and my redemption—would amount to…*nine dollars*. How often do we get the chance to right a wrong, fix a mistake, assuage a piece of our own tremendous guilt at all, let alone for the low, low price of nine dollars?

Of course I bought it.

And that is the story of the Incredible Boomeranging Coat. But, amazingly, even *this* is not quite where it ends, because before heading home triumphantly with my prize, I stopped at the local drugstore to pick up some shampoo. I was standing in line behind an older woman with a cane when something about her made me do a double take.

It was her purse. There was no mistaking it. It had been an optimistic craft fair purchase, handmade of swirling, felted wool and quite unique.

It had once been mine.

Pretty though it was, when I had finally realized I wasn't using it and likely never would, I had brought it to that same consignment shop I had just been in, where I imagine this woman had been delighted to find it.

Heck, her purchase of that purse of mine had probably just helped me pay to get Greta's coat back.

It was all so incredibly weird and coincidental. Were the gods of clutter trying to tell me something that day? I'd like to think that they were. Here is what I heard: *You may not be the sneaky parent*, they said, *you may make the occasional mistake.*

But it's okay—things will work out as they should. Keep going.

Conclusion
Some people just aren't cut out to be the sneaky parent. And that's okay.

———

Problem: The Persuasion of Stuff: Part 2
Convincing *your husband* to part with something.

Proposed Solution: The Staring Contest
From the beginning of our project, Steve had steadfastly maintained that he had "nothing" in the Hell Room. However, for some time now Greta and I had been discovering the true scope of that nothing, and it was rather impressive. Like sand dunes moving silently across the

desert, objects and boxes and random items had been wafting steadily out of the Room and into the poor, innocent
Hallway Room, blocking it up, climbing the walls, at times
obstructing the passageway altogether. Virtually all of it was
Steve's Stuff, awaiting final judgment.

As I've alluded to, when it comes to Stuff, Steve is a bit of
a walking contradiction. For him, neatness is an all-or-nothing
proposal, with things being either obsessively neat and organized (the things he pays attention to) or an unmitigated disaster (everything else). I first learned this about him when we were
dating. He amazed me with the intricate labeling system he
had devised for his photographic negatives, each with its own
archival paper sleeve and delicately filled-out labeling sticker (of
his own design). Wow! I thought. I had never met a guy who
paid so much attention to detail. It freaked me out a little, but
I was impressed. I wasn't sure what a guy like this would make
of me—I thought I was *fairly* organized, but compared to Felix
Unger here, would I end up looking like Oscar Madison?

Then I happened to see the trunk of his car. I had never
seen such chaos in such a small space. It looked like one of
our photography classrooms had been thrown into a blender:
camera bag spacers, Velcro, scattered papers, empty travel
coffee mugs, all thrown together higgledy-piggledy.

Oh. I thought. *Okay…*

Steve can have the most insanely fastidious coffee-
making process known to man, in which he uses different bean grinders depending on whether he is making an
espresso or a regular cup, and will explain in great detail
the necessity of using a *long* spout kettle for the pour-over
method of brewing. He has been known to utter phrases
such as "the key to encouraging proper bloom is in the

rousting." From the neat, shiny, and organized appearance of his various brewing apparatus, you'd be forgiven for thinking that clean but crowded corner of our kitchen is designated for performing delicate, coffee-related experiments involving lasers. At the same time, he is also the person in our house who leaves little clouds of convenience store receipts and cough-drop wrappers in his wake everywhere he goes—like Charlie Brown's friend Pig-Pen. I find these—along with cryptic notes about calculating pinhole exposure and reciprocity—on his nightstand, on top of the tall dresser, under the bed, behind his chair.

There are the things he cares to pay attention to, which he *really* does, and the things he does not pay attention to, which he *really* doesn't.

So the real question I faced was: how was I going to change the status of those items in question—boxes and boxes of them—from something he did not pay attention to to something he would?

One day I broached the subject. I knew I had to wait until lunch was over—always better to propose a disagreeable task on a full stomach. My strategy did not work.

"But!" he protested. "I have *work* to do! I need to make progress! I have a big, huge project I'm working on!"

"*Me too!*" I said. "And I can't do this part without you." Was I above mentioning the fact that I had spent the previous two mornings helping him edit photographs? I was not.

It didn't matter. There was no budging him. He did everything but plug his ears and run from the room yelling "La-la-la I *can't hear you!*" So I tried a different tack: maybe he could start by telling me what to do with all those big boxes of paper folders? And the ancient promotional handouts?

And one (*one*, mind you) of the more than two dozen camera bags we had unearthed? Taken one by one, as unseen, abstract concepts, he was able to give direction for one or two things, out of the thousand, at least.

"So that's good, right?" he said, looking quite relieved. "*That* helps, right?"

I gave him a look.

I began carrying boxes of paper folders up and down the stairs, annoyed. I fumed the whole way. How could I possibly clean up this room without him making decisions about *his* stuff? What should I do? Start building a sculpture in the living room? Open a photo supply store in the garage? Put it in a giant pile in the front yard and wait for a flood? I was at a loss.

I encountered Steve on his way back to his studio. *Look at him! Getting off scot-free,* I thought, uncharitably, *while I lug his crap around!*

"You're terrified!" I said in a tone that was joking but still accusatory.

He looked at me. "You're right," he said, seriously. "I really am. How many times have you seen me in that room?"

I thought about it. Since it had gotten *really* bad? Well...

"Like, *never*," he volunteered. "I get in the middle of all that, and I get...paralyzed."

Oh.

I am a lot of things in relation to the Hell Room: frustrated, depressed, anxious, angry, defensive, embarrassed...but *terrified*? Now I felt, you know, kind of...*bad*. Although this wasn't a get-out-of-the-Hell-Room-free card, I realized that this wasn't simply an impressive level of stubbornness I was dealing with. Getting frustrated and pushing him to deal with this head-on simply wasn't going to work. I'd have to find another way.

As it turned out the answer to that question was, as practically everything with Stuff turns out to be, a matter of context. Up in the Hell Room, and in the Hallway Room too, the problem items were easy to avoid. They practically *begged* to be avoided. *Please don't look at me!* they screamed. *I am stuff you totally don't want to deal with!* But if these items were to migrate to, say, the dining room…?

Which is of course what they did. Miraculously, box after box after box… One by one they trooped their way down to the dining room where they sat expectantly on the floor, piled up against the wall, staring at their benefactor as if, perhaps, waiting to be fed.

Greta was delighted at this development and at her dad having been caught red-handed in a contradiction. "Your pile downstairs is growing!" she announced to him gleefully. "And so is the definition of *nothing!*"

"You're grounded," he replied.

What happened next? Well, the pile stayed there. Every time we sat down to a meal, Steve would glance at it and make a comment.

Well, this is nice.

Is this all for me?

You know we can't leave all this here.

I don't have time to go through this!

You know, you can do most of this for *me.*

You know this stuff here is killing me, right?

But the stuff wasn't moving. I wasn't even nagging—the stuff did that job all by itself. After so many days had gone by that I had begun to wonder if the pile might actually grow roots and stay there forever, one day Steve suddenly acquiesced.

"Let's go through some of this after lunch," he said

pleasantly one day, out of nowhere. You could have knocked me over with a negative sleeve.

After that it was surprisingly easy—we went through the stuff like a shot. In just a few days of going through piles and boxes for an hour or so after lunch, we had taken the whole intimidating pile down to nothing. Negatives all went in one giant, save-forever, put-away box; supplies and equipment went either to the studio to be used or into the trash; camera bags all disappeared to the alternate universe that apparently exists to house all of Steve's camera bags. (I don't ask; I don't want to know.)

About fourteen times Steve was overheard to say, "Oh hey! I've been *looking* for this."

When it was all done, I was truly astounded. The pile had been *so* formidable, and my helplessness in the face of somebody else's stuff *so* complete—what would he want? What would he throw away? Eradicating that pile had come to seem like a nice idea that was never, *ever*, going to happen.

And then? In a matter of hours, it was done. Like that! Like—no big deal.

I was delighted—at first. And then I realized something else: I was jealous. *I* was the one who had been working for months, but *he* was the one who was done! Sure, he'd had a lot more than "nothing" in the room, but there was no denying it: I still was the all-time household champion of Keeping Stuff.

Rats.

Conclusion

If you can stand it, strategic placement and waiting it out just might work.

CHAPTER FOURTEEN

THE OLD HEAVE-HO

"Oh mama mia, mama mia, mama mia, let me go!"
—Queen, "Bohemian Rhapsody" (1975)

In our grand procession of Stuff problems, I've saved the best for last. In fact, this final one is so important it really seemed to require a chapter of its very own. Perhaps you've already guessed what I'm talking about.

Problem: The Deaccession of Stuff

How to find a person who can appreciate and use this item and physically get it to that person (aka *avoiding the landfill*).

Just as hard as trying to decide to get rid of something is the question of what to do with it once you've decided. I know many people who have a lot less trouble with this than I do—my husband is one of them. A significant part of our marriage has involved me picking things back out of the trash in order to deliver them to the recycling container, the composting container, or the charity box.

That's good *for something!* I say. *It's got another life ahead!*

Because we've been married for going on two decades, I'm pretty sure Steve will stop looking at me like I have three heads when I do this any day now.

I can't help it: when I imagine a perfectly good, usable thing sitting—*forever*—at the bottom of a pile of trash it makes me a little bit berserk. So finding happy homes for things has become something of an obsession.

Over the years I've made a special study of the art of getting rid of things, and of course during the year of no clutter I was getting enough practice to approach black belt status. In addition to the various good causes I've already mentioned, I'd sent boxes to family members, plied friends and acquaintances with fondue pots and bread machines, brought giant bags to clothing drives, and as a last resort mastered the fine art of putting stuff by the curb. Where I grew up, in the suburbs, doing this would've resulted in a spate of friendly neighborhood calls to the police, but around here putting something by the curb translates to: THIS IS FREE. PLEASE TAKE IT, OR I WILL CRY. And, amazingly, they do, sometimes within nanoseconds. You could put ice cubes on a paper towel out there, and I'm pretty sure someone would take them before the towel got damp.

Still, there are things that don't play well by the curb: small things, fragile things, things that can't get wet or are too heavy to get to the curb in the first place. Here are a few of the more creative solutions I have come across for these charity- and curb-resistant items.

Possible Solution #1: Use the Postal System

Many years ago, in the Pre-Kid Era, when I had time to do crazy, impulsive things like watch morning television, a particular segment caught my attention. I remember it well: the piece was touted as answering the question of "What to do with all those extra snapshots?" Or course, it was also the Pre-Digital Era, and therefore everyone who had an actual film-using camera (read: everyone) had to go have it processed at a dark, chemically smelling storefront run by teenagers.

In case you were born in the interim (in which case, stop making me feel old) or if you've perhaps forgotten the joys of this phenomenon, let me describe: after a few hours a person only slightly older than your toaster would hand you back an envelope containing twenty-four or thirty-six negatives and precisely three good photos you might actually want to keep. The rest of the envelope was filled with, to use the technical term, "poop": blurry close-ups of your pinkie, shadowy, back-lit people, people looking goofy who were not actually doing it on purpose, frustrating just-before or just-after Something Important Happened shots, and sad, pale sunsets that were always, *always* much better in person. This problem got exponentially worse when photo labs got the bright idea to start offering their customers *free duplicates*. Hooray! Now everyone could have *twice* as many blurry pinkies and bad sunsets!

No one knew what to do with all these packets of glossy also-ran photos. Wasn't that what *drawers* were invented for? Of course, many folks were able to at least discard the very worst ones—the photos that came back completely dark or hopelessly blurred. (As you have already guessed, I was not one of those people.)

So, there I was, on the edge of my couch, anxiously awaiting the pronouncement that would solve at least one of my many Thing Problems. I recognized the correspondent as a senior citizen they had brought in specifically to address issues facing older viewers. I had liked her pieces in the past—she was plucky and had a ready wit.

She began by lamenting the ubiquity of the problem—who didn't have a snapshot camera these days? And therefore a box or drawer *filled* with rejected prints? Her solution was simple, straightforward, and foolproof. Here it was: mail them to your creditors! Yes! Every time you pay a bill—electric, telephone, doctor, and so on—*slip a reject print inside*!

The anchors were dumbfounded. In my memory I picture the camera cutting to Katie Couric and Matt Lauer with their mouths hanging open. The segment was abruptly cut short, and the anchors tried to play it off as if her suggestions were a joke: "ha ha!"

But she wasn't playing along; she meant it.

I don't recall seeing the senior correspondent on the show again after that.

I think it's extremely understandable that some of us get so frustrated with our junk that we are willing to consider mailing it off to perfect strangers in order to get rid of it. The only thing that kept me from following her wacky advice was the knowledge that the poor mail-opening person at the phone or heating-oil company would undoubtedly toss the bad prints into the trash. If trash is what they were, shouldn't I be able to throw my own trash away? Why the middleman?

However, there are times when the mail can be very helpful when nothing else will do. For example, in addition to the standard "no technology" rule, many charities in our area also have a "no stuffed animals" rule, which I found maddening. After all, who doesn't like to give a kid an adorable, big-eyed stuffed animal? And what kid doesn't love that adorable, big-eyed stuffed animal for at least the next hour or two? In our house, it then it goes in the pile of adorable, big-eyed stuffed animals we have in the closet. And under the bed. And in the drawers of the spare room dresser. Eventually it begins to feel like a friendly takeover: invasion of the relentlessly winsome.

Fortunately I managed to find a charity online that collects gently used stuffed animals for children who've suffered a traumatic event. All I had to do was pay the postage. I am too embarrassed to reveal to you how many boxes I have shipped to that address, but don't worry. Even after several major rounds of culling, we *still* have closets full of delightful, furry creatures, none of whom ever get played with.

Possible Solution #2: Use the Internet

Isn't it funny how sometimes you'll do things for other people that you wouldn't think to do for yourself? Over the course of the summer, while I was losing my ever-loving mind trying to figure out where so many "perfectly good" things could be sent besides the town dump, my mother was losing her ever-loving mind trying to figure out how to squeeze two lifetimes' worth of belongings—both hers and John's—into a condominium that was already fully furnished. Every time I saw her now it was like our friends Marty and Monica all over again: "Hi, and would you like this Alaskan eggbeater? How about a stuffed iguana? Do you have any use for this old coffee pot/Christmas tablecloth/three-ton laminated bed and bookshelf unit?"[14]

It was this last thing that was causing a fair amount of consternation for my mother, and I was trying to help her with

---

14. My mother would like me to point out that she does not now have nor has she ever had a stuffed iguana.

the problem it presented. This bedroom unit was enormous—the kind of everything-welded-together, rounded-corners, super-heavy furniture unit that was very fashionable in the mid-eighties: drawers attached to bookshelves attached to bed frame attached to overhead lighting... Mom was at a loss. The charity organizations didn't have room for it; the consignment shop had already turned it down. But when she actually began talking about *paying someone* to haul the thing away I became incredulous: *pay* someone? To put perfectly good furniture in a *landfill*?!

No, no, no—there had to be a better solution than this. And that's when I remembered a wonderful thing: the Internet. After all, I had found someone who wanted *used stuffed animals* there. In Getting-Rid-of-Stuff-Land, where I now resided, this seemed an achievement tantamount to finding someone who wanted bent paper clips or the old, wadded-up Band-Aids from the soap dish in the shower. If the Internet could do that, it seemed that anything might be possible.

Larger Internet sites intimidated me, though, and also seemed impractical. What we needed was something ultra-local. I had heard from friends about a local online marketplace, but it wasn't until Mom seemed ready to burn her bedroom unit in the front yard that I thought to sign up and try it out. What's the worst thing that could happen? I'd post pictures and offer it free to anyone who would come haul the thing away. That could work, right?

Within about ten minutes I was signed up. I posted pictures from my phone. Within another ten minutes, I had a response to the post. By the end of the day we had made an appointment for the unit to be disassembled, packed into a truck, and hauled away. It was a local woman who would use the unit as new bedroom furniture for her teenage daughter. She was thrilled.

Now, I know you're probably waiting for the punch line—"and then, to say 'thank you,' she insisted on giving Mom a hot-air balloon!"—but there isn't one. This was simply something that *worked*. A connection that once would've required days or weeks via the classified ad section of the newspaper—not to mention a nominal cost—now took hours, or even minutes, and was entirely free. I had never tried this strategy before, but once I wrapped my mind around this new way of doing things, I was hooked.

It opened up a whole new horizon for me in the getting-rid-of-stuff department. After this episode, I knew what to do with a whole category of "perfectly good" things that, for various reasons, couldn't go through my normal discard channels of the consignment shops, the charity shop, and the curb.

Those weird file cabinets that had no drawer runners? Somebody *wanted* them! Those six big boxes of white pocket folders? Somebody wanted *them*! Ugly table lamp? Old dry-erase board? My leftover rug-hooking supplies? There was a perfect match out there for all of them…a good home for every "still perfectly good" thing that I was looking to foist from the clutches of the Hell Room. I felt relieved and vindicated. With a little bit of extra effort I had saved these oddball items from the garbage pile and instead given them a new lease on life. They would be *used*. Enjoyed. Loved. What more could an object want than that?

The moral of this story? Never assume there isn't someone out there who will want the thing you're getting rid of. Unless it is a shower Band-Aid.

Possible Solution #3: Use a Party!

Until a few years ago I'd never heard of a "clothing swap." When I told my friend Katrina this she almost fainted because, according to her, clothing swaps were quite possibly the best thing ever. I had been of the opinion that ramp pesto was, in fact, the best thing ever, so I felt compelled to investigate further.

As it turns out, a clothing swap is like a combination of a tiny clothing drive and a potluck dinner. If you've never been to a one, you're in for either a great treat or a total nightmare depending on your own personal perspective. I enjoy these gatherings tremendously, whereas my aunt Mill, for example, might have a medium-sized nervous breakdown. The general idea is to bring a potluck dish as well as all your family's hand-me-downs, castoffs, don't-wants and can't-stands in bags and boxes and baskets. These you cart in and dump unceremoniously onto your hostess's living room floor. Then have a lot of wine. Try the veggie chili someone brought—it's delicious. Inevitably there are fourteen mixed casserole-y type dishes of undetermined origin, and if you are in Vermont, at least three of them will involve the use of bulgur wheat.

It's fun just to sit and eat and chat with the other moms— because we're all moms here, pretty much, and definitely all women. Some bring their kids, and others take the opportunity to have the night off, so like everything else about the swap, it's a mixed bag. As we chat we cover the topics of kids, school, local news, and how good this whatever-this-is-I'm-eating-right-now is and generally just enjoy being in the random, chaotic, but utterly comforting company of other women.

At some undetermined point in the evening, after a certain tipping point of wine and food has been consumed, the pile begins to exert its gravitational pull: panther-like, the women begin to circle the gigantic pile of mostly clothing. It is usually about two feet high and sprawling in every direction like a tractor-trailer spill; the contents of it tend to blend together in one dark, unintelligible mass. Left unattended, one suspects the heap might develop sentience, rise up menacingly, and wander the house, looking for organizational self-help books to read.

But this won't happen because the pile is filled with secret, enticing potential. We who spend our lives trying to outfit children who insist on growing out of clothing before we've managed to drive it home from the store cannot resist the seduction of *free clothes*. There is always excitement in the air as the picking begins, slowly at first and then in earnest. Everyone is picking up item after item, inspecting and sorting. Rapidly, things are being tossed everywhere: into the same bags or boxes that had stood empty for the last hour or between participants ("Oh, try this!"—"Could little Andromeda wear this?"—"Check this out!") or flung back into the pile.

Yes, there are some rips here and there; there are stains. Oftentimes there's dust in the air because the clothes were stored in the garage too long, so watch out if you have allergies. But amazingly, most things are clean and ready to take home and wear the next day—which many people do.

Who knows what you might find? I've come home with things I can't imagine not having owned before. This is how I got my favorite T-shirt and my comfiest skirt. I'm amazed at how often somebody else's trash could really be your treasure. It works the other way, too, of course. That awful maroon floral blouse that *you* brought—the hippy one with the bells that jingle audibly—there's a *really* good chance that some-one, at some point in the evening, will pick it up and shriek with the thrill of conquest. She will take that thing that has been the bane of your closet since 1992, and she will give it a proper home. She will love it, and maybe, just maybe, she will even *wear* it.

There's *always* something for everyone—lots of people arrive protesting they're "just dropping off," but I've never seen anyone go home entirely empty-handed. Every time I've been to a swap I make a rule that I am definitely, positively *not* allowed to bring home more than I brought: once my bag is full I must stop. Amazingly, I always manage to find something for every member of my family. In addition to the clothes there are always odd things: a toddler airplane seat belt, a bolt of fabric, some incredible clogs that we all admire but that fit no one, and some embarrassingly racy lingerie no one will admit to bringing but that Lauren is sure to hold aloft to make everyone laugh.

"Who brought this? C'mon! *Who?*"

In the end, the pile is always decimated; all that's left are dregs. The unclaimed bits—including the clogs and the lingerie—will be taken by volunteers to a local shelter next week. Bags and boxes, all full again, get toted back to trunks and backseats, and slowly the women start disappearing into the night, with words about bedtimes and thank-yous and don't-forget-your-dish on their lips.

I have come home more than once with items that end up my new closet staples, or my kids', and all for free. Of course, there are the inevitable whoops-well-*that*-didn't-work items. Those go right back in the bin for the next swap, which I often begin the very next day. And every once in a while some mom will pause at school or at the general store and eyeing my orange pullover will say, "Hey... Where did you get...*that?*" It was hers, of course, in another life—and she's delighted. Like some funny secret we all share, like a communal closet. It makes us feel, what? Like we've figured out how to make more out of what we have *and* have great fun in the process.

Because I always come home with pretty much the same volume of stuff as I brought, technically you could argue that it effectively nullifies any net deaccessioning benefit. I'd argue, however, that I've taken outgrown and unloved clothes that were stored unhelpfully in the Hell Room or the pantry and magically turned them into clothing that will fill our closets and be worn. Ta-da!

But it's more than that. The clothing swap has helped me—just like that message the clutter gods sent me the day I found Greta's blue coat—to loosen my vice-like grip on things and realize that we are all in this together: the moms, our families, our things. I give and I get and what goes around comes around. Things even sometimes end up, mysteriously, where it seems they really ought to be.

I feel a great sense of gratitude to the ladies of the clothing swap. And, for that matter, to the people who run the online marketplaces of the world, the stuffed animal charities, and the gods of clutter themselves. They're all doing their part to get things to where they can do the most good. This helps everyone: the donor, the recipient, and the item itself, which has gone from clutter to prized possession simply through a change in ownership, an alteration in scenery.

As time wore on, I had this caterpillar-to-butterfly idea on my mind. One day I woke up and couldn't help but be

painfully aware: the end to my year of no clutter was unnerv-
ingly in sight. After so much progress, so much time spent
dealing with the many faces of my Stuff, as I gazed at the
Hell Room I could plainly see I still wasn't done.

Where the heck, I wondered, *was my butterfly?*

CHAPTER FIFTEEN

THE AUTOBIOGRAPHY RUG

"...we hold in our hands, usually weakly and loosely, but a few fringes of the tapestry of a lived life."
—Walter Benjamin, *Illuminations*

It was August. I sat in a small classroom by myself, holding a cotton magenta dress in one hand and a pair of sewing scissors in the other. As I raised the scissors to begin cutting, I thought about the literally *hundreds* of times I had worn it. About the fact that this dress was the first item of clothing I had truly picked out and bought entirely by myself. How much I had loved it, way back when.

I froze.

Every summer for the last few years, I've driven over to the other side of my state to participate in a weeklong weaving workshop. Being able to take this simple break from, well, *everything* feels like the most ridiculously luxurious thing in the world. And it is. For an entire seven days I do not plan anything, clean anything, or feed anyone. I do not drive anyone anywhere. I do not so much as pick up one renegade, under-couch sock.

Instead, I weave. The very word itself sounds relaxing, doesn't it? Kind of like a sigh: *weave*. Plus it's loads of fun. I mean, if slaving over a cranky, antediluvian floor loom in a wool-filled, attic room in August is *not* your idea of fun, I can't imagine what is. Maybe windsurfing or something.

The workshop takes place at a boarding school that would have seemed to my teenage self less like school than, say, nirvana. The school's five-hundred-acre campus sprawls across a wide, flat hill surrounded by sweeping vistas of foliage. It includes a dairy barn, a sheep meadow, several produce gardens, a blacksmith forge, and a kitchen in which all the meals are cooked—from scratch—with the assistance of a wood-fired bread and pizza oven. It's the kind of place where the solar panels have solar panels. And every Thursday morning during the school year, I am told, the students meet in the auditorium to sing a cappella from the school songbook.

Do you remember that scene in *The Grinch Who Stole Christmas* where the Whos, with Christmas bells ringing, stand hand in hand and start *singing*? I'm pretty sure that's this place.

Since I didn't go to high school here, I do what is the very next best thing: I stuff my car with yarn and books and half-baked ideas and drive over hill and dale in the hottest part of the summer like a swallow winging it's way back to Capistrano. It's time.

I could show up empty-handed—many of the students do—but instead, for weeks beforehand this year I had been gradually amassing bags and bins and piles of materials in corners—mostly clothes but also any other fabric I was at a loss as to what to do with. When the day finally came it took me awhile to get the car fully packed with all of it, but at last that was done. And then I threw in three *more* bags: three full, unwashed sheep fleeces—each one the size and weight of an enormously overstuffed laundry bag. My car was full to bursting. At that moment I swore a solemn oath to myself that I was coming home with none of it: anything that I didn't use was staying behind as a donation to the school's fiber arts program.

After arriving and dragging bag after box after bin up the three flights to the attic where we work, I took everything into an adjacent, empty classroom where I could spread out my unholy mess and have a look at it. It was really kind of ridiculous. My old uniform from the year I took tae kwon do mingled with Greta's outgrown Hawaiian print pants, my old plaid skirt from high school, faded blankets, torn sheets, an old full-length slip, an apron, the old dust ruffle from the girl's crib, all the fabric saved from when we reupholstered the couch, not to mention all the leftover fabric from every Halloween costume and sewing project I'd ever done.

Every single scrap told a story. Whenever someone happened by I'd feel compelled to tell one of them. This is the shirt I wore to Africa! This was my favorite T-shirt in college—can you imagine me wearing *this*? I wore this jumper one year when I went as Little Red Riding Hood for Halloween… Oh—here's the fabric I used to make Ilsa a giant pair of clown pants. She and her friend each went as one leg!

It was a mess, but it was a cozy, happy mess. A mess of lovely, largely happy memories. I felt lucky to have them, despite the disorder of it all, despite the fact that when people entered the spare classroom where I had spread it all out in a sort of Big Bird–sized nest they'd pause and say "oh…*wow*!" I never knew quite how to interpret that.

Most years when I arrive I have some idea in my mind what I want to make during my week, but this year I had given it much more thought than ever before. As a reformed artist, I think it's interesting to note that I never make decorative wall hangings or other objets d'art. Instead, I always make things that I will *use*: table runners, place mats, curtains. This year, for the first time, I was going to attempt my largest project ever: a rug. But not just any rug.

This was going to be my autobiography rug. It would incorporate fabrics torn from all different parts of my life. Rather than piles of memories sitting around rather uselessly, they could literally be woven together into something I'd use and enjoy every day. I had so many things I had never been able to bear parting with, but now I was going to get out a wand and be an object magician, turning these old memories into something new. Shazam!

Several years ago I had made place mats out of the leftover fabric scraps I had found in a bin at the workshop—so my new idea was essentially to do the same thing on a much larger scale with all my collected material and turn it into the world's biggest place mat. And where would this enormous autobiographical place mat go once it was finished? In the Hell Room, of course. It seemed only right.[15] The big happy mess I had brought with me felt right at home in the wonderful world of the weaving studio, which is a big, happy mess

---

15. Looking into it, I learned that scrap rugs of this sort were very popular for women to make at home dating back to the 1800s, using leftover materials from dressmaking, cotton feed sacks, and selvage scraps. I loved that sense of doubling back, touching another point in time through a handicraft, and it made me feel reassured, somehow, that my idea was a good one—despite the fact that it essentially entailed destroying all that I had brought with me.

in its own right. I know of no other place in the world like it. Every time I enter the long room crowded with floor-to-ceiling bookshelves filled with yarn, fleece, shuttles, bobbins, fabric, carders, swifts, reels, and spool racks, I feel deeply content. Former students' projects are stapled to the dormered ceiling, offering glimpses of dried flowers and ancient dyeing experiments. One entire long wall is papered with intricate weaving samples, color photocopies of brilliant patterns, and odd fiber souvenirs brought like offerings from around the world—silk pouches and elaborate examples of embroidery mingle with postcards featuring women sitting on dirt floors weaving. If you sit in one particular spot and turn your head to look directly up at the ceiling, a photocopy of a former student's face is smiling impishly down at you.

All these are just accessories, however. The real residents of the room are the looms. They occupy virtually every available bit of floor space. In order to traverse the room, sometimes you have to turn sideways in deference to them: floor looms, table looms, rigid heddle looms, and tapestry looms. And two or three are what one can only call behemoth looms. Some of them feature small brass plaques with names of donors or former owners. Just like my scraps of fabric, each and every one of these looms has a story: where it came from, who donated it, and why.

The person who can tell you every one of those stories is a lovely woman named Melissa. Educator, curator, and head storyteller of the weaving room, Melissa is one of the most brilliantly talented and yet gentle and unassuming people I have ever met, not to mention a legendary figure in the microworld of fiber. Want to learn to weave? Or knit? Or spin? Or dye? Or sew? Or quilt? Or embroider? Basically, if it has to do with fiber *in any way*, you've come to the right teacher and the right place.

Ask her about her youth in Turkey. Ask her about drop-spindle spinning or the proper mordant for dandelion leaf dyeing or backstrap weaving techniques from Peru. Ask her to untangle this ungodly mess you have made of your project. Let her show you how to remedy the snapped weft string that is giving you heart palpitations. Now it's time for her to go home: she promised her son she would make him a special batch of his favorite cookies. It's all in a day's work for a superheroic fiber goddess.

Like a character in a storybook, Melissa has been at the helm of this unwieldy but gorgeous ship, tucked up here in the attic room of this small progressive boarding school for the past twenty years, telling stories and unknotting people's mistakes, patiently teaching scores of high schoolers, and now adults in the summer program too, how to work with fiber in many ways but mostly how to weave.

Needless to say, if I wanted a better, more sympathetic companion or environment for my ambitious Stuff-transforming endeavor, I could not have found one. I would be working on one of the behemoth looms and, even so, would be weaving two lengths in a row, separating them and then sewing the two rectangles together to achieve the desired width. The resulting rug, once completed, would be substantial enough to contend with the enormous open floor of the Hell Room. With final dimensions of six by nine and a half feet, it was good I just happened to have a *lot* of material to work with.

I began the process of cutting up my many random fabrics into strips. Of course, I chose easy things first, items that didn't hurt me very much to cut up: torn sheets. A flannel nightgown so tattered it could never be worn again—not by anyone with any modesty, anyway. One of Steve's worn-out T-shirts. Couch upholstery.

The resulting balls of fabric yarn that I wound together after cutting astounded me. They were gorgeous—each one prettier than the last, which made me braver. Gradually I progressed to the Africa shirt (dusky purple Tencel) and the crib dust ruffle (mustard calico cotton). I took a breath and then took the scissors to the kilt I had bought in Ireland on the first trip I ever took without an adult along for supervision (maroon and forest green plaid wool). Then I came to a pretty important batik skirt. And I stopped.

I thought about how I had worn this skirt on the camping trip where Steve and I had met. How pretty I had felt. How exciting it all was. How, when we meandered our way back home from the camping trip together, I had come to the realization that I *loved* this guy. Which thrilled and scared me.

I took some photographs. And I heaved a sigh. Things in me were changing, I could feel it...so many months focusing on Stuff, Stuff, *Stuff* had made me bolder. What's the worst thing that could happen? I thought to myself. It reminded me of the day I finally, after ten years of kicking and screaming, took that first half a pill. To someone else it might be no big deal, but to me? It felt like jumping out of an airplane without a parachute.

It's a skirt, I thought. *A beautiful memory.* For years it had sat in a drawer. Couldn't I do more for it than that?

It wouldn't be the first or last time in this process that I froze, but this time I managed to get by it and keep going. I picked the scissors back up, ready to make something new.

The hours flew by, as they tend to do in the weaving studio. Day turns to night—is it time to go to the dining hall for dinner already? Music plays on Pandora, and the mood goes from excitement to quiet as everyone sinks into their projects. In addition to cutting up my fabric, I had to "dress" the loom before I could begin any actual weaving—first meticulously measuring out yards and yards of thread and then threading each and every individual strand through a million tiny slots, being careful not to twist a single strand or skip a single eye. This crazy process can take up to two days all by itself. I finally got up and running on my loom by the end of the second day, yet I was still unsure. Yes, the balls of fabric were looking beautiful by themselves, but was this hodgepodge of materials going to look nice *together*? Or more like a textile factory had thrown up? It was too late to worry about that now; I had to forge ahead. Off I went, shuttling my fabric back and forth, creating rows of color and pattern and texture, which, although backbreaking labor at times, strangely never fails to feel terribly satisfying. When my muscles started to cramp up I'd go back to the spare classroom next door, cutting and rolling more fabric. I proceeded like this, having no idea whether I'd like my end product, but being happy nevertheless to be making it.

Later in the week I entered the spare room, where despite my hours and hours of wrapping fabric into colorful balls, I still had a shockingly gargantuan pile of uncut fabric. I had been doing some soul searching since the previous night, and I had come to a difficult decision about another very sentimental item in the pile: my old magenta floral dress.

At the beginning of the week, this had been one of the

stories I would tell to anyone who happened to wander by, holding the dress up as if it were an archaeological specimen. *And this, ladies and gentlemen, is Early College Eve...* I told my friends and classmates about how it was the first piece of clothing I had ever bought by myself. I found it in one of those college-town shops that specialize in bulky Andean knit sweaters and incense. It was a sleeveless, pullover dress in an Indian print, very cheap and practically see-through. I distinctly recall not figuring this particular fact out until after I had worn it to the college dining hall for breakfast one morning and gotten some funny looks. I looked in the mirror of my dorm room and realized I had just walked through campus the next best thing to stark naked.

After that I wore a slip underneath. And I had worn and worn and worn the thing until it was threadbare. The day finally came when it wasn't me anymore, and I put it away, lovingly. But get *rid* of it? Never. Recently I'd had cause to dig it out of some boxes in the attic again when Greta informed me that her school was having "hippie day" and did I have anything she could wear? Ha! *Did* I?

After that it had gone in the Hell Room pile, and I had brought it along with everything else and without much thought. But every time over the past few days I had approached it with shiny scissors in hand? I had chickened out. And time was running short—the rug was going to be finished before too long, so if I wanted this piece of my history in, now was the time.

I had talked myself into it, when I arrived, fresh from breakfast at the dining hall the next morning. Or at least, I'd start with the hem and see. That's what I was telling myself, anyway, when I walked in and realized: it was gone.

Gone.

It *couldn't* be gone. That made no sense. Who would want that threadbare, shapeless dress? Who would've felt strongly enough about it to actually *take* it from a pile of someone else's stuff? I was stunned, not believing my own eyes, because it simply couldn't be true. I moved things around looking for it with increasing distress. Where was it? It had to be here. This was just stupid.

But it really wasn't there. Any other item in the entire pile could have disappeared, and I never would have even noticed. But that one dress? It was the one thing I would have missed. And it was most definitely not there.

I went to Melissa and asked her, hopelessly, if she had, maybe, seen it. I was getting upset, and she could tell. We asked around, looked in *other* fabric piles, wondered if it could have been shuffled behind something by a custodian or shoved under something by mistake. But I knew it wasn't in any of those places—if it wasn't in my pile, it was gone. That memory. That piece of me. Gone.

I went back to the empty classroom and felt a huge well of sadness fill up in my chest. It felt like some great, tragic injustice had been done to me—something deeply important ripped away that I could never have back. Why did I have to lose things? Why did things have to go away? It was like that one dress was standing in for everything that had ever been taken or stolen, lost or ruined. For the sadness of the inevitable. And even though I knew it was completely ridiculous, and I felt like an idiot, I sat on one of the tables, surrounded by big piles of my other stuff, and with sobbing breath and big heavy tears, I cried. And cried.

I cried for that dress the way you'd cry for a person.

Afterward I felt much better.

The week went on. I was still melancholy about what felt like a lost friend, but I continued ripping, cutting, rolling, and weaving my fabrics, and a sense of calm began to creep over me. It felt wonderfully therapeutic to work with these fabrics that clearly had a lot of metaphoric significance for me and *transform* them. I couldn't hold on to everything forever—no one can—but I could take these bits that I still had and make something useful and beautiful with them. I couldn't keep everything. Couldn't know what had happened to the things that went missing. But I could do *this*.

As I worked I continued to be a bit terrified in the back of my mind that it would be awful in the end, a big mishmash of nothing in particular, and there I would be, having wasted a whole week of my life destroying things I wanted to keep.

But I should have trusted the long history of women who've come before me making rag rugs from everything that wasn't nailed down because it wasn't like that at all. Instead it was like a big, incredible tapestry that just happened to—if you could decipher it—tell a million little stories from my life. I could look at it and see my old lace slip and the girls' party dresses and my high school rainbow tie-dyes, the Irish kilt and the Halloween clown pants and so many, many other things. It was all in there somewhere.

I felt like the miller's daughter in the fairy tale, the one who stays up all night spinning straw into gold. But who needs yellow metal, anyway? This was way better.

———

If you are a close reader, then right about now, you are prob-ably saying to yourself, "Hey—but what about the pledge you made to come home with nothing but the rug? To leave everything there?"

Darn it, I *knew* you'd bring that up.

Well…how shall I put this? I did still come home with *some* stuff. In addition to the completed rag rug, I brought home all the leftover fabric yarn I had made as well as two big bags of clothes I hadn't the heart to abandon after all. You're shocked, I know.

However, I did manage to leave behind quite a lot, enough so that I was counting it as a victory nevertheless. For me to leave this much behind without a second look was unprecedented. I donated more than a dozen T-shirts, piles and piles of other clothing and sheets, and all the rest of the upholstery and Halloween fabric. Also, for some ambitious future student who wanted to take on the ginormous task of washing, carding, and spinning, I left behind *all* of the unwashed sheep fleece. Yes sir, yes sir, three bags full.

CHAPTER SIXTEEN

THE WEIRDEST THINGS I OWN

"Welcome to my world! I never want to get rid of any-thing, even if I don't like it!"

—Ilsa

T he day had started out ordinary enough. The summer had at last ended, and it was a lovely, crisp, early fall day. Ilsa had been in a panicked rush to get to school, as usual, and I was annoyed that we were late, as usual. After she got out of the car, it took me a long moment to realize why she was still standing there next to the car, and why there was a look of shocked surprise on her face.

"Mom, help!" *Oh my God.* Ilsa had slammed her thumb in the car door. Quickly I opened it and she was back in her seat, wailing and bleeding, her thumb instantly puffing up purple. She cried for a solid hour after that— cried as I floored it to the nearby medical center, cried as the nurses looked at her thumb, cried as the doctor looked at thumb, cried as the radiologist looked at her thumb. And when I say she cried, I don't mean she *wept*.

Ilsa scream-cried with a vengeance as if the world had *betrayed* her.

I don't need to tell you that those kind of cries—even when we *know* everything is going to be fine, really—are the kind that cause moms everywhere to go instantly gray, break out in a full-body sweat, and vow never to be so foolish as to allow their child to touch a car door ever again.

The professionals ascertained pretty quickly that her thumb wasn't broken, and there was no edema under the nail—thank goodness. It would be pretty shades of purple and black for a while, but Ilsa's thumb would survive. Fast-forward to two months later. After turning all kinds of interesting non-thumbnail colors, like a high school senior anxious to leave home, gradually pulling away from its birth-place, Ilsa's thumbnail finally did what it had been promising to do and had fallen off in a big, mottled chunk. Ilsa looked at me.

"What should I do with it?"

Ilsa held the entire, half-inch-long thumbnail in the palm of her hand. Oh, it was *ugly*: striped and yellowed and curved in an exaggerated fashion, like a talon or a witch's nail. At the same time it was delicate, yet surprisingly strong, much like Ilsa herself.

I knew what I was supposed to say. I hesitated.

"Should I…throw it away?" Ilsa prompted. She had a look in her eye that said, *That's what normal people do with old fingernails, right?*

"*Yes*," I said firmly, because we were definitely going to do what normal people do. "Yes. Throw it away."

But she didn't move. She just looked at me, holding the thumbnail out in her palm between us like a talisman.

"I think…I think I'll keep it for a while," she said after a moment. "I'll put it…on the windowsill here."

Now, if this was another home, and I was another mother, I might have pushed the issue. I might have said, "No, put it in the trash, Ilsa" or even "Hey, keeping an old, yellow, half-inch-long fingernail on the kitchen windowsill might not be a really wonderful or, come to think of it, *appetizing* idea, Ilsa."

Instead what I said was "Okay."

"It's just…" Ilsa began.

"I know," I said. I did know. Just like my dad and the stump, she and that nail had been through a lot together. Who was I to make her part with it?

————

Because I am the kind of person who can rationalize keeping old fallen-off thumbnails, coupled with the fact that, as I've mentioned, my memory isn't always the best, I was pretty secure in the knowledge I was going to find some strange and unexpected stuff in the Hell Room. While I can't lay claim to anything as bizarre as the two-headed baby in formaldehyde that surfaced from the town house of the famed Collyer Brothers or the mummified human foot Andy Warhol put into one of his homemade time capsules, still I must confess that for a rookie I've got some decently weird stuff. I surprised even myself.

And so, without further ado, I'd like to unveil my list.

The Weirdest Things I Own

- *A box with a dead mouse in it.* I think you and Samuel have met: the dead mouse I found behind some furniture and then wrote a story about? So now it seems like he's...kind of...a friend. You don't throw away *friends*, do you? If I someday win a Nobel Peace Prize for the mouse story, won't I want to have the mouse skeleton to pose with on the cover of *Time*?

- *Santa Claus's autograph.* Inspired by a trip to Disneyland, my children now ask any costumed figure for an autograph, including Scooter the Vermont Blue Cross/Blue Shield dog. Unlike Scooter (who, to be fair, is somewhat challenged in the opposable thumbs department), the Franklin Park Mall Santa in Toledo, Ohio, graciously complied.

- *A feminist vegetarian cookbook.* Yes, the recipes are awful. The women on the back photo look appropriately dour in their button-down shirts and mannish haircuts, as if perhaps they had just finished a lovely meal of gingered broccoli stem salad and refrigerator bran muffins.

- *A Lay's potato chip bag circa 1980.* Found in the pocket of a raincoat I last wore at about age ten. The bag is emblazoned with the helpful advice to "Enjoy Lay's Brand Potato Chips with: Beverages, Fancy Salads, Your Favorite Sandwich." (Apparently this was back before people knew that potato chips could be appropriately eaten with pretty much everything, including allergy medication and wedding cake.)

- *A children's book showing an elephant on fire.* This opposites-style kid's book—originally published in French—also helpfully shows a whole elephant versus an elephant cut into pieces and the difference between a boy elephant and a girl elephant peeing. I hear the eagerly anticipated follow-up volume will illustrate the beloved elephant character getting shot by poachers, smoking crack, and having hip replacement surgery.

- *A CD featuring an operatic rendition of the poems of Winnie the Pooh.* Speaks for itself, really.
- *The only board I ever broke the year I took tae kwon do.* Helpfully inscribed: "Fall '93 (HAND)," presumably for the future curators of the Eve Museum.
- *My friend's mortgage paperwork.* Katrina? Do you even know I have this?
- *The worst art book ever.* Another outstanding nominee in the category of things so awful I have to keep them. Every image in this beautifully printed, panoramic-format book features a middle-aged male photographer wearing jeans and a T-shirt, looking bored, while pretty young female nude models lie languorously draped about the room like cashmere lap blankets. They look like they could use a good meal of gingered broccoli stem salad and refrigerator bran muffins.
- *Fur clipped from my dying cat.* So I forgot I even did this until unearthing the Ziploc bag one day in the Hell Room. *Why* did I do this? I was a little distraught. That's my answer, and I'm sticking to it.
- *A photograph of myself taken with an endoscopy camera.* Yup. I'm lying there in my hospital gown, all hooked up to a variety of oxygen and monitoring tubes, in a fisheye-lens view. I'm smiling the nervous smile of someone who hasn't yet been given the appropriate drugs that would make me fine with the idea that someone was going to send this very camera down my throat soon. As I recall, the technician was helpfully

trying to demonstrate the way the procedure would work, and when I woke up very groggily sometime later, the photo was lying next to me on the gurney, like a souvenir from the world's worst amusement park ride.

- *Every single note that was ever passed to me.* Sure, by this point you could've guessed that I have kept every letter and postcard I've ever been sent, but did you suspect that I still have all these folded-up bits of yellowing notebook paper and purple, metallic-outline pen? In the age of texting, the art of passing actual paper notes—complete with Kilroy-was-here-style doodling and goofy poems—probably seems as adorably antiquated as an appliance that only has one function. (How I ever lived without my Wireless Shoe Phone Meat Grinder I'll never know.) So I figure it's good I saved these not only for my own archives but for the collection of the inevitable Institute for the Preservation and Study of Hallway Notes. Also, these are clearly very important if I ever need to remind myself of the timeless witticisms my friends and I used to pen each other, such as, and I quote: "Math is boring, sometimes" and "All right, fine, *be* that way."

- *All my answering machine messages from sophomore year of college.* Although it's true that answering machines used to tape-record over old messages once listened to, I devised a way to keep them by recording them onto a separate cassette tape. Of course I did.

- *My appendix.* Kidding! I am kidding. Seriously, no. I mean, yes, the summer before I went to college my appendix *was* removed by a very nice surgeon just before it was about to go thermonuclear on my bloodstream, for which I am very grateful. But no, I don't have it in a little jar on my nightstand. This is primarily due to the fact that no one ever offered it to me. I distinctly recall sitting in my hospital bed the day after the operation and wondering, *So...where is it? What did they do with it?*

- *The ugliest lamps in the world.* Bought by my newlywed parents in the 1960s, back when ugly was the new pretty. Whenever people see them they invariably say: "Are you sure you want *those*?" as if, perhaps, I had temporarily lost my mind or there has been some humorous misunderstanding. The two very tall and very heavy table lamps are composed of what appears to be giant rectangles of black, welded lead and look like something out of a Jules Feiffer cartoon.

- *A genuine smitten.* Winner of the award for Most Original Wedding Present, a smitten, of course, is a single mitten knitted with two separate wrist cuffs so that you can hold hands with your beloved while still living in Vermont.

- *A ceramic sculpture featuring my husband and me as babies sharing a bottle in a jogger stroller.* A shower gift when we were having our first child, this is the hands-down winner for the Weirdest Thing I Own. The fact that we look like a two-headed monster baby? That the implication is that my husband and I are somehow *twin brother and sister*? Can I tell you how many times I've tried to throw this monstrosity away? But I am powerless against the truly awesome awfulness of it—after all, I may never receive a present this disturbing *ever* again.

CHAPTER SEVENTEEN

EVERYTHING MUST GO

"Fortunately, it turns out that being scared of yourself is a somewhat effective motivational technique."
—Allie Brosh, *Hyperbole and a Half*

T he problem was, as it so often is with a job such as this (which is to say, big, long, and that I really had no clear idea how to do), all too often there was something more urgent to be done: buy groceries! Pick up the kids! Make dinner! Do laundry! Pay bills! And always, before I knew it, it was time to do those things all over again. Strange, huh? Probably, I am the only person that this ever happens to.

So there I was, making steady progress on the Hell Room, certainly far better than any I had ever made before in my previous attempts but still not *enough* progress to convince me it was really going to get over the hump. There lingered in my head the idea that, despite my best hopes and dreams, the Hell Room wouldn't be finished any time before Ilsa went to college, and that's assuming it ever really got finished at all. What seemed far more likely was it would do what it had always done on all my previous attempts: simply slide backward, once again filling up with Stuff. It always happened slowly at first and then quickly, like when you are pouring a liquid into a bottle that tapers to a very thin neck. Before you know it—*bam!* The room looks worse than it ever did before, and you shut the door with a sigh and a shake of the head.

So what was going to make the difference this time? I kept thinking.

And that's when it happened. The universe sent me a telegram—which is to say Greta's school sent me an email. In it, tenth-grade parents were casually informed of the imminent arrival of a German exchange student this fall. Every sophomore student was required to host: no exceptions.

The gravity of the situation sunk in. Where would this young lady sleep? Greta and Ilsa already shared a room. The room next door to theirs was filled with outgrown books and toys and euphemistically termed the *playroom*. The pantry room next to that, which houses our extra freezer and is where we store things like sheets, towels, tools, extra lightbulbs, and such, was in similar, "shut the door" shape at this particular moment. The front room of our house had fallen victim to the Hell Room project and was therefore stuffed with Stuff waiting to be dealt with and dispersed: a broken chair, an old coffee machine, piles of clothes waiting to be boxed and given away, a few more camera bags and boxes I had found for Steve.

I looked around and made a terrible realization: I had been fooling myself. The Hell Room *wasn't* just upstairs. It was literally in every room of the house that we didn't sit or sleep in every day, and it was creeping into even those everyday rooms too. Now the *dining* room had boxes lined against the wall;

I was uncertain if the girls' bedroom still had a floor under all their clothes; and the nexus of the house, the living room, was like the front line—a Grand Central Station of Stuff. I regularly shoveled out the incoming: burgeoning piles of mail! Mountains of clean clothes to be folded! Random shoes strewn about! Backpacks and lunches and books and homework and musical instruments and leotards and four different kinds of tap shoes! It was as if I had been focusing on the fact that my car's windshield wipers were broken when all the while the engine was smoking and making weird grinding noises and the gas tank was leaking. I was barely managing to keep the car on the road, and I hadn't even realized it.

I looked around the house with new eyes. Sure, we had managed to live in this manner, and we still could. But for a houseguest to navigate this mess? For three weeks? A *German* houseguest?

Please don't misunderstand me; I'm not trying to promote a stereotype. Surely not all German people are neatniks. I am in large part German by heritage myself, so that disproves *that* notion right there.

I can only speak from my own personal experience, when I was an exchange high school student in Germany myself. When I went, there weren't enough American students for all the families that wanted to host, so I got to stay with two different families, each for one week. The two families were like polar opposites in many ways—one was a traditional cottage-like home with lots of dark wood. That family ate meat-and-potatoes meals, while the other family lived in an airier, more modern house and preferred "health food." But you know what they had in common? They were very orderly. Clean. Organized. To a fault.

Even to my unobservant young eyes, Germans seemed on the whole more concerned as a culture about things being in order—whether it was objects or people. I recall being baffled by things like not being able to cross the street till the light turned, even when no cars were coming, or the silent, wide-eyed head shake that my host student gave me when I put my feet up on the opposite train seat.

I had never seen such neat neighborhoods, each with its own perfect garden, lined up in a way that reminded me of dollhouses. I was amazed that every single day when we drove out of the driveway, my host father would get out of the car and go dutifully close the gate. Why not just leave it open? I thought, or, you know, just get *rid of the gate*? Looking back, I can only imagine that my host families were probably horrified at the state in which I kept my guest room.

So the exchange student wasn't coming from Jamaica or Hong Kong or Russia, she was coming from what in my limited experience was pretty much the capital of organization: Germany.

In three weeks.

Full-fledged panic might be the best way to describe what came next. The next morning I woke up on fire. I had come at last to the realization many doctors already know: every part of the patient is connected to every other part of the patient. I was dismayed to realize that my prior one-room approach wasn't cutting it. I was going to have to approach my house holistically. I saw it all at once very clearly: the pantry, the guest room, the front room, the Hallway Room, the Hell Room—they all existed like dominoes: where one went, the rest followed.

I started in the pantry—an entire small room on the first floor of the house devoted to storage, which at that moment was so stuffed that all one could manage was to crack the door an inch or two and lob some object in sideways. I almost had to get out a steam shovel at first, but by midmorning things were looking better—I had made piles of "get rid of," "give away," "sell," and "garbage" in the hall outside the door, and although Steve teased me a bit for making an enormous mess while "cleaning," I persisted. I found weird stuff that had been shoved in there on previous frantic attempts to "clean up": old mail! Clean, unfolded, previously missing clothes! By midafternoon I had the car filled with boxes and bags, and I did the rounds for the millionth time: clothing consignment shop, charity store, dry cleaner, furniture consignment shop. As in the past, my rule was *nothing comes home*, but at this point I was so disgusted with myself that for the first time I actually stuck to it.

By the end of the day the pantry was beginning to resemble an actual room that one might walk into and retrieve things from. Of course, at some point I had realized I had to reorganize the bathroom closet as well in order to make everything make more sense—so out came a procession of towels and toys and bins full of nail polish and so on. Everything I did seemed to lead me to something else; I was desperately hoping that the bathroom closet wouldn't in turn lead me to the basement or the garden shed or my neighbor's house next door because I wasn't sure I could take it.

The next day I started posting things online—free for the picking up! I made an appointment with yet *another* consignment shop that was only open by appointment. I started on the front room, which was daunting. Months after their arrival, there were still piles and piles of things from my mother's moving van—sheets and towels and comforters and small furniture everywhere. And those piles had—according to the magnetic principle of Stuff—attracted *other* things. Kids' games had made their way in here, still more camera bags, and all the bins and boxes as well as the two big trunks rescued from my dad's tag sale.

I became a woman possessed. Steve looked a little frightened of the gleam in my eye when I was holding the label maker. Whereas once upon a time my mantra had been "Don't decide...don't decide...don't decide," now everything had turned upside down. All I did every day was make decisions: broken chair? Box of embroidery floss? Extra coffeemaker?

The question was no longer "Can I use it?" or "Does it spark joy?" but "Can I possibly get rid of it?" And if I could then I did. Things I knew Mom would want got shuttled down to her. Piles of tablecloths went to the resale shop after the antique lady had passed on them. When is electronics recycling day again? Better call the town hall. When was the lady from the Internet coming to get the carpeted cat tower? I'd already contacted her, like, three times! My new mission in life became getting everything where it needed to go for its next life. I was amazed at how time-consuming this could be, but when the lady finally came to pick up the cat tower, when the guy from the chair company finally called me back to tell me the chair could definitely not be fixed, when the car, once again so overloaded that I couldn't even see out the back window, was finally empty of everything but me, I felt a tremendous, unreasonable surge of accomplishment. Who knew just plain getting rid of things was so *hard*?

As I went through these machinations I tried hard not to

look around because it was worse than horrible. Everywhere. I suspected I had upset the balance of my house. Instead of having one simply unspeakable room that was fairly easily avoided (as we'd had at the beginning of the project) or several rooms that were in less than stellar shape (due to neglect in favor of the Hell Room or way-stationing for Stuff from the Hell Room), I now had an abominable mess *everywhere*. Probably this indicated that I was making progress, but it really felt like I had opened Pandora's box, and it had exploded its contagion all over everything. There was nowhere left to hide from it.

The living room was no longer a living room. It was a launching pad. Everything that came into this room now was *leaving*, one way or another. Steve would periodically ask, "What's that soccer ball/toy bin/armadillo hide doing there?" and I'd invariably reply, "Oh, that's waiting for drop-off/recycling/Armadillo Appreciation Day."

One day we decided it was a big "free curb stuff" day. Out to the curb went battalions of belongings: several metal cabinets. Ugly lamps. Brianna's old dollhouse. Momentum was up, and I kept going, grabbing random useless items from the garage: plastic shelving! Old sorting containers, thick with dust! I had the urge to keep hauling and hauling indefinitely. I felt like Lady Macbeth: "*Out*, damned Stuff!"

The things sat by the curb as we came and went throughout our day after that, and as I always do, I worried, weirdly, that *no one would want our discards*. It's a strange feeling to want someone to come take your garbage, as if you're sending your things off for their first day at school and you want them to be popular.

But then it happened. Several things vaporized. And then one guy came back with a moving van, and he cleaned the curb out. He seemed delighted. We were delighted too: our trash was popular!

The erstwhile "playroom" next to Greta and Ilsa's bedroom would take particular attention. After several previous attempts to involve the girls in this aspect of the endeavor, since virtually everything in the "playroom" was, ostensibly, theirs, I took matters into my own hands. I went on a rampage. Games and toys that had never been popular went to the giveaway box. An enormous box was filled with stuffed animals I couldn't remember anyone actually holding, ever. Things I couldn't bear to part with that they had outgrown went into a series of large plastic bins, the kind that Marie Kondo abhors. I *couldn't* care about that anymore—sure, these were deferred decisions, but this was a matter of keeping moving. Life wasn't perfect. And I *have* an attic. So there.

At long last the smoke began to clear. My big reward was the empty space that greeted me anew in a different room each day: first in the pantry, then in the front room and living room, and finally in the playroom, which we had— presto chango—transformed into an actual guest room. That empty space was now prized as greatly as any object filling it could ever have been. I *cared* about that space. I *protected* it. Whenever anyone put as much as a half-drunk coffee cup down, I pounced like a crazed Stepford wife.

"What's *that*? What's it doing *here*? Where is it *going*? Did you just think you were going to leave that there *forever*? *Did* you? *Hmmm*?"

I had worked too hard to create that lovely bit of empty space to let it go—driven legions of perfectly good objects to new homes, talked myself out of a thousand "what ifs." I had carted boxes full of "can't bear to part with" books and toys to the attic and clandestinely shoved crates and crates of CDs into the closet at the library to patiently await their fund-raising sale next summer.

I don't even know if they *sell* CDs at the book sale. Well, I guess they do now.

So much of what I was dealing with on the first floor in preparation for our student's arrival was fallout from the Hell Room that I decided it would just have to wait patiently for me to play catch-up and try not to get too jealous. Never had I been more acutely aware of the interconnectedness of all the different functioning parts of my house: like a human body, objects moved through and were digested, used, converted to stored fat or excreted.

In this metaphor the attic of our home must be the long-term memory. One day, as I was scrounging around trying to make more storage room in the attic, I found some cool stuff. First I found some furniture I realized I was happy to part with at the consignment shop—hooray! More money with which to buy large plastic bins!—and then I came across a huge box of old comic strip books.

I was beside myself. I still had these?! I had collected and adored these slim paperback collections as a kid, reading them obsessively: *Casper the Friendly Ghost, Beetle Bailey, Richie Rich, Archie, Hagar the Horrible*... For a long time I even thought I might grow up to be a cartoonist. It felt as if I had opened up a box and a bunch of old friends had jumped out and yelled, "Surprise!"

So I was delighted but also disoriented. I suppose that was understandable because I had been going ninety miles per hour in one direction and suddenly thrown the car into reverse. I could almost hear that horrible gear-grinding noise: *but! But!* my brain sputtered in confusion. *I had been in Full Discard Mode!*

Never mind that. This was a very good find—one of those things I had known must be *somewhere* but had pretty much despaired of ever finding again. As I got out a plastic bin and neatly placed my treasured little newsprint books inside, all lined up and sorted by character, I felt terribly, inexplicably happy. With fondness, I arranged the books, flipped through them, and recalled many a childhood afternoon lying on the floor next to the radiator vent in our old dining room, puzzling over the odd deadpan humor of *Ziggy*. I took pictures and posted my buried treasure on Facebook. I found some *Mad* and *Cracked* magazines that had been my brother's in the box, so I texted him pictures of the discovery. He responded as if I had stolen a suitcase full of money from under his bed.

Hey gimme, he texted. And then, Not joking. GIMMEEE.

Once upon a time I might've been afraid to give this box of treasured old things to the girls. (Have you ever seen what three-decade-old newsprint can do? It isn't pretty.) I might've been tempted to keep them secreted away, protected. But a lot has changed in the past year.

I thought: *Keep less. Use more.*

When I was done organizing and sorting, I took the entire stash downstairs and placed it in the girls' room. At age fifteen Greta was probably not going to be enthralled by the likes of *Hagar the Horrible*, but Ilsa was just the right age. When she came home she lit up like Times Square on New Year's Eve. And then we were both terribly happy.

———

While Ilsa was making her way through yet another *Beetle Bailey Where Are You?* we finished our final preparations for our impending visitor. When Miri showed up in mid-October, we were ready. There was a neatly made bed for her to sleep in, a clean nightstand on which to place her phone or a book, an empty armchair with a folded set of towels, waiting. It all looked terribly innocent and effortless, as if, of *course* we always had this room—with its empty drawers and empty hanging space in the closet—at the ready for any guest who might happen by. Sure! Easy-peasy.

Miri, as it turns out, was utterly lovely. She's a petite little thing who got along with everybody like crazy and is fond of Converse sneakers and anything with sparkles on it. She'd always say the funniest things when we least expected it. One morning on the way to school she and Greta saw a moose in a farmer's field—which in nineteen years of living here we had *never* seen before—and after that she became moose-crazy, swooning over anything with a picture of a moose on it. Oh yes, she was fun.

As I was returning something to her room one day, I looked up and it hit me: just as Greta or Ilsa would have done in similar circumstances, she was living out of her suitcase on the floor. I smiled, thinking about those frantically excavated drawers, that hard-won closet space. It didn't matter, of course. My job, as her host, was to provide a cozy, welcoming environment with a place for her stuff, and I had done that much, despite myself. And her job, as a teenager, was to then ignore it completely.

We were both doing just fine.

CHAPTER EIGHTEEN

IT GOES SO FAST

"Guilt: the gift that keeps on giving."
—Erma Bombeck

As fall began to give way to winter, I looked back on months of desperately moving and piling and shoveling out the contents of the Hell Room, as well as the rest of the house, and never being certain I was doing anything other than, as my mother would say, rearranging the deck chairs on the *Titanic*. I was amazed to realize I'd developed a system that was, ever so slowly, working. I had found that, despite my knee-jerk tendency to keep, keep, *keep!*, there *were* many things that I could, in fact, get rid of. This was a huge revelation to me. It was not painless, of course, but with diligence, determination, and a fair amount of giving myself a good, stern talking-to, I could now shed Stuff that previously I had felt so obligated to keep it seemed that after death I would require my own pyramid.

In addition to becoming an embarrassingly familiar face at the donation door of the charity shop, I'd come to know

Diane, Stephanie, Ellen, and Jason, who run the three different consignment shops where I took well-meaning gifts,
unnecessary furniture, and mistake purchases. Were I to
reveal the sheer volume of books I've stuffed into the annual
book sale closet at the local library, they might name me an
honorary benefactor.

The routine helped me not to get bogged down—like a
shark I had to keep moving. Each place has different hours,
different rules, and I've internalized them all: who requires
an appointment, who isn't open until after eleven, who won't
even look at your things if they aren't arranged neatly on
hangers. Some afternoons I'll get ambitious and hit all of
them in a giant looping circle, always vowing never to return
home with anything but an empty car.

First stop! Diane and Stephanie's resale shop for small
housewares, clothes, and tchotchkes. Second stop! Ellen's
consignment boutique where she goes over my dresses and
purses with a fine-tooth comb before pronouncing what she'll
take. Third stop! Jason will consider consigning any larger
furniture or housewares. Fourth stop! The Health Services
Charity Shop for anything passed over by the previous three.
Last stop! The library, whose closet I fill with boxes of books
and any other media I've managed to cull.

There's nothing quite like the feeling I get when, after all
those stops, I look into the back of my car and enjoy it's sheer,
wonderful emptiness. I swell with a little bit of weird pride:
I've done my best for those objects. I've learned, too, that
it's best not to look back; I make a point of throwing away
the itemized slips everyone gives me listing the sale expira-
tion dates. If the consigned items don't sell in the allotted
time, and I don't show up to claim them, they get donated to

charity too. At the charity shop in particular, I have a strict "no entry" policy—drag and drop only. I have now made so many trips there I fear that walking in the front door of the shop might feel like walking into my own living room after some vandals had trashed the place and then labeled everything with price tags.

Amazingly, I found I wasn't obsessing about the items, as I would have once upon a time, wondering which had sold or gotten donated. For the first time, through the force of sheer stubborn repetition perhaps, I was stopping the endless cycle of self-doubt and truly letting go. Once dropped off, objects were erased from the white board of my mind. Gone.

I'd even been known to give away a box or two without removing my token "this will make it okay" item. I mean, this just wasn't like me. This was downright *normal*.

Of course, no system is perfect. Every now and then I'd have a moment of weakness and pull something back out of one of the bags or boxes. Once, it was a hat my friend Liv made for me when we were apartment-mates in college. It was a very Liv hat—floppy and floral and almost like a bonnet—kind of crazy and quirky. It was beautiful and kind of awful all at the same time, and I smiled a crooked smile when I found it—I had completely forgotten about its existence. And, of course, as I drove my car full of crap on its weekly mission, I thought about living with Liv and how she used to make all these giant collage-paintings in her room and how you almost never had to do the dishes because she was fanatical about cleaning up and how she taught me to make muffaletta.

So, of course, the kind-of-awful hat brought back all that and then the kind-of-awful hat and I were friends. I couldn't give my friend away, but it was small and I was getting rid of so much *other* stuff, I reasoned, that keeping just one thing was probably okay. After I got home that afternoon I showed Greta and Ilsa the flowery floppy hat, and they both knit their brows at me from across the room.

"What is *that?*" they said frowning, simultaneously.

"Oh, it's something my friend Liv made in college," I said. "I know—I'll never wear it. But having it is…just kind of nice."

I knew that if push came to shove, though, I could get rid of that hat. Probably. As it turned out, there was something else that was my kryptonite when it came to decluttering: baby clothes.

You will not be surprised to learn I've kept virtually all of the girls' clothes from when they were each babies and toddlers. Of course, as they were outgrown, I'd get rid of a *few* things here and there, mostly things I never liked to begin with. But really, not much. I always had this idea that I'd save them for…something. A project? Like a quilt maybe. I didn't know how to quilt, but this was entirely beside the point. After all, my mother saved *my* baby clothes, and I loved looking through them and recognizing the little cat-faced bib and the strawberry dress I was wearing in the photos in our yellowing albums.

But there was a big difference: my mother had saved, what, ten outfits? Enough to fit in one smallish box. Whereas I had enough clothes packed in a variety of large storage trunks that one could be forgiven for thinking I was planning to start several more families.

Some of these bins were in the attic, some were in the

closet of my office, and a good many of them were in the Hell Room; it was to the point where I had no idea how much we even had. I kept finding new boxes or bags of tiny, adorable clothes in sizes ranging from newborn to 5T. So far I had neither learned to quilt nor invented a space-age shrinking ray by which I could keep everything and not suffer any of the consequences. Something had to give, right?

Slowly I amassed all the baby and toddler clothing I found in the Hell Room and elsewhere into one big, enormous pile in our bedroom. One day, when I felt confident I had pretty much all of it, I sat down on the floor with the pile containing everything from cozy swaddling blankets to socks that would fit on your thumb. And I employed what has become one of my favorite techniques for winnowing stuff: I picked a container, one large plastic container, and designated it as the Baby Clothing box. I would pick and choose only the amount of clothing that would actually fit into the box. After that, I'd close, seal, and label the box and store it in the attic for the day when I suddenly had oodles of free time and got around to learning to quilt or Hell froze over, whichever came first.

Now, to be fair, I had actually already gone through this giganto-normous pile once, the day before, and managed to pull out a good three shopping bags' worth of kid clothes I truly did not care about. These were the clothes I did not even recognize as having been ours and to which none of my memories corresponded. This was ours? Really? Nevertheless, looking at what was left after that first sorting, I calculated I would still have to eliminate about half of what remained in order to fit the "keep" pile into the designated box.

So I began. Before very long the bin was full, but I was nowhere near to being done. Not even close. The problem was that I remembered every one of these items of clothing. With every jumper or footie-pajama I held up, I'd envision a tiny Greta or Ilsa laughing or swinging on a swing set or sleeping that angelic sleep that babies have.

When it comes to Stuff, this might be my worst Achilles heel of all. How often are we reminded that childhood is finite? How often do people stop to helpfully remind us as parents to "Enjoy them now! They grow so fast…"

I hate this. I mean, yes. Yes, they *do* grow quickly. But, you know, they also grow slowly. We may sometimes feel as if it has all gone by in a snap, but it hasn't. We've been here the whole time.

I think people like to say these platitudes because they feel like they are importing a tidbit of valuable advice that younger parents might have missed. They feel as if they are saying something that might inspire us to pause and appreciate our kids more than is encouraged by the hustle and bustle of everyday life.

This is what I think people *mean*. But this is not what I hear. What I hear is: "LIFE IS PASSING YOU BY! THERE'S NOTHING YOU CAN DO ABOUT IT! PANIC! GO STARE AT YOUR CHILDREN WITHOUT BLINKING UNTIL IT COMPLETELY FREAKS THEM OUT!"

To me this bit of everyday wisdom translates into a panicked inability to let go of *any* product of their childhoods, large or small. Will there come a day, I wonder, when I will *regret* throwing away this box of forgotten sketches? This neatly colored paper restaurant place mat? This Popsicle stick sculpture?

I'm torn. I want to save every tiny scrap of my children's lives and tuck them away in a childhood archive—not so much for them as for *me*. But by acting according to that principle, I realize, I am preventing us from enjoying today, *now*. I mean, how old will my girls be before they'd rather go to the mall or listen to the latest "Yeah Baby Baby" song or, really, do pretty much *anything* other than work on a project with Mom in the craft room? I know, I know. Too soon.

So I tried another approach. How about…three piles. One for the "Oo!" pieces, the most beloved ones I couldn't imagine ever parting with even under penalty of being forced to hand over my label maker. One for the "Aw" pieces, the less beloved but well remembered. The third pile was for the "Yeah, I remember this too" items.

By the end I had three piles of equal size that I regarded with despair: even parting with the "Yeah" pile seemed completely out of the question. In desperation I had started a *fourth* pile, managing to pick out only a few things to actually get rid of: *one* blanket, *one* onesie, *one* hat, and *one* jumper—a molehill next to the mountain. After going through the clothes now several times, I knew I couldn't bear to get rid of virtually any of them. It was ridiculous and kind of pathetic.

I started putting the piles into the plastic bin. "Oo!" went in first, followed by most of "Aw." I sighed. I got out a second bin, into which went the rest of "Aw" and all of "Yeah." I even threw in the tiny "eliminated" pile too.

I knew when I'd been beaten.

For much the same reason, another thing that stops me dead despite all my best efforts is adorable notes from my children. A wonderfully ironic example of this weakness of mine cropped up one day when Ilsa discovered a pile of outgrown clothing that she realized I had nefarious plans for. But instead of absconding with the contents of the pile, as she has been known to do on other occasions, instead she left me a wonderful series of handwritten, creatively spelled notes—all over the pile.

"I ware this cloths, I Don't want to get ried of it"

"you can not get ried of my cloths!!"

"ceap the Beautiful and gorgis!!!!!!!!"

"NO!!!! NO!!!! NO!!!!"

"Do Not Sakrifice the Butiey"

I managed to still get rid of most of the clothes, thank goodness, but these notes? I will most certainly be keeping them forever. How else will I remember not to sacrifice the beauty?

———

Perhaps the most daunting area of all in this entire enterprise was now staring us in the face: the Mountain of Art. And I really was not at all sure how this was going to go.

But I had hope, in the form of two empty boxes.

Somewhere in my clutter-themed reading I had come across mention of a company whose website promised to "Turn creative clutter into timeless books, calendars, pillows & more!" Although I'm naturally cautious about services purporting to reduce clutter, this one made me curious.

The deal: they send you an empty box, you fill it up with

your kid's art, and mail it back to them. They hand it over to their "professional graphic designers" who—the poor things—try to decipher which way is "up" on your kid's tissue paper collages and macaroni art, photographing and laying it all out before charging you a boatload of money and sending it back to you in a hardcover book that catalogues your child's obvious artistic prowess starting from the moment he or she put finger to paint.

But I liked their honesty. Under frequently asked questions they freely admit: "Yes, you absolutely can do all of this yourself on any photo book website. What we provide that you may or may not have is: time." And I'd had, what, oh, fifteen-plus years of children's art accumulating under my belt and Mt. Art-suvius was all I had to show for it, so it was pretty clear that allotting time to creatively photograph and lay out my children's art in a tasteful, pleasing book format was not something I was ever going to do.

But I am still a sucker for the craziness of my kids' imagination as they were growing up. And now at last we had a way to keep a souvenir of it. Surely the final books would include the picture Greta drew of our family when I was pregnant, complete with X-ray view of Ilsa in my tummy and the mysterious drawing Ilsa made of the fearsome "mowsdkrowstr," which, according to the inscription, "eats bugs and left overs that pepl aksudentuly leev." Also, "It livs in a nest hole."

These are the things that we soppy, sentimental mommies live for.

So I placed my order, and not long after that two empty boxes arrived at my doorstep. And then came a monumental day: the Sunday afternoon the girls and I trooped upstairs to the Hell Room to do no less than dismantle the art volcano.

Yes, this was one of the jobs I had anticipated to be the hardest of all. It was just like the kids' old clothes but worse. They had *made* these things! *All* of them! Drawings of imaginary animals and people that looked like potato chips with arms and legs and *I Love My Family Because* school assignments that were designed to instantly break a mother's heart into forty million pieces.

Years ago, I had attempted to sort out Greta from Ilsa and even categorize artworks by *year*, if you can believe that. I had no plan for what would happen once I had the art all sorted, organized, and presumably color-coded in rainbow order—and I had so much trouble discarding even so much as a Post-it—that I eventually gave up.

This time was different: I had a plan. First, we'd have to simply figure out *who* made *what*. So we started there: each of us grabbed a handful of papers, drawings, paintings, collages, and so on, and began sorting into three piles: "Greta," "Ilsa," and "Unknown." After a while a fourth pile arose by necessity for all the things that had silently migrated to the art pile that didn't really belong there: the birthday cards, newspaper articles, adorable little notes, and so on.

Here's what I found interesting about this enterprise: both girls seemed pleasantly mystified about the existence of so much stuff that they had purportedly created over the course of their lifetimes. What did *they* know about it? With the exception of only the most recent creations, neither one of them had memory of any of it. They were taking my word for it that I hadn't, say, outsourced the whole enterprise and had somebody else's kids make it all.

So they were bemused, convinced only when I showed them their initials in their own or their teacher's handwriting.

This, as you might imagine, took a nice portion of guilt off my shoulders—not all of it, of course, but enough that I had no trouble taking the entire stack of Unknowns directly to the recycling bin. And enough that I didn't hesitate to do the same with any identified but otherwise unremarkable artworks—for example, the colored-in-the-lines turkey handout from Thanksgiving.

Honestly, I never would've been able to do that before now. I never would have been able to discard the sixteen-page-long list of books that Ilsa read in 2013, most inscribed by me, patiently, over the course of the year so that Ilsa could receive her reading medal at the end of the year. I never could've parted with the entire pad of pastel scribbles that Greta had made in, literally, about an hour after some friends gave the pad as a gift for her third birthday. I distinctly recall thinking at the time that these drawings were brilliant. The vivacity of color! The delicacy of the line! Look how she used negative space in this one! Now I looked at them and thought, "Hmm. Scribbles." None of these things were making it into the book, and I was delighted but nervous that I felt no compulsion to keep them around otherwise. (Was I *feeling* okay?)

After we had dissembled the mountain and discarded the Unknowns, we had before us a gargantuan pile of "Ilsa" and an even larger, threatening-to-topple-over pile of "Greta" (she has had a five-year head start after all.)

Great, I thought. So far, so good. But what would happen next? Would it be the children's clothing debacle all over again? According to the company, each box could accommodate approximately two hundred artwork papers. Each kid must have had close to a thousand in her pile… Would I really be able to pick out *only* two hundred? (And did I really just say that?)

In the interest of moving forward I made a bold, arbitrary decision: one hundred artworks per kid would make up each book.

What came next was admittedly a little bit crazy, but I had no other idea how to go about the whittling-down process: I needed to *see* it. All. So Ilsa and I took her pile first and spent an entire afternoon laying out every single piece of paper, every artwork, all over the floor of the Hell Room. By the time we were through the room had a new, colorful carpet—the floor was entirely covered with Ilsa's artistic oeuvre.

In the process, we had a lovely, fascinating time, coming across all kinds of things. On an especially scribbly pencil drawing, I had written "Ilsa's very first drawing." Ilsa held it and gazed at it with something like reverence. "I just can't believe this is my *very first drawing*," she said with wide eyes.

Picking up another, she placed her hand over a hand tracing from many years ago and pronounced, "I don't like it. I want to be little again."

"I remember doing this—I thought I was a 'Monet artist'!"

"I think this is a bird and a butterfly. Mixed with a platypus."

With a little overlapping we had thankfully made it all fit within the Hell Room; I didn't like my chances if I'd had to explain to Steve why our bedroom floor was not to be walked on for the time being.

It was at this point that Ilsa found an illustrated story she had written years ago about a mermaid who was in love with a merman. It went on to read: "You are certain that this merman had a name. Well, merpeople don't *have* names." I don't know whether it was fatigue or being overwhelmed or the fact she had once written such a silly story with such an authoritative voice, but she was off in fits of giggles.

But it wasn't until we found a picture of four animals Ilsa had drawn that all hell broke loose. The drawing's animals were labeled. There was a "tiger," a "lion," a "bat," and a "snakoobatik." We took turns laughing and pronouncing it: "SNAkoobatik," "snaKOObatik"

Ilsa laughed and laughed until she wasn't making sound anymore. Tears welled up in her eyes. Just when I thought the attack was subsiding she'd erupt again into helpless peals that shook her whole body. It definitely didn't help matters when I pointed out her notation that the dreaded snakoobatik "eats raccoons and little birds."

I began to worry about her breathing, so we went downstairs and called it a day. After a good half an hour, she was still pink in the face and still emitting the occasional giggle.

"That one," she said, wiping the tears from her eyes. "That one *has* to go in the book."

Honestly, if we never got anything else out of our art organizing efforts than that lovely fit of uncontrollable laughter, it was totally worth it.

Okay, so great. Now we had one artwork for the book. Only ninety-nine more to go.

After consulting with Ilsa, we both decided that I would pick out the majority of art pieces for the book, and then she would come in and pick out the last ten or so. That seemed like a good way to get around the Ilsa indecision factor while still including her in the process.

What I realized was that it was easy to pick out the first ten or twenty—the very best, most colorful, and interesting pieces. After that…things got much, much harder. I suddenly wished I had picked a smaller number than a hundred, but it was too late for that now.

In the past I've gotten easily stymied in my attempts to organize by my fear of not doing something as well as I should—which is to say, *perfectly*. And so I'd get stuck on an unsolvable, completely unimportant problem such as how can I put these in chronological order when they aren't all dated?

Years past, this tangential conundrum would've been enough to put me off the track of completing a project indefinitely. But that was how we had gotten to where we were now, so I knew I had to find a way around such vagaries.

To counter my compulsion for chronological order I made a compromise: I set up three plastic bins in my bedroom. I didn't have to know the year precisely; all I had to do was look at the work and place it in either Early (finger paintings and scribbles), Middle (vibrant pictures of flowers and trees), or Late (caricatures and pictures of girls with large eyes). Gradually each bin filled up with chosen drawings and paintings, and before too long, it was time for Ilsa to come finish the job.

Just as I had experienced, it was easy for her at first and then suddenly very hard. She sat on my bed trying to winnow down twenty images to only ten and looked unhappy. She grimaced and complained bitterly. Without realizing it, I smiled.

"What? You find my agony funny?" she asked accusingly.

"Oh no!" I tried to explain. "No, I find it funny because… because I know how you feel."

I was going through my own agony. It was stupid of me, but there it was. Because photos were also permissible to send, and because I'm not one to leave well enough alone, I had the brilliant idea to include in the art books all of the girls' annual school portraits as well, showing them growing up over the years along with their artwork. I was thrilled by this idea, excited to finally have a place to show all these photos at once: Ilsa morphing from a delicate little pre-K doll into the strong, beautiful fifth grader with fiery red hair.

And so I had spent several additional hours riffling through the completely bewildering piles of photographs—never knowing when I might come across another school portrait. I knew I had them all; I just hadn't put them all in one place. But slowly, excruciatingly, one by one, I did find them. I lined them all up neatly on a counter in my office and enjoyed the effect of watching Ilsa grow taller, bigger, more mature in each photo. And then I'd start from the other end and go backward—watching her get progressively smaller and cuter. I was having great fun and feeling very satisfied until I made a horrible realization. One year was missing. Missing!

Everything came to a screeching halt. I was frozen in the knowledge that I couldn't show the complete set of school photos—I had looked everywhere! I tried appealing to the grandparents—surely they still had these photos tucked away somewhere? But strangely, no one else seemed to sense the urgency of this situation. I had to finish this! But how? My bedroom was clogged up with bins of artwork, boxes awaiting packing, photos covering my desk…but I was simply stuck.

Thwarted by the fact that everything has to be perfect. Perfect can be very destructive, you know.

Several weeks went by like this, the artworks getting shuffled around in my bedroom, the photos being blown to the floor in my office… *This is how it happens, despite my best intentions*, I thought. Was I really going to get this far and let everything fall back apart, with no progress made, nothing to show for all our efforts? Did I realize I was choosing to have no book at all instead of one that was a teeny bit imperfect?

That really wasn't what I wanted. Finally, I had to admit: life is imperfect. I'm imperfect.

I had arrived at my fourth mantra: "Be imperfect."

I sat down to put the artwork, and the photos, into the box.

In the middle of all the sorting and selecting of Ilsa's artworks I had happened upon a large, dusty paper art portfolio. I had no idea where it had come from or what could possibly be in it.

Ho hum, I thought. *More random crap.* When I opened it, though, my eyes got big: this was the kid artwork *my* mom had saved. I didn't even know she *had* this! True to form, just like my old baby clothes, she had saved a much smaller number of things than I seemed capable of. I counted: thirty-seven pieces of paper in varying sizes and media were in there. I had no memory of most of them. And there was no doubt even to my nostalgia-enchanted brain that the vast majority of them were meaningless to me now.

Huh.

Sorting through them I picked out half to get rid of and half to keep. Although I grew up in a crowded NYC suburb, apparently I had a predilection for painting girls holding baskets under apple trees, so those I kept. I felt sure I could've been harsher, winnowed the pile down even farther, but I didn't. This feeling of, what, acceptance? Or comfortable *detachment* was new territory for me. It felt good, strangely freeing. But, you know, I didn't want to push my luck.

CHAPTER NINETEEN

ARE WE THERE YET?

"Don't it feel like the wind is always howling?
Don't it seem like there's never any light?
Once a day don't you wanna throw the towel in?
It's easier than putting up a fight."
— "It's the Hard Knock Life," *Annie* (1977)

I t was a short and unsatisfying winter, cold enough to make you put on a coat but devoid of the things so many who live in or come to our area look forward to in winter, namely: snowflakes.

And then, just like that, it was spring again.

When I think of spring, I tend to think of beautiful, sunshiny days. These are the days when the snowdrops and daffodils are just beginning to peek above the ground and hope seems to be riding into town on a cool breeze.

But this was not that kind of spring. On this particular day, the kind of spring we were having was tumultuous, muddy, and windy. It felt far too dark to be morning, and the wind howled periodically outside as if it were part of a tale being

narrated by Vincent Price. I looked outside and had the feeling that the weather was in a confusing place, which, coincidentally, was exactly where I was too.

My project had stretched out beyond its boundaries: I had
begun in February, and the following February had come and
gone. Life went on, as it has a tendency to do, despite the fact
that things in the room were clearly not finished. The steely
resolve I'd had in our family's no-sugar project, filled with specific rules and dates and deadlines, somehow had evaporated
when it came to the Hell Room. Weeks came and went. Dinners
and loads of laundry came and went. The Hell Room weighed
on my conscience like an anvil. After so many months of work
was the room any better? Sure, it was *lots* better. But that didn't
mean it was *good*.

Shit was still everywhere. I hadn't been backsliding—I
seemed at last to have gotten over that hump—but there
were still a lot of things that hadn't quite figured out where
they belonged yet, and you know what *that* meant (dun dun
DUN): *clutter*. Still. Yeah, the floor was completely visible.
But there were still boxes here and there. Yeah, there was
actual *organization* at work now—art things in the art corner,
yarn over there in the fiber area, all the files in, or *near*, the file
cabinet along the back wall—but things still lingered. The
ginormous pile of every family photo we owned still loomed,
unorganized under the northern window. One day the floor
would be literally carpeted from wall to wall as part of the
Kids' Artwork Organization Plan, the next piles of boxes
would give way to new structures of boxes that rose and fell
like a time-lapse photo of a city skyline. As things swelled
and receded, a glacial formation of empty bins and boxes had
piled up in my bedroom; more strange stuff had migrated to

the edges of the Hallway Room. One week I spent two whole days moving heavy and awkward framed things and boxes into their new space in the back closet, falling over myself, blockading myself in and re-extricating myself over and over. Shuffle, shuffle, shuffle. Sure I'd given away, thrown away, sold, and shredded a *ton* of stuff, but the Hell Room seemed to be living up to its name: it was both punishing and eternal. It was a black hole in reverse, throwing up evidence of my life in an endless stream of useless information. Who cares? it seemed to whisper nastily to me. *Who cares?*

It was a measure of the sheer enormity of this project that I could have worked this hard and for this long on a task and have it still feel so…unfinished.

I had the "before" picture—the sheer improbable chaos of the Hell Room at its worst. What I wanted was only what every magazine editor wants: the breathtaking, beautiful, and scarcely recognizable "after" photo.

Where was my "*after*" photo, goddammit?

On days like this, I'd look around at the mess I continued to churn through like a nervous chipmunk, and I'd be tempted, like the ambivalent spring weather outside, to despair. I'd be struck by an overwhelming urge to sleep, as I usually do when I get depressed. These are the days I wish I could skip, the days when I wonder gloomily if I will ever be anything other than a sad, lower-order hoarder.

On this particular day, after giving in to temptation and lying down on my bed for a moment, suddenly my eyes opened wide. I knew I couldn't, *shouldn't* go to sleep, that was the worst thing I could do. I wasn't cheerful, but that wasn't necessary… Some part of my brain knew: it's time to get back to work. There really wasn't anything else to do but keep going.

It's a good thing that the job I'd been working on lately was brainless: document shredding. Ancient papers, bills, things with numbers, things with things on them. Everything in my overflowing file cabinets was in question, and thankfully I wasn't saving much. According to conventional wisdom, I was retaining all tax records to the beginning of time plus the past two years of anything else financial. Since I've basically never gotten rid of any paper before, *ever*, that translates to a *lot* of shredding to be done.

As it turns out, when it comes to shredding, three is the magic number. Three is how many times I can tamp down the confettied paper in the bin in an attempt to fool the machine that it is not full; three is the number of full bins I can empty into a white, kitchen-size garbage bag without spilling most of the paper confetti all over the floor; *and* three is the number of bags I can toss down the staircase before filling up the stairwell landing and blocking egress entirely.

These are the kinds of brilliant conclusions I come to as I proceed through the mounds of papers I have extricated from my bloated filing "system." Even *I* do not feel sentimental about electric bills from eleven years ago; however, the task is still fraught with peril: I might be tempted to read phone statements from back in my college days when they used to list every call made (Dunellen, New Jersey! Gainesville, Florida!) and try to guess who I had been calling there for eight minutes at 10:14 in the evening. I might stop to peruse bank statements that show old purchases, nights out at restaurants, purchases at Baby Gap…aww!

But no! I adopt a strict, sentimentality-free approach that deems old bills to be off-limits reading. Anything that might pose a question (notes from when I was vice president of the

Historical Society? The file from that time I lead Greta's third-grade Odyssey of the Mind group? My funny cartoon file?) gets shunted off to a separate pile to deal with later. It's okay—there's still plenty here to do.

I'm becoming quite the Shredding Diva. I know precisely how much paper I can add without jamming the shredder, exactly when to add the next sheets so they shred continuously without pause. I recognize the smell of heated paper that is emitted just before the motor is about to overheat. We are performing a delicate paper ballet, the piles and I.

The only problem with spending so much time in front of the shredder is that it gives me waaaay too much time to think. I might be tempted to avert boredom by reading the pages I'm shredding, which could all too easily lead to me having second thoughts, so instead I'm diverting myself with weird pep talks:

"People do things like this all the time. *I'm* just catching up!"

"These are *numbers*! I don't *care* about *numbers*!"

"I am a machine that feeds paper to another machine."

"Nobody does this! Nobody holds on to every paper they've ever touched."

"People flee countries with nothing but $5 in their pocket! Do *they* have piles of papers? No!"

I'd been shredding and filling bags and shredding and filling bags a portion of every day lately. I try very hard not to think about the landfill (I checked: shredded paper is not recyclable), and in between pep talks I apologize to the world, the earth, and the environment. I try not to worry that Steve might *need* a copy of his paid speeding ticket receipt from four years ago. I attempt not to give the shredder a nervous breakdown.

I find tiny bits of paper *everywhere*: in my hair, stuck to my socks, wedged in the spaces between the floorboards. I come to see every strand, every bit of confetti as a budding escape artist, angling to parachute to the floor rather than fall into the plastic trash bag. *Wheeeee!* whole squadrons of them cry, and when I am tired it seems more end up on the floor than in the bag. Bits of paper on the floor, I have realized, grate on my nerves, much in the way nails on a chalkboard do for other people.

Accordingly, I have developed a new, attractive tick: incessant vacuuming.

I might go on all day and into the night like this—shred, dump, vacuum, repeat—if it weren't for the fact that after a while the red warning light inevitably comes on to tell me I've mistreated my machine terribly and it needs a rest. There's no fooling the mechanism then, and it takes a good hour or so to cool the motor back down again, so this is my signal to stop for the day and turn to other things. This is good because I've begun to develop a strange pain in my right shoulder blade that I have identified as "shredder's arm."

Whole years in paper are disappearing into the greedy mouth of the shredder. Anything lacking numbers or our personal info I put in a nearby bin to recycle. With express permission from Marie Kondo, I'm delighted to throw in there an enormous stack of manuals, many of whose corresponding appliances I realize we no longer even own.

It's a relief and one that is, for once, fairly free of self-doubt and second-guessing. Getting rid of so much paper feels freeing, as if I am a Victorian woman who has just switched from wearing a whale-bone corset to a drop-waist Flapper dress. I imagine this is how so many women feel when they follow

Kondo's book to the letter and purge away an enormous percentage of their belongings. When they are done, they turn and look to their closets and shelves and see a small handful of things they love, a fraction of what had been there before, and they feel a tremendous sense of freeness.

I love Marie Kondo for this. Like other writers who have provocative, important things to say, I hear her voice in my head now when I am having a tough time struggling with my Stuff. But I also am now more convinced than ever that I don't want to cross over to that side completely.

Recently my dear friend Mary-Anne, whose four kids are grown and starting families of their own, was telling me how implementing Kondo-ism had changed her life. She told me the story of how, after they moved, she was truly horrified to see the crazy, random, and useless items they had actually paid money to move to their new home: silly hats. Old costumes. Empty containers and unloved tchotchkes.

This, plus a new, Kondo-inspired way of thinking about Stuff, inspired her to part with large amounts of old stuff, including reams and reams of old kid artwork in her garage. In particular she told me the story of a paper Santa that her daughter had made that Mary-Anne loved so much she had saved it and saved it for years, always with the intention to have it framed so she could bring it out and display it during the holidays.

Of course, she had never gotten around to it. So sitting in her garage one afternoon Mary-Anne thought about sending it to her daughter, who she imagined would be mystified to receive the old thing. *Mom? What the heck?* She could still have it framed for herself, but…did she really need one more thing to haul out at Christmastime? Really?

So, with a tiny Marie Kondo perched on her shoulder and whispering into her ear, she made the decision to throw it into the trash, along with most of the other stuff she had saved all those years. And she's delighted she did.

At least, that's what Mary-Anne says. The first time I heard this story, I believed her. The second time she told it to me, from beginning to end with no shortcuts, I began to wonder. I decided that if she ever tells me the paper Santa story a *third* time, I'll know she shouldn't have thrown it away.

Personally, I've come to understand that I haven't been on a journey to give my house a coffee enema and make it whistle-clean from top to bottom. I take way too much joy in rediscovering all those things that I've been collecting since I was a kid, always searching for things that felt "real"—things that felt genuine, had stories.

I shouldn't have to give up my love of going through old boxes and making discoveries of things I forgot existed or imagined must have been given away years ago, as if I've sent a care package to myself from some distant past I only half-remember. Suddenly, surprisingly, a box full of memories will bring it all back into sharp focus.

Sometimes it's a dusty old lava lamp that makes me laugh—I had a hard time getting rid of *this?*—before I send it on its way. Sometimes it's my old Hard Rock Cafe shirt with the neck hem cut out that looks remarkably good considering that in the T-shirt world it's probably old enough to start collecting social security. And sometimes it even comes in a little bit handy, as my fifth-grade report card did.

A few years ago we hosted a party at our house to celebrate several friends' birthdays, and I have to say, it was just about the highlight of my hoarding life. The theme we decided upon was the eighties, and as you can imagine, I was ready. While everyone else went to the thrift shop in search of a costume, I went to my attic and pulled down bins of some of the worst clothing imaginable: dresses with shoulder pads and crepe balloon skirts, leather miniskirts, scores of black rubber bracelets, my studded belt with handcuffs, and my old jean jacket with safety pins all over it from my Cyndi-Lauper-Meets-Sid-Vicious phase.

I hauled out my dusty record collection—Men at Work! The Jackson Five Victory Tour! Duran Duran!—which not so long ago I had considered so embarrassing that if I were someone else I would have gotten rid of it... Now I was ecstatic. I hung up forty-five covers that folded out into posters. I left period-correct comic books with references to Pong and Jazzercise on the coffee table. But I was frustrated too: there was more up there, I *knew*. Where were my Michael Jackson posters? What about my old pin collection? But I didn't have the *time*, darn it. I knew I had a copy of *The Valley Girls' Guide to Life*, if only I had another month or so to find it!

I was also curious: was I forgetting anything? So I looked online at "eighties party ideas," and I was *horrified* at what I saw: this stuff wasn't like the eighties! You can't just put "Awesome" and "Totally" all over everything and call it "the eighties"! Clearly, these party supplies were based on a bad, misinformed caricature of the decade as designed by someone born nowhere near it. Probably this is exactly how my parents feel when we ask them about sock hops.

What I learned, though, was this: people *loved* seeing all my real eighties stuff. I was proud to still have it. And yet everyone else did pretty great too. Betsy showed up in overalls with one strap hanging loose, Bob came in a track suit and gold chains looking like a Beastie Boy, and Scott showed up as a preppy complete with his collar turned up. Cori made a sheet cake that replicated the screen of a Pac-Man arcade game. People came with their memories of the eighties with all kinds of different references I had entirely forgotten about, and with them brought the thrill of shared recognition: "oh my God, remember *that*!?"

Mandy arrived wearing her actual, original prom dress and pointed out that she should get bonus points because, in bringing her husband Jed, she had also brought her actual, original prom *date*. As if that weren't enough, Jed actually shaved his hair into a dramatic, standing-straight-up Mohawk just for the event. I don't even want to know what makes a person's hair stay in ramrod spikes like that: Elmer's? Gorilla Glue? Talk about authenticity.

With our real stuff, as well as with our fake, borrowed, and bought recreations, we celebrated the fact that we had all been there, and we all remembered. Although I enjoyed bringing all my stuff out of the attic tremendously, I also could step back and recognize that having everything be, not just authentic, but literally mine from when I was fourteen was not entirely…*necessary*.

Is this obvious? To me it hadn't been. My deeply, fanatically literal nature has caused me confusion on more than one occasion.

One time when Greta was very small we were visiting Steve's parents. They had brought out a bouncy rocking horse for her to play on: an ancient honking thing with squeaking springs and too dangerous in about forty-seven different ways to ever be sold today. They called it "Thunder," and everyone referred to it as "the same one" that Steve and his brother

Chris had played on when they were little, and so that is what I literally thought it was. It seemed rather unlike Sharon and Bill to hold on to a large child's toy like that for so long, but I guessed this one thing had been so beloved that they made an exception.

Later, when I was perusing the family snapshot album, I saw pictures of Steve riding "Thunder," and I was astounded to realize it was entirely different: different color, different construction. Sure, it was a plastic horse that bounced, but the similarity ended there. Steve didn't understand my confusion.

"Sure, it's not *exactly* the same one, but Dad *found* it! The same one! They haven't sold those kind of bouncy horses for years!" he explained. Steve's father had been delighted to happen upon it at the Salvation Army or perhaps a tag sale. To Steve and his Dad it was like the difference between two identical stamps on a roll: if one was gone, you used another. What was the difference? The function, in the end, was the same.

So, did it *matter* whether the plastic horse was the selfsame one that Christopher and Stephen had *actually* ridden in those fading pictures from years ago? For that matter, did it matter so very much whether the rubber bracelets I wore to our eighties party were recent imitations or the very ones I purchased at the mall with my babysitting money in 1983?

To me, at least, up until this year, that was like asking whether it matters if the copy of the Declaration of Independence you're looking at is really the one touched and signed by Thomas Jefferson. (*Matters?* Of course it matters! It's *everything*!) But over the course of this year, I've come to realize there are other ways of looking at such things. A plastic bouncy horse is not the Declaration of Independence, and it needn't be. We can still remember, even when the signifiers aren't genuine. Yes, I prefer them to be genuine, to be *real*. But it isn't the end of the world—usually—when they are not.

Which lessens the burden significantly when you're trying to decide if the world may continue to spin if you free up some Hell Room space by getting rid of an old bridesmaid dress. I now know that, if someone throws a "wear your most hideous bridesmaid dress" party, rather than throwing myself into a paroxysm of remorse, I'll simply go to the thrift shop and have a lot of fun trying to pick out the worst one I can find. Can I forgive myself for giving away the world's most hideous bridesmaid dress that I actually owned? Well, don't I have better things to worry about?

I love looking back, but a large part of this year for me, I am realizing, is not just about getting rid of stuff or even changing how I do things. It's about realizing that it does me no good to live with my eyes glued to the rearview mirror. It's about forgiveness—of myself, of the world—for not being perfect, any of it. It's about accepting that sometimes when you want the Declaration of Independence, you get postage stamps. One Thunder can be as good as another, or close enough.

They say close only counts in horseshoes and hand grenades, but that isn't true. The Hell Room was close, really close, to not being a Hell Room anymore, and that counted for so much in my mind that it was enough to make me giddy one day and a neurotic wreck the next. I could *see* it. I could *feel* it—we were on the verge. I wandered around the house preoccupied—I was asking Steve to repeat himself a lot because I could only focus on one question in my mind: what more was it going to take?

CHAPTER TWENTY

THE ROOM FAIRY

"That's the whole meaning of life, isn't it? Trying to find a place for your stuff."

—George Carlin

I was sitting in a comfortable armchair next to the window, and it was raining outside, causing the steel roof to generate a continual pittery-pattery background noise. I was in that Hallway Room I've described so many times, just outside the Hell Room, that acts as a little library for our collection of books, which I could actually *see* now. It was gray out, and I had taken up my long-lost knitting, which, I realized in retrospect, I had put down when the Hell Room project began.

It was, I realized, an incredibly peaceful, happy moment.

Greta had come upstairs the other day and exclaimed for about three minutes straight how amazing it was to see the Hallway Room empty at long last. Nothing waiting to go anywhere, nothing awaiting last judgment.

"*Seriously,*" she said. "It is very weird to have that library space. I feel the compulsion to...*put* something there," Greta laughed to me, gesturing like she was shoving some imaginary objects against the walls, walls that had previously been lined with so many bizarre and ever-revolving iterations of our Stuff.

The new not-so-cluttered reality was going to take some getting used to.

Of course, still, the Hell Room was not completely done. Even this, the Hallway Room, was not yet completely done. But it was done enough that I could sit in a chair and put my knitting book on the end table, which, given its history up until now struck me as nothing short of miraculous. I had a light next to me on the end table, a ceramic lamp decorated with butterflies that I have never really liked but which reminds me of my grandmother because it used to be hers.

I realized that for me, not everything is going to spark joy. Some of the books on the shelves around me are there because they spark guilt. Or good intentions. Or because I *read* them, damn it, and I am proud of that fact.

I'm part of the way there, to Kondo's land of the immaculate, joy-sparking place, but I also know that I will forever be an exile to that land. I can get on the bus that is supposed to go there as much as I like, but I will forever be taking weird, unexpected detours at the last minute. Because I'm the kind of person who keeps her daughter's fallen-off fingernail in a box.

But I felt deeply okay about this right then because I had a place to sit and a light to knit by. When I went looking, I found my needles and yarn right away because amazingly, there is a place for them now.

Would I ever get to the end of it? I wondered. Had I crested the hill yet?

"*No*. No way," Steve says emphatically.

"Do you realize what that would mean?"

It is after dinner, and Steve and I are taking a walk in the crisp early May air. Greta is off at an activity, and Ilsa is now old enough to stay home by herself these days…something I've yet to get used to. Everything seems fresh and damp and brisk; all the trees are still like sticks, refusing to bud yet. Next to the road and down the bank the Mettawee River rushes by, beautiful and clear, looking like the textbook definition of *cold*.

Ever since my deadline came and went in February I'd been like a lost soul, searching for a way to end my Year of No Clutter. What would that even mean? I'd been grasping for a hold I couldn't seem to find… I had decided the only way for it to *really* be done was to complete something big, something I never thought possible before this all began.

So I've told Steve I think it is time: I want to pull all the carpet out of the Hell Room. *That* will be the way I know it is really done.

Although everyone agrees the carpet is disgusting and needs to be taken out at some point, Steve argues that the room simply isn't ready: yes, it is one thousand times better than it was, but for a task like this? The room would need to be basically *empty*. He explains that means *everything*—every single, solitary last thing—would have to come out of the room. The remaining two very heavy file cabinets, and all the art and fiber shelves we've so carefully culled and organized and placed. The built-in table? Unscrewed from the wall. As we walk along he very politely gives me the distinct impression he thinks I've lost my mind. Maybe I have. I'm clawing the walls to find a solution.

"You know," he says, "HGTV isn't going to come in here and give you a room makeover. And even if they did, I don't think that would be nearly as interesting as what you've done."

"What have I done?" I argue. I feel like I'm swimming or trying to punch my way out of a hot-air balloon. "I've made progress…but it's never enough! I need a *wow*! I need a decisive moment."

"Don't you see? This is just like the Year of No Sugar with the peanut butter cup!"

I have no idea what he's talking about. I mean, yes, on New Year's Eve at the stroke of midnight, a Reese's peanut butter cup was the sugar-thing I chose to have to mark the moment. After an entire year writing and talking and obsessing about sugar like nobody's business, it was the one thing I just *wanted*. Once I had it, the best way to describe that moment would be incredibly…*anticlimactic*. Like, yeah, okay. And?

But what did that have to do with the Hell Room?

"Don't you see?" he went on. "The next day we woke up and, what? It wasn't like we were visited by the sugar fairy who restocked all our shelves overnight. Or brainwashed us into not knowing what we knew now. It's not like we suddenly started going to restaurants and behaving as we did before. Everything was different. Even though according to the calendar the project was 'over,' it really wasn't. We had changed. Do you see?"

I was starting to, but it was hard. I was sunk so far down the sinkhole of "How can this ever be done?" that it was taking me some time to try to climb out to see his point.

"If there's one thing I've learned about home ownership," he went on, "it's that it's a job that's never over."

"Kind of like…eating?" I ventured.

"Yes!" He was proud I was following. "Clutter isn't a thing that you finish with…because it's something you always contend with. Same as food. *You're* never *done!*

"I've watched you this year, the past few months in particular. You've changed. Sure, our home will never be featured in *Architectural Digest*, but you can't spend more than a year focusing on something like this without having it change you. Change how you do things, how you look at things.

"Look," he said, trying to give me a for instance. "What did you do this morning?"

"Cleaned my office," I answered. I had dusted, vacuumed it, thrown things away, recycled, and filed. Much of it had been cleaning up actual dirt and putting-things-away mess, and some of it had been making decisions about clutter too.

"Right. You never used to clean your office. The kitchen? The bathroom? Sure. But not the office. And why did you do that? Because you were going to work. You've made that connection between clutter in your environment and clutter in your life and clutter in your mind."

I thought about how the other day I had at last brought Ilsa's big box filled with artwork to the shipping store—a box that contained literally her entire lifetime of creations, not to mention all those years of beloved school portraits, and represented hours of work that went into choosing, assembling, numbering, and packing it besides. I had handed it off to the man at the mailing store. No hesitation. Like it was nothing.

I thought about that morning when it rained and me, sitting in the cozy Hallway Room, surrounded by books. Since then Steve and I have started bringing our coffee up there most mornings and sitting in the armchairs talking before we go off to work. I find myself thinking about the books on the shelves—the ones I've read and the ones I want to read. It changes the conversations we have and the things we talk about—being surrounded by all those books.

I thought about the moment, perhaps a month or two ago, when I realized that a seismic shift in the Hell Room had occurred: the room had gone from looking like the world's worst storage closet to resembling, without a doubt, a Real *Room*. I knew this because the girls had started to *use* it. I'd encounter Ilsa or Greta's latest craft project strewn on the floor; markers and scissors and yarn were regularly being found, used, and *sometimes* even returned to their designated spots. I'd call to find out where the kids were, and they'd answer from upstairs…in the room. And they'd stopped calling it the Hell Room.

"Where are you going, Ilsa?" I'd asked her one afternoon recently.

"To the art room," she'd answered breezily.

The art room, I thought.

I thought about the children's story of the Velveteen Rabbit, a stuffed animal who is turned into a real rabbit by the magic fairy. I wondered: do you think there's a room fairy?

"You don't have to bring in the TV makeover people or tear out the carpet to prove you've changed," Steve said. "You already have."

"But…how do I know I won't just go back to recreating a Hell Room all over again once the project is really over?" I asked. And then I had a thought that had never occurred to me before: was I prolonging the project, making it stretch beyond the boundaries of the original year, simply out of fear and mistrust of myself?

"You won't," Steve replied confidently. "You've worked too hard to get here."

_____

And once I understood it. I admired the wonderful symmetry of it all: where once I held on to objects so tightly I nearly strangled both my past *and* my present, now I've held the Year of No Clutter so tightly that I nearly strangled it as well.

I told you: I'm nothing if not consistent.

So, once again, I'm practicing trying to follow my own admonitions, the lessons the Hell Room has taught me: to trust myself. Keep less, use more. Be imperfect. Doing these things feels like stepping off a cliff into thin air, but it's paid off before when, after ten years, I finally took the medication; when, after eighteen years, I finally opened the Hell Room door in earnest and decided to tell the world my ugly secret; and when, every single time over the last year, I made a decision to keep (*What if I'm a hoarder?*) or a decision to discard (*What if I'm filled with regret?*). No decision that we make about anything in life is 100 percent safe, and I know now *that's* what kills me.

In the end the room wasn't as much a Hell as it was a purgatory—a Room of Indecision—and I have transformed into a person who, rightly or wrongly, *can* make decisions. Somewhere along the way I came to a startling conclusion, which is both the bad news *and* the good news at the same time: at the end of my life no one is going to show up and give me an A+ if I did enough things right.

I still have work to do: a lot of work. The Mountain of Snapshots and Family Photos still looms under the north window, waiting to be wrangled with, and all the files aren't completely contained in the cabinets yet. Now that I have a sewing table again, I can work on the two unfinished beanbag chairs I promised to make the girls more than a year ago. I have big plans to put them on top of the crazy multicolored autobiography rug and—here's an idea—have a place to sit besides the floor.

And that stained old carpet *is* coming out... It's just a matter of time.

So I'm still afraid. It's a big part of who I am, just like my things. But it isn't *who* I am, and that is what makes all the difference.

All this time I'd been searching in the Room for my "after" picture...it had never occurred to me until just now: the "after" picture is me.

P.S.

"None of this stuff belongs to us. We just happen to get to use it for a while."
—Stephen Gaskin, *Monday Night Class* (2005)

I have to tell you something. Thank you.

I couldn't have done this without you—quite literally. It was because you were here, in my head, reading about all our adventures as I put them down, that I was able to confront the demons that otherwise would've been left behind a closed door indefinitely. It's an unsettling thought, but who's to say I wasn't just a few years' accumulation away from graduating to becoming a true, textbook hoarder? The kind you *can't* hide from your friends and family? I'm grateful, and confident enough now, to say we'll never know the answer to that question.

Cross fingers.

And now that we have arrived at the end of the book, I can confirm a suspicion I've had all along: there is really no such thing as a Year of No Clutter. Not in my life anyway. I'll always have clutter because I love *things*—the evidence of our lives and our experiences—so very much. I'll always endeavor to make better sense out of them, to have better organization, more efficient storage, to jettison that which can possibly be parted with and to give the rest a logical place to go, a place where it belongs. This last is, as we've discovered, the trick to transforming an item of "clutter" into something else: a belonging, perhaps. A memento. A keepsake.

I know now that it's an ongoing forever process. I've learned that I can survive it—making decisions for better or worse—and it really is all okay. Someday we're all going to that great big antique shop in the sky, and the things we leave behind us are as likely as not to be bizarre and incomprehensible to anyone but ourselves. We just do the best we can with it all.

This spring, as I was having my "*is it done?*" crisis about the Hell Room, Greta was acting in a local production of Tracy Letts's Pulitzer prize–winning play *August: Osage County*. In it, the patriarchal character of Beverly delivers a monologue about life and, incidentally, the objects we live it with. Of course, because I'm the grand poobah of my daughter's fan club and because no one could really stop me, I went to see the production multiple times. Every time I heard the actor come to a particular part of the monologue, I sat up straight in my chair. I always had the weird feeling Letts had written these few sentences specifically to me:

"Y'know…a simple utility bill can mean so much to a living person. Once they've passed, though…after they've passed, the words and numbers just seem like…otherworldly symbols. It's only paper."

Important. It's all terribly important. Until suddenly, one day, it isn't. Who knew all along I had been wrestling with the impermanent nature of life itself? Accept it or don't, but I'm not solving that one anything soon, am I?

"Be well, do good work, keep in touch," Garrison Keillor reminds me from my car radio every morning.

To that I might add: "Enjoy your things."

RESOURCES

Plumprint is the online company that photographs and reproduces your child's artwork in book form. They did a terrific job on Ilsa's book—titled *Art is Interesting!*—which now proudly sits on our living room coffee table. And they returned all artwork and photographs in a nice, neat box that I can put in the attic for posterity to discover at some later date. Voilà! No more art volcano!

(Well, except for Greta's. That's next.)

S.A.F.E. (Stuffed Animals for Emergencies, Inc.) collects and distributes stuffed animals to children in emotional or traumatic situations. You can cut back on the plush madness while someone else gets a much-needed new stuffed friend: everybody wins! Greta's comment? "That's the most amazing thing I've ever heard!"

Visit their website at http://www.stuffedanimalsforemergencies.org/ to find out where you can donate your clean stuffed animals by mail.

ACKNOWLEDGMENTS

Writing a book and cleaning a room are quite similar practices in some ways: they're both a process of continuous sifting in which things are kept and things are lost. You'd be amazed by the number of stories that *didn't* make it into this book—like the story of my dad's fifty-pound sculpture made of compressed aluminum pans, or how my aunt Mill periodically mails me belongings from her house like a never-ending estate distribution for someone who hasn't died yet. The process of creation, I suppose, necessarily entails exclusion, which is to say, when something is made there's always something lost too. It couldn't be otherwise. Probably there is a scientific name for this like the Law of Conservation of Verisimilitude or something.

Knowing what you do now about my cluttering tendencies, I suspect you can begin to appreciate just how hard it might be to edit one of my manuscripts. In this regard I have an enormous debt of gratitude to my editors Shana Drehs and Grace Menary-Winefield for doing to my manuscript what I did to the Hell Room, and then some: no easy task. Truly, when I was lost in the woods, it was these two wonderful women who lit lanterns so I could find my way back to a meaningful path.

Extreme thanks are due to my agent Angela Miller, without whom my harebrained schemes might never see the printed page. She has a keen eye, a ready wit, and makes one hell of a delicious goat cheese. You do not know it yet, Angela, but I am knitting you a superhero cape.

I cannot overstate the impact my therapist has had upon my life. It is to her that this book is dedicated, because without her none of my current life would be possible. Surely, neither therapy nor medication is for everyone, and certainly they each need to be implemented with care, attention, and—I'd argue— love. But, I'd really like to think that out there, somewhere, is a person who will be helped by the story of how I came to stop being quite so darned stubborn, and accept help. Although it took years, I finally came to understand that suffering in silence, when alternatives may exist, is neither noble nor necessary.

When you are friends with a writer, you never know when something you have said or done might end up in a book somewhere. I would like to thank everyone who is my friend anyway, but especially the many, many folks who shared their stories of Stuff with me; I was amazed to realize that almost everyone I meet has a story to tell on the subject of Stuff. And of course, special appreciation is due to those whose stories ended up being included here.

Thank you to Annette and Stan for trusting me with the story of their friend, Gary.

Thank you also to Marty and Monica Kravitt, Terry and Karen Ogden, Mary-Anne Van Degna, Debbi Zuckerman, and Cara Allen for their wonderful Stuff stories. Most of all on this account, my gratitude to my dear friend Miles

Kelly—the one with the figurative balls of steel—for sharing with me an ongoing, lifetime conversation about the agonies and the ecstasies of Too Much Stuff. Everyone should have a person like Miles in their life to call up and say, "You *know?*" and have them respond, "I know."

Every writer should have a crack team of super-friends who will drop everything and weigh in on subjects as pivotal as whether the pee joke is funny or just kind of gross. On this account, thanks to Miles Kelly, Gretchen Hachmeister, Robin Kadet, Noreen Hennessy, and Rhonda Schlangen. I am a fortunate person indeed to have such wonderful, intelligent, and supportive friends.

I count myself a very lucky person to know Melissa Johnson, the high priestess of all things fiber, as well as my longtime weaving cohorts Carol McGorry and Deedee Alton. Rather than laugh, they hugged me while I cried about missing an old, stupid, cotton dress.

Thank you to the church pastor and to Jacob Park—for asking right questions at the right time. And big appreciation to Chuck Schaub for your expert legal advice.

It is possible that Marie Kondo may yet parachute into my backyard to tell me I am doing this Stuff thing all wrong. When that happens, I will seize the opportunity to enthusiastically shake her hand and thank her for giving us brilliant new ways to think about our Stuff. Even if I may never quite make it to the spare and beautiful land of Kondo-ism, I love that it exists, and that she dedicates to our objects so much time, thoughtfulness, and respect. From one Stuff-obsessed person to another, I salute her.

Much love and appreciation to my dad, my brother, and Uncle Jim, for unwittingly being party to my ad hoc DNA research group on clutter. Thank you in advance for not dis-owning me. Probably.

Love and thanks also to my mom for putting up with my many, many kid collections and all my corresponding clut-ter, the burgeoning signs of a hoarder-in-training, no doubt. Thank you for letting me be me.

I must thank my beautiful and amazing daughters Greta and Ilsa: you teach me so many things. Without your help, I certainly never could have faced down the dreaded Hell Room, and without your ever-present senses of humor I wouldn't have enjoyed it half as much. I fervently hope that when you grow up you will be glad you had an eccentric mom who not only kept things like your fallen-off fingernail in a box, but had to write a book to tell the whole world about it too.

There are husbands, and then there are husbands. I couldn't possibly thank Steve enough for the love and support he gives not only to me, but to my writing career, which seems to consist mainly of turning our family home life upside down in various ways. Whether it is excess anxiety or excess stuff, thank you, Steve, for being there and giving me the time and space to figure it out, always. If it weren't for you, this book might never have found its ending.

Would it be weird for me to thank my Stuff? Probably. Nevertheless, I will. For all the things I live my life with and the things that give me joy, the things that help me remember and interpret the story of my life, I am very grateful to them, all of them. Whether you ended up in a recycling bin or at the consignment shop, woven into a rug, given away, or stuck into a bin in the attic for me to discover a few decades from now—I hope I have done justice to you all.

And for the record—I actually love Edith Piaf.

ABOUT THE AUTHOR

Serial memoirist Eve O. Schaub is the author of *Year of No Sugar* (2014), a book about her family's attempt to live and eat for a year without any added sugar in their food. Her memoir joins an expanding global conversation about the impacts of sugar on our health. To date, Schaub considers not hyperventilating on national television one of her greatest accomplishments.

She has been made by her daughters to swear, among other things, that her next book will not be:

- *Year of No Boyfriends*
- *Year of No Cheese*
- *Year of No Shampoo*

She lives in Vermont with her family and an ever-fluctuating number of chickens.

www.eveschaub.com
@eveschaub